HOMES OF THE FIRST LADIES

For Granddaughter Mackenzie

*May your future husband aspire to be
First Husband of the Land*

HOMES OF THE
FIRST LADIES

A GUIDE TO
PUBLICLY ACCESSIBLE HOMES, MUSEUMS,
AND RELATED SITES

by

William G. Clotworthy

The McDonald & Woodward Publishing Company
Granville, Ohio

The McDonald & Woodward Publishing Company
Granville, Ohio
www.mwpubco.com

HOMES OF THE FIRST LADIES: A GUIDE TO PUBLICLY ACCESSIBLE
HOMES, MUSEUMS, AND RELATED SITES
A McDonald & Woodward Guide to the American Landscape

© 2011 by The McDonald & Woodward Publishing Company

Printed in United States of America
by McNaughton & Gunn, Inc., Saline, Michigan

Mixed Sources
Product group from well-managed
forests and other controlled sources
www.fsc.org Cert no. SW-COC-002283
© 1996 Forest Stewardship Council

First printing, first edition: October 2010

10 9 8 7 6 5 4 3 2 1
19 18 17 16 15 14 13 12 11 10

Library of Congress Cataloging-in-Publication Data

Clotworthy, William G., 1926-
  Homes of the first ladies : a guide to publicly accessible homes, museums,
and related sites / by William G. Clotworthy. — 1st ed.
    p. cm.
  Includes bibliographical references and index.
  ISBN 978-1-935778-00-4 (pbk. : alk. paper)
  1. Presidents' spouses—Homes and haunts—United States—Guidebooks.
2. Dwellings—United States—Guidebooks. 3. Historic buildings—United
States—Guidebooks. 4. Museums—United States—Guidebooks. 5.
Presidents' spouses—United States—Biography. I. Title.
  E176.2.C58 2010
  973.09'9—dc22

                                                        2010027624

Contents

Contents

Section III

Additional Information

Section I

In Recognition of the First Ladies

Introduction

I live a very dull life here and know nothing that passes in the town. I never go to any public place . . . Indeed, I think I am more like a state prisoner that anything else. There is certain bounds for me which I must not depart from . . . and as I cannot do as I like, I am obstinate, and stay at home a great deal.

— Martha Washington, October 23, 1789[1]

I have a forum. I won't have it always. The time is now.

— Laura Bush, 2001[2]

While researching my book *Homes and Libraries of the Presidents* I realized that, while the focus was on presidents, at the same time I was studying their wives, those women who did not seek nor run for office but were, through marriage, destined to become our nation's First Ladies. Who were they? What were their backgrounds? What influence, if any, had they on their husbands as these men made often monumental decisions? The answer to the last question may never be known, although history has speculated that in some cases the influence of these women was significant. The other questions, however, are more easily answered.

After all, many of the residences included in *Homes and Libraries of the Presidents* belonged to a **couple**. Mount Vernon was the home of George **and** Martha Washington. Lawnfield was the residence of James **and** Lucretia Garfield and Spiegel Grove was the residence of Rutherford **and** Lucy Hayes. The ladies made them homes, whether the magnificent Mount Vernon in Virginia, the rustic ranch house of Lyndon and Lady Bird Johnson in the Texas hill country or the modest home of Harry and Bess Truman in mid-America. All of these structures reflect the honest American values of their occupants — hard work, respect, marital devotion and deep, abiding love.

By visiting them, we may be able to better understand the men who attained America's highest political office and the women who stood by their sides as they led our nation through years of struggle and growth to America's pre-eminence in the world. Together.

First Ladies, then, have been and continue to be important. Edith Mayo, Curator Emeritus of the National Museum of American History, once said, "She represents the kinder, gentler side of the presidency, and I think she has always been a voice in the country for those who don't have a political voice."[3] That may be true of more recent First Ladies although it was not always so. After all, President Martin Van Buren didn't even mention his wife and family in his autobiography! Nowadays presidential wives are in the news on a daily basis, and they speak out on issues, formulate fashion and at times cause controversy. Over two centuries have passed between the rather plaintive quotation of Martha Washington and the forceful comment of Laura Bush as she vowed to use the stature and power of her unofficial position to speak out on issues of importance.

First Ladies. What an interesting, eclectic group — shy or ebullient, cosmopolitan or countrified, healthy or infirm, wealthy or poor, well-educated or unschooled, ambitious or passive; each has represented, in her own way, a social stratum of the nation and the political beliefs of her husband, at least publicly. It's impossible to categorize them easily and ill-advised to try to do so as expectations and opportunities have significantly changed over the last two centuries. Early First Ladies, although widely admired, functioned mostly in the background and would undoubtedly be shocked by the attention, adulation, fame and, certainly, the outspokenness of their modern White House counterparts.

These women might even be surprised by the unofficial title now in common use. Martha Washington was referred to as "Lady Washington" by General Washington's troops during the Revolutionary War, a sobriquet carried over from our British royal heritage, a sincere mark of respect that continued through Washington's presidency, although the term made Martha uncomfortable. Her own use of the term "first lady" in a letter to a friend, inadvertently prophetic, bore fruit in 1849 when President Zachary Taylor, at the death of Dolley Madison, eulogized, "She will never be forgotten because she was truly our First Lady for a half-century."[4] Taylor's remark was the first recorded use of the term which, thereafter, disappeared until 1860 when *Leslie's*

Illustrated Newspaper referred to Harriet Lane, President Buchanan's niece and White House hostess, as "First Lady." The publication may have simply intended to make a distinction between a president's wife and another person who served as hostess but the term was used, only infrequently, until 1877 when reporter Mary Clemmon Ames referred to Lucy Hayes as "First Lady" at the inauguration of husband Rutherford B. Hayes. Somehow, that time, the term caught on to become a fixture of American lexicon, the commonly accepted title for the wife of the President of the United States.

Author Kati Marton once wrote:

> *The First Lady is one of our most cherished institutions. We're a deeply traditional people, and maybe out of some residual nostalgia for the monarchy that we fought so hard to shed, we really set up the White House and the presidency as sort of semi-monarchical.*[5]

That's true considering the American fascination with royalty and celebrity as exemplified by our interest in, for example, princesses Grace and Diana, and with such entertainment royalty as Count Basie, Duke Ellington and Elvis the King. There is, of course, commercial royalty as exemplified by king- and queen-sized beds, princess phones, Burger King and Dairy Queen.

There is no constitutional job description for the First Lady as it is not an elected position. In fact, women were not granted suffrage until 1920, during the presidency of Woodrow Wilson, when Tennessee became the thirty-sixth state to ratify the Nineteenth Amendment that granted women the right to vote.

Since 1789, when George Washington became our first president, the role of the First Lady has evolved. Prior to the Civil War, wives (including a president's wife) were expected to remain in the background, voices and opinions stifled; content, perhaps, to act as a proper eighteenth- or nineteenth-century helpmeet — docile, dutiful — and silent. Those early First Ladies were, in fact, highly diverse individuals. Before her marriage to George Washington, Martha Dandridge Custis was a wealthy plantation owner and slave holder in her own right. Abigail Adams was a prolific writer and documentarian of the colonial social and political era. Elizabeth Monroe, in Paris with her husband, James, then ambassador to France, was instrumental in saving the Marquis de Lafayette's wife from the guillotine. Sarah Polk acted as her husband's private secretary, confidante and political advisor. Dolley

Madison, raised as a modest Quaker, became the nation's arbiter of taste and fine living, while Margaret Taylor, annoyed that husband Zachary ran for the presidency in the first place, demonstrated her independence by refusing to participate in the social milieu as First Lady. She remained in the family living quarters, eschewed all social responsibilities and left the White House only to attend church.

Things changed around the time of the Civil War. With the invention of the telegraph and improvements in photography, newspaper coverage of the war was more timely and extensive, leading to increased public interest in current events, especially political matters. The personal lives of the presidents and First Ladies became more interesting and widely known; the beliefs, fashions and hairstyles of the First Ladies, for example, became popular topics of conversation. There were early twinges of interest in women's rights as exemplified by such pioneer activists as Elizabeth Cady Stanton, Susan B. Anthony, Clara Barton and others. It was not until the twentieth century, however, that Edith Roosevelt, Helen Taft, Edith Wilson and Florence Harding began to shatter the mold of First Lady reticence which led to the social activism of Eleanor Roosevelt, Betty Ford, Rosalynn Carter and Hillary Clinton. Media coverage — newspapers, magazines, radio and especially television — thrived on presidential pictures, personalities and peccadilloes. The personal lives of the President and First Lady became public property.

As a group, our First Ladies have only one thing in common — marriage to a President of the United States. The single exception to this generalization in this book is bachelor President James Buchanan's niece and ward, Harriet Lane, who served as his White House hostess and full social partner. Also, it would be proper to recognize that four wives listed here — Martha Jefferson, Rachel Jackson, Hannah Van Buren and Ellen Arthur — passed away before their husbands' presidencies began. While technically not First Ladies, it is clear that their early influence on their husbands was profound.

For all their differences, there are similarities between some First Ladies. For example, Martha Washington spent many winters with her husband in military encampments, Julia Grant and Lucy Hayes spent a great deal of time at military camps during the Civil War, and Eleanor Roosevelt, Pat Nixon, Barbara Bush, Hillary Clinton and Laura Bush visited troops stationed near combat zones in Europe, the South Pacific, Vietnam and the Persian Gulf. Mary Lincoln and Jacqueline Kennedy experienced, first-hand, the horror of presidential assassination. Lucretia Garfield, Ida McKinley, Anna Harrison, Margaret Taylor, Florence Harding and Eleanor Roosevelt were widowed when their husbands died in office.

Letitia Tyler, Caroline Harrison and Ellen Wilson died while residing in the White House. Julia Tyler, Frances Cleveland and Edith Wilson married sitting presidents and Barbara Bush and Abigail Adams share the honor of producing sons who would assume the same high office once held by their husbands.

Most First Ladies have been admired, some revered — and several vilified. Mary Lincoln, Edith Wilson, Eleanor Roosevelt, Rosalynn Carter, Nancy Reagan and Hillary Clinton absorbed more than their share of criticism, deserved or not — for being overly active, overbearing, demanding, political or extravagant. The most maligned was undoubtedly Mary Lincoln, the object of a hate campaign so vicious that, following President Lincoln's death, her behavior became so erratic that she was committed to a mental institution for a brief period.

Eleanor Roosevelt and Hillary Clinton were heavily criticized for their social activism, while Sarah Polk, Mary Lincoln and Helen Taft, albeit behind the scenes, were equally active in promoting (some say pushing) their husbands' political careers. Conversely, several First Ladies were passive, confined to inactive roles. Eliza Johnson, Letitia Tyler and Ida McKinley were unable to perform many duties expected of First Ladies due to illness.

First Ladies are, then, a disparate group, and a fascinating one. Excepting Sarah Polk, Mary Lincoln, Helen Taft and Hillary Clinton who harbored dreams of political grandeur, or those who married sitting presidents, the others hardly visualized residence in the White House. They were young women who married their husbands then working as farmers, attorneys, military officers, tailors, newspaper publishers, schoolteachers, haberdashers, congressmen, government bureaucrats or mining engineers. One even was working as a motion-picture actor.

By studying First Ladies, we also study presidents, for their influence on one another was significant. Sarah Polk was her husband's private secretary, and Eliza Johnson spent her newlywed days in husband Andrew's tailor shop, where she helped tutor the poorly educated young man in reading and mathematics. Eleanor Roosevelt became husband Franklin's eyes and ears — and legs — when he was struck with polio, and newlywed Lady Bird Johnson used an inheritance to finance Lyndon's first campaign for Congress.

Rosalynn Carter and Hillary Clinton were their husbands' full political partners, and Edith Wilson was nicknamed "The Presidentress" when she became a conduit between her husband, the Congress and the nation after her husband became physically incapacitated by a severe stroke.

In 1960, President Harry S Truman wrote, "I hope someday someone will take time to evaluate the true role of the wife of a president, and to assess the many burdens she has to bear and the contributions she makes."[6]

It was not until 1995, however, that former Canton, Ohio, school teacher Mary Regula, unable to find good reference material about First Lady Mary Todd Lincoln, realized how little the nation knew about First Ladies. Thereupon, she decided that America needed an organization devoted to the study and historical significance of the nation's First Ladies and founded the National First Ladies' Library, its purpose to compile a bibliography of works on First Ladies.

By 1998, a web site featuring the bibliography was complete. First Lady Hillary Clinton honored its dedication by writing:

> *At this exciting time in our history, as we look forward to a new century and the next millennium, the National First Ladies' Library preserves a very special part of our nation's political and social history. The electronic library allows you to browse through a comprehensive bibliographic database exhibiting the enormous contributions made by forty-three remarkable women . . . The items contained in this library help us to understand our nation's past and, with that understanding, to meet the future with confidence.[7]*

At the same time, it was clear that the organization needed a larger physical location. Providentially, the Canton, Ohio, family home of former First Lady Ida Saxton McKinley, owned by the National Park Service, had office space available. The National First Ladies' Library had found a home. A major refurbishing effort was undertaken; the interior décor was brilliantly recreated to represent the Victorian period of the Saxton family residency (see page 145) with several rooms set aside for exhibits on First Ladies — and the William McKinleys who had resided in the house for many years following their marriage.

The library venture was so successful that it led almost immediately to further expansion. Thus, in September 2003, the National First Ladies'

Library Education and Research Center (see page 147) opened in a seven-story building only one block from the Saxton McKinley home that remains open as a house museum. At the dedication of the Education Center, as she witnessed her dream come true, president and founder Mary Regula said:

> *Now, with this state-of-the-art research facility and library, and a beautifully restored Victorian museum, someone searching for a role model, researching a speech or defending a maligned First Lady has a place to come to document the truth. This will become a home for scholars, schoolchildren, authors and armchair historians alike to finally fill the void in American history.*[8]

The guest of honor at the dedication was First Lady Laura Bush who remarked:

> *As a former teacher and librarian and a First Lady, I am glad to be here to commemorate the opening of this center for history, 'her-story' and for learning . . . This is a national archive which chronicles the lives and legacies of America's first ladies and the significant political and social contributions they've made . . . The First Ladies' Library, like thousands of libraries across America, stands as a beacon for education and information. If we have a question about the world, the library is the place to find the answer. And someone will always be here to help us find the answer — our dedicated librarians. Thanks to the librarians and docents here today for helping to educate and inform the public — and for inspiring people to learn their history.*
>
> *It is vitally important for every American — and particularly for young people — to learn about our democracy. An understanding and appreciation of history makes every American a more engaged citizen. John Adams said, 'Liberty cannot be preserved without a general knowledge among the people,' and what knowledge we can gain from the stories of these great women.*
>
> *The stories of First Ladies are a vivid reflection of American women and of American history. Their stories deserve to be told and remembered. As Edith Roosevelt honored first ladies before her by displaying their portraits in the White House, the National First Ladies' Library honors the lives of these great women. John*

Adams' wife, Abigail, once reminded her husband to 'remember the ladies.' Thanks to the First Ladies' Library, the history of America's First Ladies will continue to be told — one remarkable woman at a time.[9]

The nation owes a debt of gratitude to Mary Regula for her vision and dedication and to the hundreds of volunteers and professionals who have made the National First Ladies' Library possible. According to Edith Mayo, a member of the Board of Directors, "What you get is women using everyday life and everyday materials to structure a really important role created out of a vacuum. It's quite a stunning achievement."[10]

The focus of this study is, in general, the identification of homes of the First Ladies that are accessible to, and managed for, public visitation. By examining the backgrounds of the First Ladies and by being able to visit and experience the places where these women lived, we may expand our knowledge and sense of these women and the places that helped shape them and now interpret them. Regretfully, many homes once occupied by these women have been lost and it is only recently that preservationists and historians have become active in locating, restoring, and interpreting these structures. Girlhood or other pre-marital homes of Abigail Adams, Dolley Madison, Mary Todd Lincoln, Julia Grant, Lucy Hayes, Ida McKinley, Edith Wilson, Grace Coolidge, Bess Truman and Mamie Eisenhower have survived and are open for public visitation. Many other homes that the First Ladies shared with their husbands, along with presidential libraries and museums, are repositories of important historical information and provide valuable insight into the backgrounds, lives, careers and influences not only of the men but, increasingly, also of their wives.

The first formal effort to recognize and protect a residence because of its historical significance as the former home of a First Lady, rather than a residence or other site primarily associated with her president-husband, was undertaken by the Abigail Adams Historical Society. Formed in 1947, the society's singular purpose was to save and restore the birthplace home of First Lady Abigail Adams. With the cooperation of the town of Weymouth, Massachusetts, plus countless volunteers and restoration experts, the society initiated a multi-year restoration project that was not completed until 1958! It was well worth the wait, as its authenticity is faithful to the history of the house and the era of its early occupants (see page 27). Then, in 1968 the

Kentucky Mansion Preservation Foundation was formed to preserve, restore and maintain Kentucky's historic properties that included the once-dilapidated childhood home of Mary Todd Lincoln in Lexington (see page 97). At the same time, dedicated citizens in Chillicothe, Ohio, formed a foundation to preserve the childhood home of First Lady Lucy Hayes which opened to the public in 1996 as the Lucy Hayes Heritage Center (see page 125).

And, in 1970, a restoration committee in the small town of Boone, Iowa, was formed to save the birthplace home of its favorite daughter, Mamie Eisenhower, a house which opened to the public in 1980 and was to become Boone's favorite tourist attraction (see page 208). The most recent manifestation of the effort to preserve homes of the First Ladies is that of the Edith Bolling Wilson Foundation of Wytheville, Virginia, which has purchased and is restoring and interpreting the birthplace of one of the nation's most interesting, influential and controversial First Ladies (see page 167). Another effort, more modest but nonetheless important, is that of Champlain College in Burlington, Vermont, which acquired First Lady Grace Coolidge's girlhood home. This house is now in use as an administrative office, but it remains open to the public and features a special display area honoring Mrs. Coolidge (see page 179).

Appropriately, one truly extraordinary First Lady has been honored with her own National Historic Site — and the cottage called Val-Kill (see page 198) is the centerpiece of the Eleanor Roosevelt National Historic Site in Hyde Park, New York. In May, 1977, President Jimmy Carter signed a bill creating the site in recognition of the historic contributions of the woman known as "First Lady of the World."

Despite these important efforts, surely other opportunities exist for the identification, preservation and interpretation of homes or other features associated with a First Lady. Citizens in Guilford County, North Carolina, for example, saved some logs from the rude birth cabin of First Lady Dolley Madison when it was torn down in the nineteenth century, qualifying that undertaking as perhaps the earliest effort to preserve at least a part of such a "First Lady-related place" for its historical value (see page 39).

In the following pages, readers will find a short biography of each First Lady — including one of Harriet Lane and those four women who died before their husbands became president — followed by a description of her now publicly accessible home(s) (Figure 1, Table 1). In some cases, associated

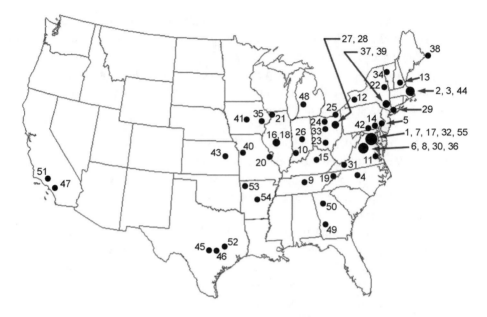

Table 1. Homes, museums, and related sites described in this book that commemorate the First Ladies.

1. Mount Vernon
2. Abigail Adams Birthplace
3. Adams National Historical Park
4. Greensboro Historical Museum
5. Todd House
6. Montpelier
7. James Monroe Museum and Memorial Library
8. Ash Lawn-Highland
9. The Hermitage
10. Grouseland
11. Sherwood Forest
12. Fillmore House Museum
13. The Pierce Manse
14. Wheatland
15. Mary Todd Lincoln House
16. Lincoln Home National Historic Site
17. President Lincoln's Cottage at the Soldiers' Home
18. Abraham Lincoln Presidential Library and Museum
19. Andrew Johnson National Historic Site
20. Ulysses S. Grant National Historic Site *and* Grant's Farm
21. Ulysses S. Grant Home State Historic Site
22. Grant Cottage State Historic Site
23. Lucy Hayes Heritage Center
24. Rutherford B. Hayes Presidential Center
25. James A. Garfield National Historic Site
26. President Benjamin Harrison Home
27. First Ladies National Historic Site

Table 1, *continued*

28. William McKinley Presidential Library & Museum
29. Sagamore Hill National Historic Site
30. Pine Knot
31. Edith Bolling Wilson Birthplace Museum
32. Woodrow Wilson House Museum
33. The Harding Home
34. Goodhue Home
35. Herbert Hoover Presidential Library and Museum
36. Rapidan Camp
37. Home of Franklin D. Roosevelt National Historic Site *and* Franklin D. Roosevelt Presidential Library and Museum
38. Roosevelt Campobello International Park
39. Eleanor Roosevelt National Historic Site
40. Harry S Truman National Historic Site
41. Mamie Doud Eisenhower Birthplace
42. Eisenhower National Historic Site

43. Dwight D. Eisenhower Presidential Library and Museum
44. John F. Kennedy Presidential Library and Museum
45. Lyndon B. Johnson National Historical Park and Lyndon B. Johnson State Park and Historic Site
46. Lyndon Baines Johnson Library and Museum
47. Nixon Presidential Library and Museum
48. Gerald R. Ford Presidential Museum
49. Jimmy Carter National Historic Site
50. Jimmy Carter Library and Museum
51. Ronald Reagan Presidential Library and Museum
52. George Bush Presidential Library and Museum
53. Clinton House Museum
54. William J. Clinton Presidential Library and Museum
55. The White House

facilities — such as museums or presidential libraries that are open for public visitation — that contain interpretation, reference material and gallery displays related to First Ladies also have been included. Several of these sites are featured in the sixteen color plates that depict rooms and gardens in which the women lived and worked, and museum galleries that interpret and celebrate their lives. Collectively, the homes and other sites identified and described below allow the reader and visitor to better understand the places that helped shape the character and legacy of this group of important American women. Maps identify the general location of each of these sites.

While every effort has been made to ensure the accuracy of visitor information presented in the book — such as the location of the sites on maps, directions for reaching the sites, visiting hours, phone numbers, admission fees and facilities for the disabled — much of this information is subject to change. When planning a visit to any of these sites, it is suggested that visitors call, write or log on to the appropriate web site to obtain the most current information and consult detailed maps or current directions for actually reaching the sites.

I would have a "position" but not a real "job" . . . There is no training manual for First Ladies . . . Each carved out a role that reflected her own interests and style and that balanced the needs of her husband, family and country. So would I . . . I had to decide what I wanted to do with the opportunities and responsibilities I had inherited. Over the years, the role of the First Lady has been perceived as largely symbolic. She is expected to represent an ideal — and largely mythical — concept of American womanhood.

— Hillary Rodham Clinton[11]

Section II

Homes and Related Sites
of the First Ladies

Martha Dandridge Custis Washington

First Lady, 1789–1797

Born: June 2, 1731, New Kent County, Virginia
Died: May 22, 1802, Mount Vernon, Virginia

> *My heart is made up, my heart is in the cause;*
> *George is right; the general is always right.*

— Martha Washington[12]

Martha Dandridge, one of eight children in a well-to-do Virginia plantation family, received education and social training commensurate with the then-prevailing customs as regards females. Her mother instilled strong religious belief coupled with insistence on proper deportment and social training. Thus, Martha did what well-to-do girls did — studied with a tutor, learned to embroider and play the spinet and ordered her wardrobe from England. She was up at dawn to study her letters and rules on manners and to take lessons on plantation crafts and management. Martha learned how to dance, manage servants, entertain and feed guests and how to decorate with flowers and scents. In other words, she was prepared for an acceptable marriage.

At eighteen she married Daniel Parke Custis, a wealthy planter twenty years her senior. He passed away seven years later, leaving Martha with two young children, thousands of acres of prime tobacco land, fine houses (her main residence, ironically, was called White House), almost three hundred slaves, household silver and considerable pounds sterling.

Without question the most desirable widow in Virginia, she met George Washington in 1758, he already a military hero and soon-to-be member of the Virginia Assembly. There must have been an immediate attraction for he called on her formally only once before proposing marriage which took place at her home on January 6, 1759. While modern sensibilities may question the brevity of the courtship, it was not unusual in the eighteenth century as men and women married when young and often were widowed at an early age. There has been controversy as to whether George and Martha loved one another or if the marriage was merely one of convenience, but as the Washington marriage lasted over forty years, it is fair to believe that love grew when nurtured with fidelity, understanding, mutual dependence, consideration, respect and affection.

Martha once described herself as an "old-fashioned Virginia housekeeper, steady as a clock, busy as a bee, cheerful as a cricket."[13] She was neat as a pin, a bit over five feet tall, with a stubborn streak and strong will that stood her in good stead in the difficult years ahead — years of personal loss and grief, long separations from her husband and, later, attention, adulation and civic responsibilities far beyond her wildest dreams.

Martha needed that strength as life in the eighteenth century was rarely easy. Many diseases were incurable, with life expectancy only into the forties. Infant mortality was particularly high and anesthesia for medical or dental surgery was unknown. While Martha's general health was excellent, she nursed husband George through several near-death ailments and lost close friends and beloved family members at early ages. Martha herself lost two children as toddlers, teen-aged daughter Patsy died of epilepsy and son Jacky passed away of camp fever before he was thirty. When she visited her husband during the Revolutionary War, Martha witnessed the ravages of disease and hardship amongst the troops, yet never hesitated to join General Washington wherever he might be. It was difficult to be away from Mount Vernon, but the loneliness was eased by the knowledge that her presence was important to her husband and his troops.

In 1775, George Washington traveled from Mount Vernon to Philadelphia to attend the Second Continental Congress where he was appointed Commander-in-Chief of the nascent Continental Army, then a disorganized band of militiamen and others who had surrounded a British army in Boston. Washington immediately left for the north, but not before the normally staid General wrote Martha a letter in which he expressed affection and concern for her welfare:

I should enjoy more real happiness and felicity in one month with you, at home, than I have the most distant prospect of reaping abroad, if my stay were to be Seven times Seven years . . . My unhappiness will flow, from the uneasiness I know you will feel at being left alone — I therefore beg that you will summon your whole fortitude, and pass your time as agreeably as possible — nothing will give me so much sincere satisfaction as to hear this, and to hear it from your own Pen.[14]

The General asked other family members to look after Martha in his absence, but as the first year of the war dragged on, rumors and fears that the British might kidnap Martha as a valuable hostage were rampant. Taking no chances, Washington sent word for her to join him at his headquarters in Cambridge, Massachusetts. She set off on a month-long trip through sometimes unfriendly and dangerous territory. The journey north was a new and sometimes uncomfortable experience for a woman who had never been out of Virginia, but whose native grace and solid social background helped overcome the difficulty of the journey. Cambridge would be the first of seven such trips.

Martha and the family reacted with unrestrained joy when the war ended and the General returned home on Christmas Eve, 1783. They enjoyed Christmas dinner together for the first time in many years, and Martha prayed that it would be the beginning of the retirement she and the General had dreamt of for so long.

The conclusion of the war had been bittersweet. In 1781, her son Jacky, only twenty-seven, died of camp fever immediately after the British surrender at Yorktown. George and Martha, who were childless, arranged for the custody of two of Jacky's children, ages two and four. Daughter-in-law Eleanor, widowed at twenty-three, had older children as well, and was in no condition, physically or emotionally, to care for them. The children were not legally adopted, but the Washingtons had supervised the rearing of Nelly and young "Wash" at Mount Vernon since their births.

The next few years rolled by peacefully. Martha performed her plantation duties and reveled in the instruction and care of the grandchildren, thus she was unprepared for George's call to the presidency. Almost fifty-eight, she was not eager to uproot her life again although it was clear that, despite her protestations, she recognized her duty to serve at her husband's side.

She did not attend George's inauguration but arrived in New York a month after the event. The Governor of New York welcomed Martha and led a great parade in her honor to the Executive Mansion at 3 Cherry Street. No First Lady has ever experienced such an outpouring of love and honor.

George Washington once referred to his presidency: "I walk on untrodden ground. There is scarcely any part of my conduct which may not hereafter be drawn into precedent."[15] So it was with Martha, who found it difficult to be on constant display, with little time for old friends and personal affairs. For eight years she lived in New York and Philadelphia, dutifully exercising responsibilities with regard to social calls, entertainment and management of the President's House. All the while, she cared for her grandchildren and in two dramatic instances, nursed the President through almost-fatal illnesses.

While she appreciated the approbation that came to George, Martha was more circumspect about her own station. In a letter to a friend, she wrote:

> *With respect to myself, I sometimes think the arrangement is not quite as it ought to have been, that I, who had much rather be at home, should occupy a place with which a great many younger and gayer women would be prodigiously pleased. — As my grandchildren and domestic connections made a great portion of the felicity which I looked for in this world — I shall hardly be able to find any substitute that would indemnify me for the Loss of a part of such endearing society. I do not say this because I feel dissatisfied with my present station — no, God forbid: for everybody and everything conspire to make me as contented as possible in it; yet I have too much of the vanity of human affairs to expect felicity from the splendid scenes of public life. I am still determined to be cheerful and to be happy in whatever situation I may be, for I have also learnt from experience that the greater part of our happiness or misery depends on our dispositions, and not upon our circumstances; we carry the seeds of the one, or the other about with us, in our minds, wherever we go.*[16]

Martha Washington, with her strong religious belief, solid training in the social graces and an innate belief in marital fidelity and personal propriety, set an example of dedication, duty and responsibility through eight years of war and eight years of her husband's presidency that has served as an inspiration to the First Ladies who have followed her shining example.

Mount Vernon

MOUNT VERNON, VIRGINIA

I cannot tell you, my dear friend, how much I enjoy home after being deprived of one so long, for our dwelling in New York and Philadelphia was not home, only a sojourning. The General and I feel like children just released from school or from a hard Taskmaster and we believe that nothing can tempt us to leave the sacred roof-tree again.

— Martha Washington, letter to Mrs. Henry Knox[17]

George Washington and Martha Custis were married at White House Plantation, her home on the Pamunkey River north of Williamsburg, Virginia, on January 6, 1759. Honeymoon trips were uncommon in the eighteenth century, so the newlyweds stayed at White House before traveling to Williamsburg where George, a new member of the Virginia House of Burgesses, attended a session of the Virginia Assembly.

Afterward, the Washingtons, accompanied by her two children, a number of slaves, and laden with a wagon train of personal goods and furniture, made their way to Mount Vernon (Figure 2, Plate I). The house at Mount Vernon, once a modest dwelling of 1½ stories with a central hall and four small rooms on the first floor, had been a typical Virginia plantation home — small, practical and perfectly comfortable for a bachelor farmer, but inadequate for a family. Before Martha and her children arrived, Washington had the house raised to 2½ stories and extensively redecorated.

The Mount Vernon plantation was a major agricultural enterprise with thousands of acres under cultivation requiring constant attention and hard work. There were overseers and slaves to feed, clothe and tend. There were cattle and hogs to raise for milk and food, and fish to catch and salt. There were horses to breed and wagons and carriages to maintain. There was grain to mill and wells to dig. There were taxes to pay and accounts to keep. To be profitable, the plantation had to be self-sustaining on a large scale.

Martha's responsibilities were in the realm of household management that included supervision of the slaves who worked in the smokehouse, wash house, spinning house, kitchen and manor house. A large staff was required to cook and serve meals, to manufacture, launder and clean clothing

Figure 2. Mount Vernon, Mount Vernon, Virginia. Mount Vernon, overlooking the Potomac River, was the plantation home of George and Martha Washington. Photograph courtesy Mount Vernon Ladies' Association.

and serve as nannies for the children. As such, attention to their training and daily work efforts, as well as consideration of their health and well-being, were extremely important facets of Martha's duties. She was also called upon to be a gracious hostess and helpmeet for her husband; her background and training proved invaluable as she supervised the transformation of Mount Vernon from bachelor estate into a family home.

The Washingtons' elegant residence, situated on a bluff overlooking the majestic Potomac River, fell into a state of deterioration by the mid-nineteenth century, but since has been restored to its earlier glory by the Mount Vernon Ladies' Association which has owned and operated the estate since 1860 and brilliantly preserved the lifestyle, heritage and glory of George and Martha Washington. From the color of paint on the walls to the actual arrangement of furniture, the interior has been replicated to appear as it did during George and Martha's last years. Fourteen rooms are open to visitors, each filled with original Washington-era pieces — furniture, paintings, silver, porcelain and bric-a-brac — and each vibrant with rich window hangings, decorated ceilings, carved mantels and polished woodwork. Bright green and vivid blue walls, handsome wood grains and dimity and satin window hangings reflect the ambience of that historic time and the taste and influence of the house's master and mistress.

The outbuildings where Martha supervised the daily work of the household have been preserved, and a four-acre exhibition area serves to demonstrate George Washington's pioneering farming efforts, including a reproduction of a unique sixteen-sided wheat-threshing barn he designed. Mount Vernon, an excellent example of colonial architecture with indications of other influences in Palladian windows and originality of the wide front portico as it evolved over a 100-year period, is white, simple, uncluttered and relaxed. It is America's most popular historic home, recognized as one of our nation's greatest treasures, an evocation of eighteenth-century plantation life and the retreat, haven, home and final resting place of the country's guiding spirit, George Washington, and the woman who stood by his side for over four decades.

In 2006, Mount Vernon dedicated two new buildings — the Ford Orientation Center and the Donald W. Reynolds Museum and Education Center — both of which concentrate on George Washington as a dynamic, fascinating hero rather than the popular-elder-statesman icon, illuminating his early years and his military and political careers which cannot be covered in depth by a tour of the estate which focuses on life at Mount Vernon. When visitors enter the grounds, they pass through the Orientation Center to be greeted by life-sized bronze sculptures of the Washingtons and two of their grandchildren, and are then treated to a dramatic 18-minute mini-epic film featuring pivotal moments of Washington's life. Another popular attraction is *Mount Vernon in Miniature*, an authentic, one-twelfth-scale replica of the mansion which prepares visitors for what will be experienced in the actual home.

The Museum and Education Center features 25 gallery and theater experiences — many of them with interactive technology — that illuminate the Washingtons' life story. Over 700 objects offer an intimate glimpse of some of their personal possessions — clothing, military equipment, silver, porcelain, china services and other artifacts. Many items, such as clothing worn by the Washingtons and a chair cushion (one of twelve) worked in cross-stitch by Martha over a period of thirty-six years, are examples of those displayed in rotation to protect them from damage by light and other environmental conditions. Miniature portraits of George and Martha and her children, Patsy and Jacky, form an important part of the Mount Vernon art collection, and complement the larger portraits on display in the manor house.

When Washington died in 1799, Congress voted to prepare a special crypt in the Capitol building in Washington, DC, although his body was interred at Mount Vernon pending preparation of the crypt. Martha passed away in 1802, laid to rest next to her husband. At that time, remaining family members decided against moving the bodies to the capital, a proper decision. Mount Vernon is, after all, the place where George and Martha Washington belong. Together.

DIRECTIONS: By car: Mount Vernon is at the south end of the George Washington Memorial Parkway, 8 miles south of Alexandria, Virginia, and 16 miles from downtown Washington, DC (Figure 3). **By rail or bus:** For schedules from Washington, DC, contact *Metro Bus and Rail* in Washington, (202) 637-7000 or visit *http://www.wmata.com/default.cfm. Gray Line Bus Tours*, (202) 289-1995 or *Tourmobile Sightseeing Tours,* (202) 554-5100 also serve the Washington and Mount Vernon area. **By boat:** The motor vessel *Spirit of Mount Vernon* sails from Washington, DC, between mid-March and late October. Call (866) 211-3811 or log on to *www.spiritofwashington.com*

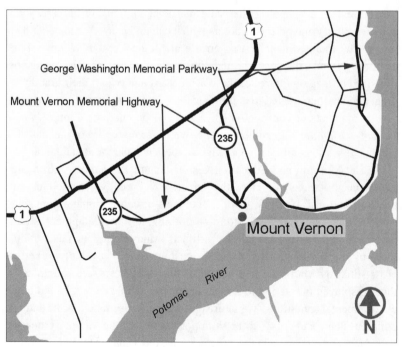

Figure 3. Location of Mount Vernon, Mount Vernon, Virginia.

for schedules and prices. *Miss Christin* sails from Alexandria from early April through late October. Call (703) 684-0580 or log on to *www.potomacriverboatco.com* for schedules and prices. Fares for both ships include admission to Mount Vernon.

PUBLIC USE: Season and hours: Mount Vernon is open seven days a week, every day of the year, including holidays: April-August, 8 AM-5 PM. March, September, October, 9 AM-5 PM. November-February, 9 AM-4 PM. **Admission fee:** Yes, with discounts for groups, seniors and students. **Food service:** Food and drinks are not allowed on the grounds, but a full-service food court and more formal restaurant are located in the Mount Vernon Inn complex just outside the main gate. **Gift shops.** *The Shops at Mount Vernon* are also in the complex. **For people with disabilities:** A limited number of wheelchairs are available on a first-come, first-served basis. The first floor of the mansion, the Ford Orientation Center, the Donald W. Reynolds Museum and Education Center and many of the outbuildings are accessible. Material for the hearing impaired is available.

FOR ADDITIONAL INFORMATION: Contact: Mount Vernon Ladies' Association, Box 110, Mount Vernon, Virginia 22121, (703) 780-2000. **Web site:** *www.mountvernon.org*. **Read:** (1) Charles Cecil Law, *et al.* 2001. *Mount Vernon: A Handbook*. (2) Helen Bryan. 2002. *Martha Washington: First Lady of Liberty*. (3) Patricia Brady. 2005. *Martha Washington: An American Life*.

Abigail Smith Adams

First Lady, 1797–1801

Born: November 11, 1744, Weymouth, Massachusetts
Died: October 28, 1818, Quincy, Massachusetts

> *In the new code of laws, which I suppose it will be necessary*
> *for you to make, I desire you would remember the ladies and be*
> *more generous and favorable to them than your ancestors.*

— Abigail Adams, letter to John Adams, March 31, 1776[18]

Abigail Adams, wife of one president and mother of another, was a most remarkable woman. At a time when many females did not attend school, she was tutored at home by her parents and other family members and became a highly intelligent observer, literate commentator, prolific correspondent and superb chronicler of American political history. Thousands of letters to friends, political figures, family members and especially to her husband are one of the great repositories of historical knowledge regarding the Revolutionary era and birth of the new republic. She spoke out passionately for women's rights long before suffrage became a reality in 1920.

Abigail married attorney John Adams when she was not quite twenty. The newlyweds set up housekeeping in a small saltbox farmhouse next door to the house, then occupied by John's widowed mother, where he had been born in Braintree (now Quincy), Massachusetts. John transformed a downstairs room into a law office while he continued to work the farm. The relationship of John and Abigail was both physically and intellectually passionate. John appreciated her intelligence and depended on her political and emotional advice throughout their marriage.

Except for a short period of residency in Boston and several years in Paris and London on diplomatic assignments, the Braintree house was the Adams' primary residence for over twenty years. While John was in Europe or in Philadelphia in the service of the fledgling nation, Abigail remained in Braintree with child care and farm management left entirely in her hands. Separations covered almost half of their fifty-four-year marriage.

Life in the eighteenth century was difficult and problems faced by the Adams family were not unusual. One daughter was stillborn, the result of Abigail's toxemia. Disease was rampant and often fatal. The entire family underwent painful smallpox inoculations, and Abigail experienced anxiety and deep emotional strain when sons John Quincy and Thomas traveled to Europe with their father. She experienced agonizing periods of fever and illness. Son Charles died of alcoholism and daughter Abigail ("Nabby") entered into a difficult marriage, then fell victim to breast cancer. Yet Abigail persevered — her love for John and belief in his work and the cause of liberty never wavered. The realization that his diplomatic and intellectual role was essential to the cause of independence and the formation of a new nation sustained her through periods of difficult physical, emotional and financial stress. Their voluminous correspondence is a valuable historic record, a testament to an unusual eighteenth-century husband/wife partnership based on love and mutual respect.

Abigail Adams Birthplace

WEYMOUTH, MASSACHUSETTS

Abigail Smith was born and reared in a manse built in 1685 for the pastor of the First Church of Weymouth, who was succeeded by Abigail's father, Reverend William Smith, in 1738. Abigail was the second of four children in a family known for its progressive outlook, especially regarding educational rights for females. Abigail was tutored at home by her parents, relatives, friends and, most notably, by her grandmother Quincy who became an especially positive influence on the eager young scholar.

The Weymouth house (Figure 4), scheduled for demolition in the late 1940s, was saved by the Abigail Adams Historical Society which moved the run-down structure to a town-donated plot at the intersection of North and Norton streets and initiated a daunting reconstruction effort. The house was

Figure 4. Abigail Adams Birthplace, Weymouth, Massachusetts. Photograph courtesy Abigail Adams Historical Society.

stripped to its frame, a central chimney with four fireplaces and a beehive oven in the kitchen were rebuilt, paneling in the front rooms was redone using panels from an old Braintree home and the kitchen beams and wall panels were resurrected from a tavern in Hingham, Massachusetts. Of particular interest is the bedroom, furnished with a rope-strung bedstead and baskets for bonnets as it might have been when occupied by Abigail and her sisters. Other furnishings and artifacts date to the period of the Smith residency and serve to illustrate what home life was like in the mid-eighteenth century.

DIRECTIONS: Weymouth is a suburb south of Boston. **By car from Boston:** Take Route 3A southbound and turn right on North Street in Weymouth. The Abigail Adams Birthplace (Figure 5) is on the right side of the street at the intersection with Norton Street. **By MBTA from Boston :** Take the Red Line to Quincy Center and transfer to the bus (Route 222) to Weymouth and depart at the corner of North and Norton streets. The Abigail Adams Birthplace is on the corner of North and Norton streets next to the cemetery.

PUBLIC USE: Season and hours: The Abigail Adams Birthplace is open by appointment only. Call (781) 335-4205 for reservations. **Admission fee. For people with disabilities:** The first floor is accessible.

FOR ADDITIONAL INFORMATION: Contact: Abigail Adams Historical Society, Box 147, Weymouth, Massachusetts 02191-0002, (781) 335-4205. **Web site:** *www.abigailadamsbirthplace.org.* **Read:** (1) Natalie S. Bober. 1995. *Abigail Adams, Witness to a Revolution.* (2) Phyllis Lee Levin. 1987. *Abigail Adams.*

Adams National Historical Park

QUINCY, MASSACHUSETTS

Following their wedding in October, 1764, John Adams brought Abigail to a "saltbox" farmhouse in Braintree (renamed Quincy in 1792) next door to the similar house in which he had been born, a building typical of New England homes of the late seventeenth century — a house framed with huge beams secured with wooden pegs, floored with wide planks, and covered with clapboard siding over brick-filled walls to ward off the rigors of New England winters (Figure 6A). The houses were utilitarian and comfortable with multiple fireplaces built around a central chimney. John and Abigail's house consisted of two upper and two lower rooms, one of which became John's law office and noted as the place where John and others framed the Massachusetts State Constitution, the primary model for the Constitution of the United States.

When John was called to Philadelphia in 1774 to attend the first Continental Congress, Abigail remained in Braintree to supervise the farm and begin her life-long correspondence with John and others, writings treasured as the most perceptive home-front observations made during the War for Independence and which included her incisive and intelligent comments on early American political thinking.

Life was not all correspondence and farming, however. Abigail and young son John Quincy witnessed the Battle of Bunker Hill from nearby Penn's Hill and, later, at General Washington's invitation, she visited his headquarters in Cambridge. In 1776, she traveled to Boston to witness a reading of the Declaration of Independence.

The years in Braintree dragged on as John was absent many times attending to political responsibilities in Philadelphia and Europe, and it was not until 1784 that Abigail and daughter Nabby joined John and son John Quincy in France, then on to England. While there, the couple finalized the purchase of a farm back in America, only 1½ miles from their home in Braintree. In 1787, they returned to America to the farmhouse they called "Peace field" (Figure 6B, Plate II) in honor of the Paris Peace Treaty that John helped negotiate.

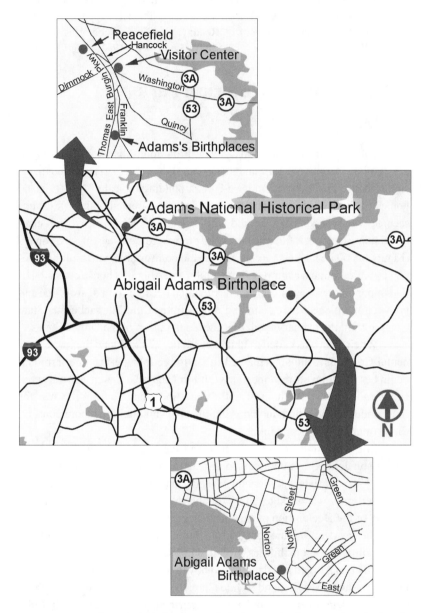

Figure 5. Location of Abigail Adams Birthplace and Adams National Historic Park in Weymouth and Quincy, Massachusetts.

Figure 6. (A) The saltbox house in Braintree is where John Adams was born, making this one of the oldest extant birth structures of an American president. A similar, adjoining house is the one that John and Abigail moved into after they were married. **(B)** Peacefield, the larger farm home that the Adamses purchased while he was on diplomatic assignment in Europe. Photographs courtesy National Park Service, Adams National Historical Park.

The Adamses began to furnish the house with furniture brought to America from John's overseas missions and many of those items remain, but almost before they could unpack, John was called to New York City as George Washington's Vice President and it was another twelve years before he retired to Massachusetts permanently. During those years of absence, Abigail for the most part remained in Braintree where she supervised major improvements to "Peace field" that included the addition of an east wing. Other additions, including use of the nickname "Old House," were made by Adams descendants, and by 1927 the original house had expanded into a twenty-one-room mansion.

At the end of the Adams presidency, John and Abigail were, at long last, able to enjoy their garden, books, children and grandchildren. "I long for rural and domestic scenes," he noted, "for the warbling of birds and the prattle of my grandchildren."[19] Abigail wrote to a friend, "All my desire and ambition is to be esteemed and loved by my partner, to join with him in the education and instruction of our little ones, to sit under our own vines in peace, liberty, and safety."[20]

Much has changed at "Peace field" over the last two hundred years, but the garden's fragrance and beauty offers a link to the splendor and serenity of an earlier day. A white York rose brought from England by Abigail still thrives, and a walk on the gravel path through the orchard and colorful blooms engenders a renewed sense of the history, tradition and quietude of Peacefield, the commonly accepted modern version of the house's name.

Visitors to Peacefield are often moved by the President and First Lady's bedroom where Abigail passed away in 1818. John's adjacent study includes the desk upon which he wrote peace treaties and where he corresponded with his friend Thomas Jefferson. And it is the room where he passed away on July 4, 1826, the fiftieth anniversary of the adoption of the Declaration of Independence. It was, remarkably, the same day that Jefferson died at Monticello.

The United First Parish Church is located near the National Park Service visitor center. In 1822, John Adams donated the interest from certain lands he owned, and provided granite from his quarries, to build a new church building that was dedicated in 1828, with then-President John Quincy Adams in attendance. The bodies of John and Abigail Adams were transferred to crypts in the new church and the bodies of John Quincy Adams and his wife Louisa joined them in repose; he in 1848, she in 1852.

A handsome bronze statue of Abigail Adams with her hand on the shoulder of son John Quincy as they stood watching the Battle of Bunker Hill, stands beside the church. A stone cairn on nearby Penn's Hill marks the actual spot from which they viewed the battle.

DIRECTIONS: By car from Boston: Take I 93 (Southeast Expressway) southbound to Exit 7 (SR 3 southbound, a left lane exit). The first exit will be Exit 19 (Washington Street/Quincy Adams T/Quincy Center) that flows into Burgin Parkway. Proceed straight on Burgin Parkway and turn right at the seventh light onto Dimmock Street. Turn right at the next intersection, Hancock Street. The Adams National Historical Park Visitor Center is on the left in the Galleria at Presidents Place (Figure 5). **Northbound from Cape Cod:** On Route 3, take Exit 19 (Quincy Center/Quincy Adams T) which merges with southbound traffic from Boston, then follow the above directions. **By MBTA from Boston:** Take the Red Line train outbound to the Quincy Center Station. Depart the station via the Hancock Street exit. Cross Hancock Street to reach the visitor center.

PUBLIC USE: Season and hours: The park is open daily April 19-November 10, 9 AM-5 PM. Visitors must join guided tours, conducted on a first-come, first-served basis, starting at the visitor center and lasting 2 hours. The last tour begins at 3:15 PM. November 11-April 18 the historic homes are closed but the visitor center is open Tuesday-Friday, 12 M-4:30 PM. **Admission fee:** Yes. Youth under 17, free. Admission includes entry to all three houses. **Book store. For people with disabilities:** The lower floors of Peacefield are accessible with a picture book available to help interpret the second floor. There are two-step entries to the Franklin Street houses. The National Park Service provides free trolley service between the visitor center, Peacefield and the Franklin Street homes.

FOR ADDITIONAL INFORMATION: Contact: National Park Service Headquarters and Administrative Offices, Adams National Historical Park, 135 Adams Street, Quincy, Massachusetts 02169, (617) 773-1177 (or) Adams National Historical Park Visitor Center, 1250 Hancock Street, Quincy, Massachusetts 02169, (617) 770-1175. **Web site:** *www.nps.gov/adam*. **Read:** (1) Paul C. Nagel. 1983. *Descent from Glory: Four Generations of the John Adams Family.* (2) David McCullough. 2001. *John Adams.*

Martha Wayles Skelton Jefferson

Born: October 19, 1748, Charles City County, Virginia
Died: September 6, 1782, Charlottesville, Virginia

Martha Wayles Skelton, a twenty-three-year-old widow, married Thomas Jefferson at her ancestral home, The Forest, in Charles City County, Virginia, on New Year's Day, 1772. Described as a beautiful woman "with a lithe and exquisitely formed figure, with a graceful and queenly carriage,"[21] Martha was well-educated, with a superior mind and an inherited capacity for business. She was also an accomplished musician with a lovely singing voice. A possibly apocryphal story about her courtship with Thomas Jefferson tells of two suitors calling on the desirable widow, but when they heard her singing and playing the harpsichord, accompanied by rival Jefferson playing the violin, they shrugged, turned around and left, realizing the romantic game was up.

For the first few months of their marriage, the South Pavilion, the first building constructed at Monticello, was their home. The Monticello mansion itself, half as large as today's structure, was in a constant state of construction turmoil but Martha managed the domestic household, kept the account books and, in ten years of marriage, bore six children, three of whom survived infancy. Never robust, her health began to deteriorate following the last pregnancy and it became clear that her physical condition was terminal. Thomas remained at her bedside for four months and when she succumbed, was so overcome with grief that he kept to his bedroom for almost a month.

Tradition holds that Jefferson made a deathbed promise to never remarry, a controversial request during those days of sometimes early widowhood and remarriage. There has been speculation that Martha, who had a troubled emotional childhood — her own mother passed away a few months after her birth, and she had two stepmothers by the time she was thirteen — might have caused concerns about her own children's upbringing by another woman.

Regretfully, Jefferson, devastated by the death of "the cherished companion of my life," destroyed all of their correspondence. In his autobiography, he described the marriage as a period of "unchequered happiness"[22] but rarely referred to it for the rest of his life. Sadly, not a single portrait of Martha has survived, and Monticello displays precious few artifacts associated with her — a few pieces of silver from her first marriage, a daily journal and a music book.

It is clear from what little is known that Martha Jefferson, had she lived, would have been an outstanding First Lady — gracious, charming, well-read and beautiful. During his eight years in the White House, Jefferson often called on Dolley Madison, wife of the Secretary of State, to act as his hostess. His daughters Maria and Martha, married to Congressmen John Wayles Eppes and Thomas Mann Randolph, respectively, also served as White House hostesses for their father on occasion.

Dolley Payne Todd Madison

First Lady, 1808–1817

Born: May 20, 1768, Guilford County, North Carolina
Died: July 12, 1849, Washington, DC

It may have been an error on the part of the county clerk, but the name on her birth certificate was **Dolley**, not "Dolly" nor "Dorothea." The unusual spelling is but one misconception about Dolley; for example, some considered her a decorative, flighty "hostess with the mostest." In fact, she was a warm, intelligent, perceptive woman with a natural flair for decorating and entertaining, and she and husband James Madison had a deep and lasting relationship based on love and affection. It can be truly said that they lived for one another.

Shortly after Dolley's birth, her family moved to Hanover County, Virginia, where — although undocumented — they may have lived in the home of her mother's cousin, Patrick Henry, for a short period while their own farmhouse was under construction. The Paynes were Quakers who adhered to certain moral restrictions. No dancing or other worldly diversions were allowed to take young minds off the rule of the Spirit. No music was allowed at home or in the nearby Meeting House. The women wore drab, full dresses with white collars and high necks. Colored ribbons and jewelry were forbidden. Although those restrictions were surely frustrating to a lively young woman, Dolley did not rebel either morally or spiritually.

In 1783, in protest over the issue of slavery, her father moved the family from Virginia north to Philadelphia where he began a starch business. The transition from the relative isolation of farm life to the crowded and bustling city of Philadelphia must have been a culture shock and, when the starch business failed, Dolley's father, burdened with guilt, withdrew to his room and began a lifetime of bitterness. Dolley's mother was forced to take in boarders to keep the family solvent.

At twenty-one, Dolley married fellow Quaker John Todd and soon gave birth to two children, but a severe yellow fever epidemic in 1793 took the lives of her husband and baby, leaving Dolley a twenty-five-year-old widow with a two-year-old son. Young and attractive, she had many desirable suitors, but chose forty-three-year-old bachelor politician James Madison whom she married in September, 1794. Gossips remarked that she had married solely for convenience and security, and it is true that the Madisons were an unlikely combination. Although marriages of convenience were not uncommon in those days of early widowhood, history has proved the Madison marriage to be a true love match. As in the case of George and Martha Washington, perhaps love developed and blossomed with time and nurturing.

Dolley Todd Madison was "read out of meeting" by the Quakers for marrying an Episcopalian, yet Dolley, in spite of her restrictive upbringing, so loved people, entertaining, decorating — and her husband — that she had no qualms about casting aside the social restrictions of her faith. Her natural, outgoing personality endeared her to James' elderly parents, for example, and she adored the bucolic life at the family home at Montpelier Plantation.

When husband James was Secretary of State during the administration of Thomas Jefferson, Dolley assumed many of the functions of White House hostess. President Jefferson and Vice President Aaron Burr were both widowed, and Jefferson's daughters remained, for the most part, back home in Virginia. Thus Dolley, as wife of the highest-ranking member of the presidential cabinet, became more and more responsible for decorating the White House and often took care of the ladies at social functions. When her husband became president in 1809, she assumed an even more active role, all the while setting high standards for entertaining, her aim being to assure that the administrations of both Thomas Jefferson and husband James be politically successful and socially brilliant. James in the office and Dolley in the drawing room was a formidable combination. Her sixteen years as White House hostess was not only an incredible span of years, but set a standard of behavior, social nicety and glamour that was not equaled, perhaps, until the tenure of First Lady Jacqueline Kennedy.

Dolley Madison proved to be an astute politician as well as social arbiter. She had a photographic memory for names and personal information and visited Capitol Hill frequently to pass the time of day. Her conversations and actions with politicians prompted presidential historian and later Secretary of State James C. Blaine to remark that "she saved the administration of her husband, holding him back from the extremes of Jeffersonianism."[23]

During the Madison presidential years, writer Washington Irving was a guest at one of Dolley's levees, after which he described her as "a fine portly, buxom dame who has a smile and pleasant word for everybody."[24] Whatever her influence, Dolley Madison shall forever be remembered as one of our most dynamic First Ladies — her wit, charm, political acumen and caring nature set a standard rarely accomplished.

Dolley's most dramatic contribution as First Lady was in August, 1814, during the War of 1812. British invaders nearing the capital forced President Madison and Dolley to evacuate the White House. The President left to join the defenders of the capital while Dolley remained behind to pack important papers. The most famous story is of Dolley saving the Gilbert Stuart portrait of George Washington that hung in the East Room. She removed it from its frame and packed it on a fleeing wagon as the British approached and guns boomed nearby. When the British arrived, they dined in "Mrs. Madison's dining room" before torching many buildings, including the President's House. But one of America's most prized possessions, the Washington portrait, had been saved, due to the foresight and courage of First Lady Dolley Madison.

James Madison left the presidency in 1817 and the couple retired to Montpelier, the Madison ancestral estate near Orange, Virginia. James and Dolley would not visit Washington again during his lifetime. Until his death, he spent his time as a visionary farmer and political correspondent. His health, never robust, was of great concern to Dolley, who nursed James through occasional periods of rheumatism and other ailments. They continued to enjoy lavish entertaining, however, and worked together to edit Madison's voluminous papers which were later sold to the federal government.

The great negative burden of Dolley's life was her son, Payne. Accepted by James Madison as his own, he was, nonetheless, indulged by his mother and turned out to be a profligate and wastrel. His constant gambling and other debts were paid by the Madisons, but to no avail. Payne was never able to find permanent employment.

After the President's death in 1836, Dolley was forced to sell Montpelier for financial reasons and move to a small house on Lafayette Square in Washington where she remained highly popular. As the capital's social doyenne, Dolley Madison was entertained at the White House and elsewhere and continued to receive dignitaries and other callers until death called in 1849. For almost fifty years, Dolley Madison had been America's "First Lady."

Greensboro Historical Museum

GREENSBORO, NORTH CAROLINA

The Greensboro Historical Museum (Figure 7), whose focus is on the history of Guilford County, North Carolina, offers special exhibits devoted to Dolley Payne Todd Madison who was born near present-day Guilford College in Greensboro. Her birth cabin was torn down in the mid-nineteenth century but some of the logs were saved because of Dolley's fame. Using some of those logs, the historic Isley House, a structure with architectural

Figure 7. Greensboro Historical Museum, Greensboro, North Carolina. Photograph courtesy Greensboro Historical Museum.

characteristics similar to the original Payne cabin, was restored on the grounds of the Greensboro museum. The house will be opened to the public in 2011 for guided tours that will allow visitors to see furnishings typical of those found in Piedmont North Carolina in the early part of the nineteenth century.

The Dolley Madison display area in the museum features reproductions of two of Dolley's fabulous dresses (the originals are too fragile for display) plus signature headdresses. The section also contains one of the most complete collections of Dolley's belongings, purchased at auction from a private collector nearly forty years ago by a group of Greensboro citizens interested in honoring and further expanding our knowledge of one of Greensboro's favorite daughters.

The collection includes such items as an 1850 portrait of Dolley by John Vanderlyn and an 1848 daguerrotype of her. Dolley's calling card case, silk slippers, snuff box and handwriting samples are included in this very special display.

DIRECTIONS: From I 85 (Exit 122) or I 40 (Exit 218), take Freeman Mill Road into downtown Greensboro where, just past McGee Street, the name changes to Edgewood Street. Continue on Edgeworth to West Market Street, turn right onto West Market, then left onto Davie Street which deadends at Summit Street. The museum is on the right just past the Greensboro Cultural Center (Figure 8).

PUBLIC USE: Season and hours: Tuesday-Saturday, 10 AM-5 PM; Sunday, 2 PM-5 PM. Closed national and City of Greensboro holidays. **For people with disabilities:** Accessible.

FOR ADDITIONAL INFORMATION: Contact: Greensboro Historical Museum, 130 Summit Avenue, Greensboro, North Carolina 27401, (336) 373-2043. **Web site:** *www.greensborohistory.org.* **Read:** Holly C. Shulman and David B. Mattern, eds. 2003. *The Selected Letters of Dolley Payne Madison.*

Todd House

PHILADELPHIA, PENNSYLVANIA

In the 1780s, Philadelphia, the largest and most important city in the loose confederation of states, was a hotbed of political activity and social history. Young Quaker Dolley Payne was undoubtedly dazzled when her family moved from the country to a city with brick houses, paved roads,

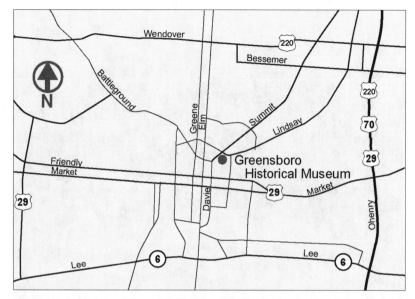

Figure 8. Location of Greensboro Historical Museum in Greensboro, North Carolina.

street lamps, busy ships and docks, a hospital, volunteer fire department and, in particular, the stuff of history — the Betsy Ross House, City Tavern and Independence Hall where the Continental Congress debated and wrote the Constitution of the United States. The Robert Morris House on High Street was the home of President Washington, and young Dolley often saw him pass by in his colorful carriage.

The Payne family moved in with Quaker friends before they settled in their own house at 231 New Street where Dolley's father began a starch business. He had no head for business and the family soon felt the pinch of poverty, necessitating that part of the house be rented to boarders. At about the same time, Dolley, courted by Quaker attorney John Todd, stood with him at the Pine Street Meeting House where they pledged themselves as man and wife. The newlywed Todds set up housekeeping in a house on Chestnut Street and as John prospered, they purchased a handsome brick home at 4th and Walnut streets (Figure 9).

The Quaker Meeting House and the early Payne and Todd homes are gone, but the second Todd House, saved from demolition by the National

Figure 9. Todd House, Independence National Historical Park, Philadelphia, Pennsylvania. Photograph courtesy Independence National Historical Park.

Park Service, remains as part of Independence National Historical Park. The Todd House is a restoration that reflects the life style of eighteenth-century Philadelphia's middle-class. It is typical of the period, an end-of-row type with the front door on the side and a colorful garden in the rear. A complete inventory of its furnishings was discovered during the restoration, and the house contains period furnishings of the types that were likely used by the Todds, based on the inventory and further historical research.

John Todd died in the yellow fever epidemic of 1793 leaving Dolley as a desirable young widow with a small son. She caught the eye of confirmed bachelor-congressman James Madison, and it was in her parlor that she first met "the great little Madison,"[25] beginning one of the most productive and loving relationships in American political history.

DIRECTIONS: The Todd House is at the corner of Walnut Street and 4th Street within Independence National Historical Park. The Independence National Historical Park Visitor Center is located at 6th and Market streets (Figure 10).

PUBLIC USE: Season and hours: Independence Visitor Center; open year-round, 8:30 AM-5 PM. Most park buildings are open 9 AM-5 PM. Closed Christmas Day. **Admission fee:** Free, although tours of the Todd House require tickets that are available at the visitor center on a first-come, first-served basis. **For people with disabilities:** Accessible.

FOR ADDITIONAL INFORMATION: Contact: Independence National Historical Park, 143 S. Third Street, Philadelphia, Pennsylvania 19106, (215) 965-2305. **Web site:** *www.nps.gov/inde/todd-house.htm*. **Read:** Noel B. Gerson. 1975. *The Velvet Glove: A Life of Dolly Madison.*

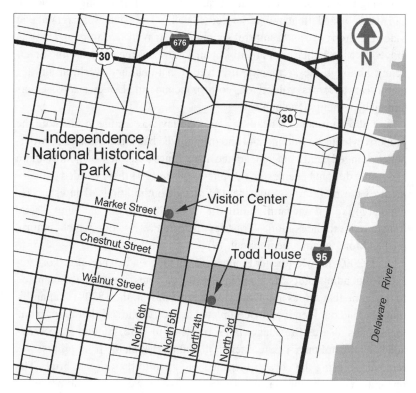

Figure 10. Location of Independence National Historical Park and the Todd House in Philadelphia, Pennsylvania.

Montpelier

MONTPELIER STATION, VIRGINIA

I wish you had just a country home as this.
It is the happiest and most independent life.

— Dolley Madison[26]

The Montpelier property was settled by the Madison family in 1723. The house itself (Figure 11) was built around 1760 by James Madison's father. James himself enlarged it twice — in 1797 and in the 1810s. James and Dolley Madison spent a great deal of time in Philadelphia and Washington, returning to Montpelier again and again throughout their long, productive and distinguished life in public service (Plate II). The estate was a retreat that Madison referred to as "a squirrel's jump from heaven."[27] James and Dolley moved to Montpelier permanently upon James' retirement from the presidency, although they remained involved in national and world affairs for many years as James' voluminous correspondence and Dolley's lavish entertaining kept them in the public eye.

Following James's death in 1836, Dolley was unable to maintain the property which she sold in 1844 and then moved back to Washington. Montpelier changed hands and appearance many times until then-owners William and Annie duPont began extensive alterations in 1901 that included enlargement of the main house and the addition of outbuildings. The estate remained in the duPont family until 1983 when Marion duPont Scott's heirs transferred it to the National Trust for Historic Preservation which, in turn, opened Montpelier to the public in 1987.

In 2003, the Montpelier Foundation, an independent non-profit organization that administers Montpelier, announced plans to restore the mansion to the home that James and Dolley Madison knew in the 1820s. That ambitious architectural renovation, completed in 2009, removed alterations made to the mansion after President Madison's death in 1836, including the wings added by the duPonts. Plaster facing, including that on the front pillars, was removed to bring the core of the mansion down to the original brick. The restoration reduced the mansion from fifty-five to twenty-two rooms.

The Foundation has currently (2010) turned its attention to refurnishing the mansion and recreating the interior décor as enjoyed by James and

Figure 11. Montpelier Mansion, Montpelier Station, Virginia. Photograph by Kenneth M. Wyner, use courtesy The Montpelier Foundation.

Dolley Madison. Unfortunately, Dolley had sold many original furnishings to pay the debts of her son, Payne. Thus, the Foundation has initiated a "Presidential Detective Story," searching courthouses, libraries, collections of papers and the internet, looking for diaries, letters, visitors' accounts, newspaper articles, estate inventories, tax lists, receipts, bills — anything that might provide a clue to the location of original Madison pieces. Some furniture has been discovered and moved back into the mansion which helps bring the era of James and Dolley Madison to life, offering visitors a unique first-hand encounter with America's heritage through the eyes of one of its most famous presidential couples.

Visits to Montpelier begin at a modern visitor center that features a short film presentation describing the restoration and architectural detective story that led to Montpelier's remarkable transformation, with the emphasis on the Madisons' life at Montpelier. There is a gallery, *Treasures of Montpelier,* featuring James Madison's miniature by Rembrandt Peale, his spyglass, a brace of pistols, Dolley's diamond engagement ring and a reproduction of her favorite red gown.

Many other features remain in place on the 2700-acre estate grounds: (1) the Madison family cemetery, the final resting place for James and Dolley; (2) the slave cemetery; (3) the James Madison Landmark Forest, a 200-acre old-growth forest that has been designated a National Natural Landmark and is the best surviving remnant of the original hardwood forests that once blanketed the Virginia Piedmont. The mature tulip poplars in the forest, known colloquially as the "Big Woods," are 250 years old and date to President Madison's lifetime. A series of interlocking trails, about two miles in length, open the natural treasure to visitors; (4) a formal garden. James and Dolley enjoyed a four-acre garden designed by a French gardener. In the early 1900s, Annie duPont designed a two-acre garden on the same site. Traces of the original Madison garden survive in the scheme of the paths and parterres; (5) a landscape arboretum. Madison corresponded with horticulturists throughout America and Europe and imported a number of exotic plants. Two large Cedars-of-Lebanon and a row of walnut trees date to the Madison residency.

At an exhibit opening at Montpelier in 1998, First Lady Hillary Rodham Clinton said:

> *We need to be educated and inspired time and time again by the American story written here by James and Dolley Madison . . . because it is only by understanding where we came from — looking squarely at our past, appreciating the sacrifices and difficulties others endured for us to be enjoying what we enjoy today — that we can hold dear those ideals and values that should be cherished, and pass them on to our own children and grandchildren.*[28]

DIRECTIONS: Montpelier Station is 4 miles south of Orange, Virginia, alongside Route 20. **From Charlottesville:** Take US Route 29 northbound to Ruckersville, turn right onto Route 33 eastbound. At Barboursville, take a left onto Route 20 towards Orange. The entrance to Montpelier is 8 miles farther on the right. **From Washington, DC:** Take I 66 westbound to Gainesville, then US routes 29/15 to Culpeper and US Route15 southbound to Orange, picking up Route 20 southbound. Go about 4 miles to Montpelier on the left (Figure 12).

PUBLIC USE: Season and hours: April-October, 9 AM-5 PM. November-March, 9 AM-4 PM. Closed Thanksgiving Day, Christmas Day. **Admission fee:** Yes, with discounts for groups, students and seniors. **Picnic area. Gift shop. For people with disabilities:** The second floor is not wheelchair-accessible.

FOR ADDITIONAL INFORMATION: Contact: James Madison's Montpelier, PO Box 911, Orange, Virginia 22960, (540) 672-2728. **Web site:** *www.montpelier.org*. **Read:** (1) Ralph Ketcham. 1990. *James Madison: A Biography*. (2) Jeannette Covert Nolan. 1958. *Dolley Madison*.

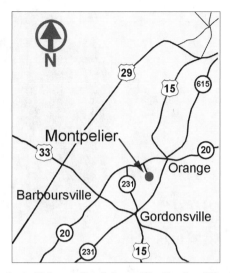

Figure 12. Location of Montpelier, Montpelier Station, Virginia.

Elizabeth Kortright Monroe

First Lady, 1817–1825

Born: June 30, 1768, New York, New York
Died: September 23, 1830, Aldie, Virginia

Harry Ammon, a biographer of James Monroe, described Monroe's wife Elizabeth as:

> *A remarkably beautiful woman, with a much-admired taste in dress and decoration. In public her formal manners left an impression of coldness and reserve, but in private she was a devoted wife and doting mother, possessing to the full the domestic virtues then so highly prized — a complete absorption in the affairs of her family and household and a total detachment from the world of politics and business. She was in many ways the image of the conventionally reared eighteenth-century woman . . .*[29]

Elizabeth Kortright, daughter of a New York City merchant with Tory leanings who lost his fortune in the Revolution, was seventeen when she married James Monroe, then a member of the Continental Congress meeting in Philadelphia. After Congress dissolved in 1786, the couple settled in Fredericksburg, Virginia, where they lived in a house owned by James's uncle, Judge Joseph Jones. James opened a law office, served on the City Council, and progressed to a distinguished career as a public servant, eventually holding more major offices than any other president — United States Senator; Minister to France (twice), England and Spain; Governor of Virginia;

Secretary of State; Secretary of War; and, of course, President of the United States. With each assignment there were new homes to find and furnish, new friends to make, and new responsibilities to accept. Adjustment was especially difficult when he was stationed in Europe, but the Monroes adapted brilliantly.

In 1795, during the French Revolution, Monroe was Minister to France when Madame de Lafayette, wife of the Marquis de Lafayette, America's favorite Frenchman, languished in Le Plessis Prison in Paris. Rumors swirled about that as a member of the nobility, she faced the guillotine. A daring and extremely dangerous plan to save her was hatched, its success dependent on the beauty, fame, reputation — and steel nerves — of the American Minister's wife. The lovely and petite (she was a mere 4 feet, 11 inches tall) Elizabeth Monroe, known to the French as "La Belle Americaine," and dressed in her best finery, rode up to the gate of Le Plessis in a splendid carriage with prominently displayed American insignia. She announced to crowds of surprised Parisians and astonished prison guards that the wife of the American Minister was calling on Madame de Lafayette and would it be possible to see her?

The guards brought out a tearful Adrienne de Lafayette who surely thought she was on her way to her execution, but was instead embraced by Elizabeth Monroe. After a short visit, Elizabeth made it clear in a loud voice that she would return in a few days, a message obviously received by the proper authorities for within days, husband James was able to secure the release of Madame de Lafayette and her two daughters, supply them with American passports and send them off to join the exiled Marquis in Prussia. The guillotine had been foiled, thanks to the courage and nerve of Elizabeth Monroe.

That incident notwithstanding, the Monroe residency in Paris was elegant. The couple developed European tastes in manners, food, clothing and furniture. They learned to speak fluent French and filled their embassy home with French furniture, silver, porcelain, tapestries and carpets, much of which was brought back to Virginia for use at their home in Charlottesville, and later in the White House.

Monroe had been recalled from Paris in 1796 and for the next number of years the Monroes divided their time between Albemarle County, Virginia, where they constructed a house named Highland, and Richmond, Virginia, where James served as Governor from 1799 to 1803. That year, President Thomas Jefferson appointed Monroe Minister Envoy Extraordinary and Minister Plenipotentiary to France. This second mission to France was brief but spectacular as James conducted successful negotiations with Emperor Napoleon for the Louisiana Purchase. For the next four years, the Monroes alternated residences in London and Paris, where Elizabeth acquired many jewels and gowns that have survived and are on exhibit at the James Monroe Museum and Memorial Library in Fredericksburg.

When the Monroes returned to the United States in 1807, they spent most of their time at Highland until 1811 when James began to serve another term as Governor of Virginia, a term cut short when he was appointed Secretary of State by President James Madison. Thus he and Elizabeth resided in Washington during much of the next thirteen years while he served as Secretary of State and President. They frequently returned to Highland, especially in the summer, not only to escape Washington's heat but to oversee operations of the farm.

Elizabeth's life was dependent in large measure upon James. Perhaps taking a cue from his close friend Thomas Jefferson, Monroe made almost all family decisions, including those involving furniture selection and home decoration. As President, James made social customs fit his ideas, terminating many he considered frivolous. Practiced as a political wife, dutiful as befitted a proper nineteenth-century companion, and schooled in proper European social customs, Elizabeth had a formal manner that made her appear aloof and suspect as White House hostess. Her reputation deteriorated even further when she abandoned the practice (at her husband's insistence, probably) of the president's wife calling on wives of congressmen and diplomats, either on a return basis or otherwise. Of course, that reputation was exacerbated by the fact that she had succeeded casual and extroverted Dolley Madison as First Lady.

During Monroe's second presidential term, Elizabeth, increasingly troubled by illness, turned more and more social responsibilities over to daughter Eliza, and as the President's popularity increased in what was called the "Era of Good Feelings," White House receptions became well-attended. When the Monroes left Washington in 1825, they retired to their country home, Oak Hill, in Aldie, Virginia, where Mrs. Monroe passed away in 1830.

> *It is a remark, which would be unpardonable to withold, that*
> *it was improbable for any female to have fulfilled all the duties of*
> *the partner of such cares, and of a wife and parent, with more*
> *attention, delicacy and propriety than she has.*

— James Monroe[30]

James Monroe Museum and Memorial Library

F REDERICKSBURG, V IRGINIA

From 1786 to 1789, James and Elizabeth Monroe resided in Fredericksburg, Virginia, where James practiced law in a building located on what is now the site of the James Monroe Museum and Memorial Library (Figure 13).

While living in Paris in the 1790s, the Monroes purchased several suites of exquisite Louis XVI furniture that are on display at the museum, as is a particularly popular piece, the Louis XVI desk upon which Monroe signed his annual message to Congress in 1823, part of which became known as the Monroe Doctrine. Also fascinating is Mrs. Monroe's impressive gem collection (especially the tiara she wore to the coronation of Emperor Napoleon in 1803), formal clothing worn by the couple at the Court of Napoleon and early miniature portraits of James and Elizabeth rendered during their stay in Paris.

Figure 13. James Monroe Museum and Memorial Library, Fredericksburg, Virginia. Photograph courtesy James Monroe Museum and Memorial Library.

In addition to the furniture and other personal items brought from Europe, visitors see the formal dinner and dessert china that the Monroes purchased for entertaining at the White House and learn of the couple's complex relationship with Washington society.

Other galleries at the museum feature changing exhibits such as *The Making of a Revolutionary, Americans in Paris: Monroe as Diplomat* and *The Era of Good Feeling: The Monroe Family in Washington* when James and Elizabeth Monroe were responsible for establishing the style of living in the White House that remains the standard. Special events are also offered by the museum.

DIRECTIONS: From I 95 Exit 130, exit onto Route 3 eastbound. Follow Business Route 3 to William Street to Charles Street and turn right onto Charles. The museum is ahead on the right/west side of the block (Figure 14).

PUBLIC USE: Season and hours: Monday-Saturday, 10 AM-5 PM; Sunday, 1 PM-5 PM. During December, January and February, the museum closes at 4 PM. **Admission fee. Museum shop. For people with disabilities:** Accessible.

FOR ADDITIONAL INFORMATION: Contact: James Monroe Museum and Memorial Library, 908 Charles Street, Fredericksburg, Virginia 22401-5801. (540) 654-1043. **Web site:** *www.umw.edu/jamesmonroemuseum.* **Read:** (1) James Monroe. 1959. *The Autobiography of James Monroe.* (2) Lee Langston-Harrison. 1992. *Images of a President: Portraits of James Monroe.*

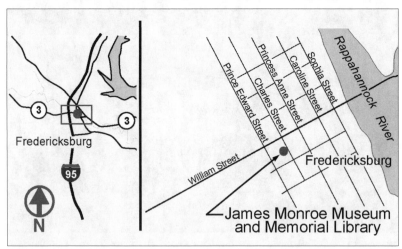

Figure 14. Location of the James Monroe Museum and Memorial Library in Fredericksburg, Virginia.

Ash Lawn-Highland

CHARLOTTESVILLE, VIRGINIA

Ash Lawn-Highland, an historic house museum (Figure 15, Plate III), is the centerpiece of a 535-acre working farm, the home of James and Elizabeth Monroe for almost twenty-five years. The Monroes named it "Highland" to differentiate it from "Lowland," their farm in Albemarle. The name was changed to Ash Lawn by a subsequent owner and combined with Highland.

The Monroes moved to the area at the urging of Thomas Jefferson, who admired the Monroes and wished to create a social and intellectual community near his home, Monticello. Compared to that masterpiece, Ash Lawn-Highland is unimposing. The original house was a modest frame building, although additions have increased its size to almost 4,400 square feet. Like most farms and plantations of the time, it was a self-contained community that employed the services of resident craftsmen and slaves. There were numerous outbuildings, mills, orchards, vineyards and fields that totaled 3,500 acres.

Figure 15. Ash Lawn-Highland, Charlottesville, Virginia. Photograph courtesy Philip Beaurline, Ash Lawn-Highland.

The Monroes sold Ash Lawn in 1826. In 1931, then-owners/philanthropists Jay and Helen Johns opened it to visitors and, in 1974, bequeathed it to Monroe's alma mater, the College of William and Mary, "as a historic shrine for the education of the general public."[31] The period rooms are filled with Monroe possessions and mementos; Hepplewhite and Sheraton furniture stand beside Louis XVI and French Empire furnishings and English accessories brought back from France. French wallpapers and period paintings provide a background for Monroe treasures from their diplomatic service in France — exquisite furniture and ideas, tastes and manners of the Continent.

The house grounds extend to the Monroe barn site and other farmyard areas where archaeological research continues to identify historic features, roadways, buildings, an ice pond and mill sites. Particularly popular is a stroll through a distinctive boxwood garden and onto a spacious lawn enlivened by colorful, strutting peacocks.

DIRECTIONS: Ash Lawn-Highland is 2½ miles south of Monticello near the intersection of routes 53 and 795 (James Monroe Parkway). From I 64, take Exit 121 in Charlottesville, exit to Route 20 and proceed southbound to Route 53 and turn left. Route 53 will wind up the mountain past Michie Tavern and Monticello. After passing Jefferson Vineyards, turn right on Route 795 for one-half mile to Ash Lawn-Highland on the right (Figure 16).

PUBLIC USE: Season and hours: April 1-October 31, 9 AM-6 PM. November 1-March 31, 11 AM-5 PM. Closed Thanksgiving Day, Christmas Day, New Year's

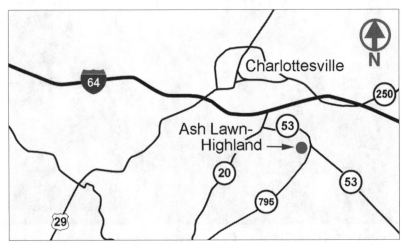

Figure 16. Location of Ash Lawn-Highland near Charlottesville, Virginia.

Day. **Admission fee:** Yes, with discounts for groups, students and seniors. **Picnic area.** Catered lunches for groups are available by advance reservation. **Museum shop. For people with disabilities:** Fully accessible, including Braille material for the blind and special facilities for the hearing-impaired.

FOR ADDITIONAL INFORMATION: Contact: Ash Lawn-Highland, 1000 James Monroe Parkway, Charlottesville, Virginia 22902-8722, (434) 293-9539. **Web site:** *www.ashlawnhighland.org.* **Read:** (1) James E. Wootton. 1987. *Elizabeth Kortright Monroe.* (2) Ash Lawn-Highland. 1999. *Ash Lawn-Highland: A Guide.* (3) David L. Holmes. 2006. *The Faiths of the Founding Fathers.*

Louisa Catherine Johnson Adams

First Lady, 1825–1829

Born: February 12, 1775, London, England
Died: May 14, 1852, Washington, DC

Louisa Johnson, the only First Lady born outside the United States, grew up in London where her father represented American tobacco and other commercial interests in Europe. During the Revolutionary War, her family moved to Paris, then returned to England after the conflict when Mr. Johnson was appointed the first American consul. Their London home thus became a mecca for visiting Americans, one of whom was young diplomat John Quincy Adams, who courted and married Louisa in 1797.

John Quincy Adams was an over-achiever, reared by perfectionist — some say domineering — parents, John and Abigail Adams, whose constant, well-intentioned advice deprived the young man of self-confidence. Fanatic about work and achievement, he believed that females should be delegated to a subordinate place in marriage and society, and compounded his innate chauvinism with indifference and a graceless lack of understanding. His general attitude was, in today's parlance, insufferable. Louisa, educated in London and Paris, possessed wit, beauty and literary knowledge. John Quincy Adams biographer Paul Nagel wrote:

> She was as complex and impressive a human being as her
> husband. Her achievement went beyond the feat of living with
> John Quincy Adams for half a century . . . Had she received a

college education, Louisa Catherine Johnson might easily have become the scholarly superior of her spouse. Tucked away in her papers is the evidence of her keen interest in literature, medicine and music. Where he was often disorganized and superficial, she was disciplined and rigorous.[32]

She played the harp, had a sweet singing voice and drew a number of eligible suitors and, from the perspective of 200 years, it's difficult to understand such an odd pairing. Yet she chose John Quincy, and the marriage lasted fifty years — fifty years of inattention on his part and forbearance on hers. As they approached their golden anniversary, she told their son Charles:

He is a man with whom you cannot temporise, and the didactic tone is the only one which can be operative. The little attentions which are mere commonplaces in this world are utterly lost upon a man who thinks it is a great deal of offence to be asked to change his coat or put on a clean shirt.[33]

Life with John Quincy Adams must not have been easy.

The couple honeymooned in Germany where John Quincy was posted as American Ambassador. During four years in Berlin, Louisa suffered four miscarriages before she bore George Washington Adams shortly before John Quincy was recalled to America. It was Louisa's first trip to the United States, although she considered herself thoroughly American. After all, her uncle, Thomas Johnson, had been a signer of the Declaration of Independence and her London home had been a gathering place for many Americans. If she were intimidated by the prospect of meeting the Adams family, especially her outspoken mother-in-law, it was not evident. It may have been initially difficult for both women, but history assures us that Louisa and Abigail produced a close and endearing friendship.

John Quincy, out of favor in the Jefferson administration, returned to the practice of law in Boston. Then, in 1803, the voters of Massachusetts sent him back to Washington as a member of Congress. In 1809, he was appointed United States Ambassador to Russia by President James Madison, a post he accepted without consulting Louisa. He announced to her imperiously, and characteristically, that she would accompany him to Saint Petersburg, but that their two oldest sons, ages eight and six, would remain in America to live with his Aunt Mary and her husband. Only two-year-old Charles Francis would accompany them to Russia. Outraged, Louisa dutifully followed orders although her letters speak of the "agony of agonies" in deserting her children when they most needed a mother's influence. She never forgave her husband, although once settled in Russia, she performed the duties of a diplomat's wife with grace. Her mastery of the Russian language, her musical ability and innate common sense endeared her to the Czar's court, her dour husband notwithstanding.

In 1814, John Quincy left Saint Petersburg to attend peace negotiations in Ghent, Belgium, designed to end the War of 1812. When it was signed at Christmas, he wrote (ordered?) Louisa to join him in Paris. Author Christine Sadler described her journey:

> *Louisa set out by carriage with her youngest son, now almost eight years of age, two servants, and assorted helpers hired for the trip. It was in the dead of winter and would have been a hazardous journey at best, but all Europe now was in a chaotic uproar caused by the news that Napoleon had escaped from Elba. Stuck in snowdrifts, robbed, and nearly thrown in jail, Louisa and her little party pushed south and west. As they entered France, the roads were clogged with veterans rushing to join their returning emperor, and Louisa's Russian drivers decided they should hasten back home. It was harrowing, but at last Louisa swept into Paris along with the veterans after having shouted 'Vive L'Empereur' to the point of exhaustion.*[34]

Her journey across Europe to join her husband is the stuff of heroic legend, and history has noted the bravery of Louisa Johnson Adams.

From Paris, the Adamses moved to London where John Quincy served as American Ambassador to the Court of Saint James before President Monroe called him home as Secretary of State. As a cabinet member's wife, Louisa gave weekly parties, returned calls and was considered an excellent hostess. When John Quincy ran for president in 1824, she rallied behind his candidacy by hosting theater parties and making public appearances. Once her husband was elected, Louisa's hospitality as First Lady was gracious and proper as befits someone trained in London and Paris and exposed to the grand courts of Europe. As her husband found all social activities oppressive, she undoubtedly struggled through them.

The three Adams sons lived in the White House, as did niece Mary Catherine Hellen, who married middle son John in 1828. Their first son was born in the White House and brightened the lives of grandparents John

Quincy and Louisa in the latter part of his single term, although the Adamses did not leave the capital for good. In 1831, John Quincy Adams was again elected to Congress from Massachusetts, becoming the first ex-president to serve in Congress.

Upon the death of John Adams in 1826, Peacefield was inherited by John Quincy Adams and he and Louisa used it as the summer White House during his presidency. See Adams National Historical Park (pages 29–33) and figures 5 and 6B.

Rachel Donelson Robards Jackson

Born: June 15, 1767, Pittsylvania County, Virginia
Died: December 22, 1828, Hermitage, Tennessee

In the late-eighteenth century, Rachel Robards, unhappily married and separated from her husband, fell in love with Andrew Jackson, a young attorney boarding at her mother's log-cabin rooming house on the Tennessee frontier. Rachel's husband had moved to Kentucky and when her mother sent Rachel to Natchez to live with friends, Jackson accompanied her. Robards sued Rachel for divorce late in 1790 on the grounds of desertion and adultery and, in the belief that her husband had obtained a divorce, she and Jackson married in 1791, only to discover two years later that Robards had filed only an intention to divorce. Technically, Andrew and Rachel were living an adulterous relationship. The divorce was legitimized in 1793 and she remarried Jackson in January 1794, yet accusations, political and otherwise, about the so-called adultery plagued the couple throughout their marriage.

Rachel was the product of a wealthy, well-known family. Her father, Colonel John Donelson, was a member of the Virginia legislature, surveyor, militia leader and prominent citizen who led his family to central Tennessee as part of an expedition intending to settle that area. Her father had passed away by the time Rachel married Andrew Jackson, thus she brought not only a substantial inheritance to the marriage, but an extended family of brothers, sisters, nieces, nephews and others who were constant visitors and sources of support and connections. The childless Jacksons even adopted one of Rachel's twin nephews, naming the child Andrew Jackson, Jr. They also raised as their own an orphaned Indian child whom the General had discovered on the battlefield at Tallushatchee in 1813.

Rachel Jackson, shy and retiring, was the one constant in her husband's life. She made a home at The Hermitage, even assisting in the management of the plantation with great skill and success during Andrew's frequent absences as commander of Tennessee militia in the Creek War, Major General in the United States Army in the War of 1812, the Seminole War in 1818, and as Governor of Florida in 1821. Rachel even traveled to Louisiana and Florida to join him when he asked. Always pious, she tended to become deeply religious as she grew older, especially as she prepared to leave for Washington for Andrew's presidential inauguration.

Even though the adultery stories were widespread and patently political, one story relates that Rachel overheard some women bemoaning the fact that such a woman as she didn't belong in the White House. Rachel experienced a panic heart attack so intense that it may have contributed to her death only three months before her husband's inauguration as seventh President of the United States. Andrew Jackson certainly believed it did.

Devastated by her death, as Rachel had been his pillar of strength for over thirty-five years, the President-elect commissioned a copy of her portrait from The Hermitage and hung it on the wall facing his bed in the White House where "it might be the first object to meet his eyes when his lids opened in the morning and the last for his gaze to leave when they closed in sleep at night."[35] In the belief that scurrilous talk contributed to her death, he had her tombstone inscribed:

> *Her face was fair, her person pleasing, her temper amiable, and her heart kind . . . To the poor she was a benefactor, to the rich an example, to the wretched a comforter . . . She thanked her creator for being permitted to do good. A being so gentle and yet so virtuous, slander might wound, but could not dishonor.*[36]

During Jackson's two terms in the presidency, Emily Donelson, one of his wife's nieces, and Sarah Jackson, wife of the President's adopted son, served as White House hostesses.

The Hermitage

The 425-acre plantation purchased by Andrew and Rachel Jackson in 1804 was a far cry from today's Hermitage. At that time there was merely a clump of log cabins — storerooms, slave quarters and a two-story farm-house, although the latter featured decorative paneling downstairs and French wallpaper on the upper floor. In 1821 they built a fashionable house in the popular Federal style, its symmetrical façade embellished only by a fan-lighted entry. Two wings and a colonnade were added after Mrs. Jackson's death.

In 1834, The Hermitage was partially destroyed by fire, the upper floor lost and the ground floor severely damaged. Jackson had it rebuilt within the framework of the original walls and foundation, changing the roofline and adding columns to the portico in the Greek Revival style. The interior was totally renovated by enlarging rooms and adding new wallpaper, furniture and carpeting. To unify the elements and complete the Greek Revival look, the front brick walls were painted white, although the other three sides remained natural.

Visitors to The Hermitage (Figure 17, Plate IV) enter a sprawling visitor center that houses a gift shop, restaurant and an impressive museum containing original Jackson artifacts, memorabilia and graphic displays tracing his career and the history of The Hermitage. Self-guided tours begin with the screening of a twenty-minute orientation film before moving to the mansion where trained interpreters answer questions, the most frequently asked about the panoramic wall paper covering the entire front hall. Scenic paper was popular in fine homes of the period — in this case the paper depicts the epic legend of Telemachus searching for his father Odysseus on the Island of Calypso. The paper was severely damaged in the 1834 fire, but Jackson purchased a new set in his wife's memory as it had been chosen by her. Much of the furniture was destroyed when the house burned but there are several original pieces including Jackson's desk, two card tables, two sets of drawers and the dining table. Another popular item is the original portrait of Rachel Jackson that hangs over the mantel in the President's bedroom.

The grounds at The Hermitage are lush and manicured. The path from the visitor center to the mansion winds past a guitar-shaped driveway bordered by cedar trees planted in 1838. Tragically, a devastating tornado in

1998 destroyed many of the old cedars and hundreds of other trees, but the cedar drive has been replanted. On one side of the mansion is "Rachel's Garden," an excellent example of a Southern plantation garden. Over an acre in size, it is maintained with the same species of flowers available when Rachel Jackson gathered bouquets for departing guests or made floral arrangements

Figure 17. The Hermitage, Hermitage, Tennessee, looking across Rachel's garden toward the north front of the structure. Photograph by Paige Swope.

for the house. There are over fifty varieties of flowers, shrubs, herbs and trees; the central beds are arranged in a formal geometric design with brick borders. At the southeast corner is the Andrew and Rachel Jackson Tomb, a stone monument built along classic Greek lines supporting a copper dome atop fluted columns.

To the rear of the mansion are a number of outbuildings including a one-story slave cabin and the original Hermitage — a two-story blockhouse of three rooms — one on the ground floor and two upstairs. The great room was at once kitchen, dining room, sitting room and parlor. According to guest Mrs. James K. Polk, "the large table that stood in the middle of it was capable of seating twelve to fourteen people comfortably and was always set."[37] Tulip Grove, the residence of Andrew Jackson Donelson, Rachel's nephew who acted as Jackson's private secretary, is located nearby, as is the Old Hermitage Church, built on land donated by Jackson in 1823. Mrs. Jackson was extremely religious, and President Jackson fulfilled a deathbed promise he made by joining the church in 1838.

DIRECTIONS: From I 40, take Exit 221 (The Hermitage) to Old Hickory Boulevard North (CR 45). The entrance on the right is prominently marked. From I 65, take Exit 92 (Old Hickory Boulevard South) (Figure 18).

PUBLIC USE: Season and hours: April 1-October 15, 8:30 AM-5 PM. October 16-March 31, 9 AM-4:30 PM. Closed Thanksgiving Day, Christmas Day and the third week in January. **Admission fee:** Yes, with discounts for groups, students and seniors. **Food service:** There is a public restaurant on-site, plus two outdoor picnic areas. **Museum shop. For people with disabilities:** Accessible, with the exception of the second floor of the mansion and Tulip Grove Plantation.

FOR ADDITIONAL INFORMATION: Contact: The Hermitage, 4580 Rachels Lane, Hermitage, Tennessee 37076-1344, (615) 889-2941. **Web site:** *www.thehermitage.com*. **Read:** (1) Patricia L. Hudson. 1990. "Old Hickory's House." (2) Katherine Cruse. 1994. *An Amiable Woman: Rachel Jackson.*

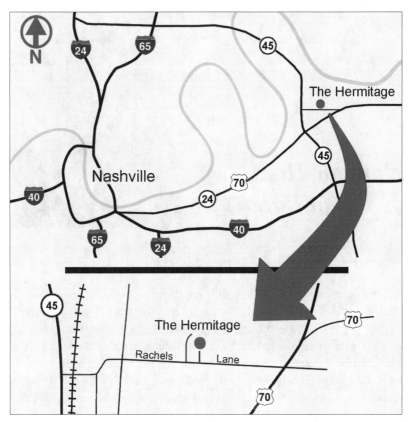

Figure 18. Location of The Hermitage, Hermitage, Tennessee.

Hannah Hoes Van Buren

Born: March 8, 1783, Kinderhook, New York
Died: February 5, 1819, Albany, New York

Little is known about Hannah Hoes, the cousin whom young attorney Martin Van Buren married in 1807. They were products of Dutch Reformed clannishness and shared the same social status. She has been described as small, slim and religious, with a "lack of pretence, her unruffled disposition and her thoughtfulness were just what her husband needed after the constant stress of the courtroom . . . she made no demands on him."[38] Hannah passed away in 1819, only thirty-six years of age. Her legacy was the four Van Buren sons she bore.

When Martin Van Buren moved into the White House, the social tempo of the presidency changed radically from the rough Jackson occupancy, as the widowed Van Buren and his sons were known for urbanity and social polish. Dolley Madison, by then an aging Washington doyenne, was appalled by a White House with the lack of a woman's touch, however. A longtime matchmaker, Dolley arranged a meeting between her niece, Angelica Singleton, and President Van Buren's eldest son, Abraham. The match worked, and the young couple married in November, 1838. Angelica, descendant of wealthy Carolina aristocrats and a graduate of a posh Philadelphia finishing school, was well-suited for the job of White House hostess and filled the position with great charm.

Anna Tuthill Symmes Harrison

First Lady, March–April, 1841

Born: July 25, 1775, Morristown, New Jersey
Died: February 25, 1864, North Bend, Ohio

When William Henry Harrison was inaugurated as President in 1841, his wife was confined to their home in Ohio by illness. Doctors forbade her to travel until the weather improved and she was still recuperating when the President died of pneumonia after only a month in office. During that brief period, White House social duties were handled by the Harrison's widowed daughter-in-law, Jane Irwin Harrison, and her aunt, Mrs. James Findlay.

Anna Harrison might have been an outstanding First Lady. Born into a distinguished New Jersey family, she attended Clinton Academy in Long Island and Isabella Graham's finishing school in New York City before moving to Ohio where her father had invested in agricultural acreage. Army Captain William Henry Harrison, in command of Fort Washington near present-day Cincinnati, met Anna in 1795 and they fell in love. Her father objected to an army marriage, but when he was out of the house one day, Anna calmly walked out and married her captain.

The young couple constructed a four-room log cottage near Fort Washington, but after Harrison was appointed Governor of Indiana Territory in 1800, they moved to Vincennes and initiated construction of a mansion above the Wabash River. Its design, based on Harrison's birthplace, Berkeley Plantation in Charles City, Virginia, was named Grouseland for the birds on the property.

Harrison resigned from the Army in 1814 and the couple moved to North Bend, Ohio, where Anna's father had bequeathed them 2,000 acres of lush farmland. They moved their original log house to the farm, covered it with clapboard and added to it until there were twenty-two rooms, all in use, much like Grouseland. Harrison became a full-time farmer until his election to the House of Representatives, then to the United States Senate and, finally, the presidency.

Anna Harrison lingered well into the Civil War years as a respected and popular resident of North Bend. She deplored the military conflict, but was gratified that her grandsons were fighting for the Union. One grandson, Benjamin, had volunteered as a second lieutenant of the Indiana Volunteers and rose to the rank of brevet Brigadier General. His election as President of the United States in 1888 made Anna Symmes Harrison the only woman to be the wife of one president and grandmother of another.

Grouseland

VINCENNES, INDIANA

In 1800, William Henry Harrison, Governor of Indiana Territory, the western frontier of the United States, began construction of a house similar in appearance to his boyhood home in Virginia, Berkeley Plantation (Figure 19). He and wife Anna were accustomed to quality eastern living, thus the home brought a visible symbol of civility and style to the frontier. Structural differences were made, however, to accommodate the requirements of frontier living. Due to the threat of Indian raids, for example, the outer walls of Grouseland were eighteen inches thick and the walls and ceilings reinforced against the stress caused by the weight of the extra-thick walls. Grouseland and its dependency, separated by a covered walkway, contains seventeen rooms and ten fireplaces (Plate V), the rooms always full as the Harrisons had four children when they moved in, they had four more while living there, they entertained frequently, and they created a haven for their neighbors in the event of an Indian incursion.

After the Harrisons moved from Vincennes to North Bend, Ohio, in 1812, Grouseland underwent many changes of occupancy, including periods of private residency, thirty years as a less-than-four-star hotel, ownership by the Vincennes Water Works, and later ignominy as a grain storage facility. By

1909, it had started to decay. Scheduled for demolition, it was saved from the wrecker's ball by the newly-formed Frances Vigo Chapter of the Daughters of the American Revolution, which was granted custody of the historic home. The ladies restored the house, filled it with genuine Harrison possessions and other period pieces and opened it for visitation in 1911.

The first floor contains six rooms. The central hall features a winding free-standing cherry staircase, and to the right is the dining room with a

Figure 19. Grouseland, Vincennes, Indiana. Photograph courtesy Grouseland Foundation.

Sheraton sideboard, an original Harrison piece. To the left is the council room which features another original artifact, a round cherry table. A contemporary portrait of General Harrison hangs above the fireplace.

The second floor of the Mansion contains six bedrooms. A front bedroom, located over the dining room, contains two double beds, one of which belonged to the Harrisons, as did a blanket chest, candle table and bamboo chair. All of the other rooms have been furnished by donations from Harrison descendants or others, and serve to reflect the graciousness of the Harrison family.

The basement serves as a museum, and a dependency utilizes space for historical displays, war materiel, uniforms, maps and other artifacts delineating the life and career of the outstanding military figure who served our young nation with distinction, yet led it as our ninth president for only thirty-one days.

DIRECTIONS: Vincennes is on the southwestern edge of Indiana at the junction of US Routes 41 and 50. **From US Route 41 from the north:** Take US Route 41 (Business) into downtown Vincennes and turn right on Saint Clair Street. At Second Street, turn left and continue south. At Harrison Street, turn right. At First Street, turn left, then right onto Scott Street. Grouseland is on the right. **From US Route 41 from the south:** Exit at Hart Street and turn left (north) to First Street. Turn right on First Street, continue over the railroad tracks and turn left on Scott Street to Grouseland on the right (Figure 20).

PUBLIC USE: Season and hours: March-December, Monday-Saturday, 9 AM-4 PM; Sunday, 11 AM-4 PM. January and February, daily, 11 AM-4 PM. Closed Thanksgiving, Christmas, New Year's Day. **Admission fee:** Yes, with discounts for groups, students and seniors. Children under five, free. **Museum shop. For people with disabilities:** No special facilities.

FOR ADDITIONAL INFORMATION: Contact: Grouseland Foundation, 3 West Scott Street, Vincennes, Indiana 47591, (812) 882-2096. **Web site:** *www.grouselandfoundation.org*. **Read:** Freeman Cleaves. 1990. *Old Tippecanoe: William Henry Harrison and his Time.*

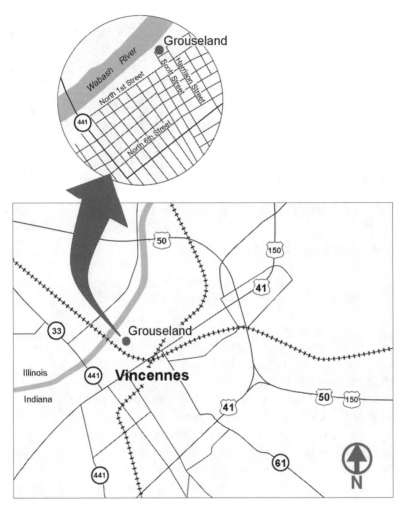

Figure 20. Location of Grouseland in Vincennes, Indiana.

Letitia Christian Tyler

First Lady, 1841–1842

Born: November 12, 1790, New Kent County, Virginia
Died: September 10, 1842, Washington, DC

At 5 AM on April 5, 1841, two dusty, fatigued riders pounded on the front door of a modest house in Old Williamsburg, Virginia. They had ridden for twenty-four hours to bring Vice President John Tyler the shocking news of President William Henry Harrison's death. Tyler blinked in sleepy shock for only a moment before he roused the household, and within hours the new President was on the road to Washington.

Mrs. Tyler and the Tyler daughters followed weeks later, a move complicated by the fact that the new First Lady, Letitia Christian Tyler, was a victim of paralysis, having been confined to a wheelchair for the previous three years. Author Christine Sadler quoted Letitia's daughter-in-law Priscilla:

> *She must have been very beautiful in her youth, for she is very beautiful now in her declining years and wretched health . . . She is the most entirely unselfish person you can imagine. In her own home she had continued to regulate all the household affairs, and all so quietly that you can't tell when she does it.*[39]

In the White House, too, she lived quietly, attended by her family. She avoided excitement and made only one semi-public appearance, that to attend daughter Elizabeth's wedding in the East Room in January, 1842.

Letitia, born to a prominent Virginia family, brought property and influence to her marriage to John Tyler in 1813. As the daughter of a wealthy Virginia planter and wife of an ambitious young attorney, she was expected to be modest, demure, pious and self-effacing, content to remain in the background while her husband climbed the political ladder — United States Senator, Governor of Virginia, Vice President and President.

Their engagement was proper and prolonged. Five years. Three weeks before the wedding, he is reported to have said that, not until then had he "ventured to kiss her hand on parting, so perfectly reserved and modest had she been."[40] Nonetheless, Letitia bore him eight children, several of whom lived with the Tylers in the White House, including eldest son Robert, his wife Priscilla, and their infant daughter.

President Tyler asked twenty-four-year-old Priscilla to assume the duties of White House hostess. A professional actress before she married Robert, Priscilla was charming, witty, attractive, socially prominent and more than capable in fulfilling the social responsibilities of First Lady. Her second daughter, born in the White House, was named Letitia Christian in honor of the invalid First Lady. Priscilla was a reluctant White House hostess, however, as she and Robert were anxious to leave the White House as he hoped to launch a legal career in Philadelphia. Their chance came sooner than expected as President Tyler married Julia Gardiner in June, 1844.

Julia Gardiner Tyler

First Lady, 1844–1845

Born: May 4, 1820, Gardiners Island, New York
Died: July 10, 1889, Richmond, Virginia

Julia Gardiner, a striking twenty-three-year-old from a wealthy and distinguished New York family, was in Washington to enjoy the 1843 social season. At a White House social function she met the widowed and considerably older President, and there was an immediate attraction. Concern over their age difference and the propriety of honoring a proper mourning period, however, made the couple circumspect about a romantic relationship.

In early 1844, Julia and her father were guests of the President on a Potomac River cruise aboard the *USS Princeton*, during which the firing of a new on-board cannon was to be demonstrated. The President and Julia were dining below decks when the cannon blew up and killed several spectators, including Julia's father. However tragic, the incident brought the lovers closer together. Julia was quoted, "After I lost my father, I felt differently toward the President. He seemed to fill the place and to be more agreeable in every way than any younger man ever was or could be."[41] They married in New York City in June, 1844, the first time a President had married while in office.

Julia worshipped her husband. She admired everything about him — his writing, his speaking voice, his causes — all became part of near hero-worship. Author Paul F. Boller wrote:

> *After he signed the joint resolution of Congress taking Texas into the Union, she vowed she would always wear 'suspended from*

my neck the immortal gold pen with which the President signed my annexation bill. [42] *She became as ardent a states-righter as her husband and, if anything, even more impassioned than he in defense of the South and critical of the North as the nation began to slide into divisive controversy. She even learned to speak and write like a southerner. Tyler reciprocated the adoration. 'She is all I could wish her to be . . .' he told one of his daughters, 'the most beautiful woman of the age and at the same time the most accomplished.* [43]

There is no record of the response of the Tyler children.

Julia Gardiner Tyler was First Lady for only eight months, yet they were exciting. Under her influence, White House entertainment was lavish, although some critics considered it overly regal. After the White House, the Tylers retreated to Sherwood Forest, a plantation on the James River where the former President became a gentleman farmer and Julia presented him with seven children. Added to the eight children from his first marriage, the number made John Tyler the most prolific President in history.

By the time the Civil War began, Julia was a passionate secessionist, a northern woman with southern principles. Outspoken in detestation of her own heritage, she once told her mother she was "utterly ashamed of the State in which I was born, and its people."[44]

John Tyler passed away early in 1862, and Julia did not re-marry. She converted to Catholicism, settled in Richmond and died of a stroke in 1889, coincidentally in the same hotel where her husband had passed away years before. Julia is buried next to John Tyler in Richmond's Hollywood Cemetery.

Sherwood Forest

CHARLES CITY, VIRGINIA

During the first year of his presidency, John Tyler purchased a James River plantation called Walnut Grove, not far from where he'd been raised. Tyler was nominated for a second term by the northern branch of the divided Democratic party as a third party candidate while James K. Polk was nominated by the Kentucky branch. When Tyler refused the nomination, it enraged Henry Clay, the nominee of the Whigs who had counted on a Democratic party split. He compared Tyler to the outlaw Robin Hood retiring to his

Sherwood Forest, a political insult which pleased Tyler so much that that he changed the name of the plantation from Walnut Grove to Sherwood Forest.

Sherwood Forest, a Georgian clapboard structure (Figure 21), renovated in 1845 to the Greek Revival style, was increased in size by connecting the kitchen and laundry to the east wing by a colonnade, then connecting the law offices to the main house with a sixty-eight-foot-long ballroom. Three stories high and only one room deep, the completed house ended up with a 300-foot façade, making it the longest frame house in America.

A large house was necessary to accommodate John and Julia's seven children, in addition to two from his first marriage, who were living there. The spacious rooms include a family sitting room occupied by a 200-year-old ghost, the Gray Lady. Legend tells us she descends the staircase each night and rocks till dawn in a non-existent rocking chair. Presumably she is the only ghost to haunt a presidential home.

The Gray Lady notwithstanding, Sherwood Forest has been continuously occupied by direct Tyler descendants and remains a working 3,500-acre plantation with a manor house that is a repository of family heirlooms

Figure 21. Sherwood Forest, Charles City, Virginia. Photograph by Bradley Olmar, Sherwood Forest.

from the eighteenth and nineteenth centuries. The grounds, open to the public, comprise twenty-five acres of terraced gardens, woodlands and lawns designed by noted landscape architect Andrew Jackson Downing in the early-nineteenth century. The formal garden contains a bird bath placed there by Julia Gardiner Tyler in 1847 and there are over eighty varieties of century-old trees on the property, including one of the first Ginkgo trees from Japan, presented to former President Tyler by Captain Matthew C. Perry when he returned from the Orient in the 1850s after opening the Trade Route with Japan. The plantation yard features an original seventeenth-century tobacco barn, garden house, milk house, smoke house, law office, kitchen/laundry building, an 1829 slave house and an overseer's house.

DIRECTIONS: Sherwood Forest is on the John Tyler Memorial Highway (SR 5), 35 miles east of Richmond and 18 miles west of Williamsburg. Historical markers direct visitors to Sherwood Forest (Figure 22).

PUBLIC USE: Season and hours: *Grounds*: daily, 9 AM-5 PM. *Mansion*: By advance reservation only. **Admission fee.**

FOR ADDITIONAL INFORMATION: Contact: Sherwood Forest Plantation, 14501 John Tyler Memorial Highway, Charles City, Virginia 23030, (804) 829-5377. **Web site:** *www.sherwoodforest.org*. **Read:** (1) Robert Seager II. 1962. *And Tyler, Too.* (2) Bruce Roberts. 1990. *Plantation Homes of the James River.*

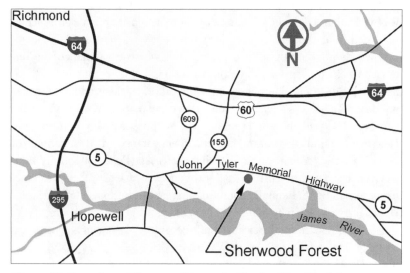

Figure 22. Location of Sherwood Forest in Charles City, Virginia.

Sarah Childress Polk

First Lady, 1845–1849

Born: September 4, 1803, Murfreesboro, Tennessee
Died: August 14, 1891, Nashville, Tennessee

Sarah Polk was arguably the first politically active First Lady as she had been husband James' secretary, advisor, helpmeet and promoter throughout much of his political career. While not necessarily in the forefront of causes or controversy, she was Polk's intellectual equal and he sought her advice on most important matters.

For a woman of the time, Sarah Childress was well-educated. Her family was well-to-do and Sarah was tutored at home, attended a private girls' school in Nashville, and completed her education at the Moravian Female Academy in Salem, North Carolina. She met James Polk when he was clerk of the Tennessee House of Representatives in Nashville. A story recounted by Sarah herself was that Polk, commiserating with Andrew Jackson about his lack of political success, was advised to settle down and marry. "Which lady shall I choose?" Jackson advised, "The one who will never give you no trouble. Her wealth, family, education, health and appearance are all superior. You know her well." "You mean Sarah Childress?" asked Polk thoughtfully. After a brief pause, he started off. "I shall go at once and ask her."[45] She accepted his proposal, but only on the condition that he run for the state legislature. He ran, he won, and they married shortly after.

Sarah Polk became her husband's confidential secretary, privy to everything that came across his desk during his fourteen years in the United States Congress — including three as Speaker of the House — then Governor of Tennessee and President of the United States. She was careful and circumspect to not express an opinion publicly as the times would not permit her to overstep the bounds of feminine propriety and social acceptance.

She was an impressive First Lady — articulate, charming, well-read and experienced in the social and political world of Washington, DC, although she was sometimes criticized for austerity and religious fervor. Mrs. Polk, a deeply committed Sabbatarian, banned playing cards and dancing in the White House and served no wine except at state dinners. On Sunday morning, she would carry the President's hat and gloves into the parlor and announce to the President and any guests that it was time for church. Word soon got out, and people began to avoid visits to the White House on Sunday mornings.

James K. Polk pledged to serve but a single term as President. Consequently he worked prodigiously, disdaining vacations or indulgence in wasteful activities. While official presidential entertaining was necessary, the Polks cut such social activities short so they might return to the office, no matter what the hour. There seems to be little question that the burden of the presidency contributed to his death, as he died only a few months after leaving office. Secretary of State James Buchanan said, "He was the most laborious man I have ever known; and in a brief period of four years had assumed the appearance of an old man."[46]

Mrs. Polk, only forty-six when her husband passed away, dedicated the rest of her life to memorializing her husband's life and legacy. She resided in "Polk Place," a mansion in Nashville, and turned the house into a Polk museum where James' study was preserved as he'd left it. She also managed, in absentia, a 1,000-acre cotton plantation in Mississippi. She received callers on a regular basis, but did not leave the house except to attend church.

During the Civil War, she entertained Confederate officers, but when Union forces occupied Nashville, she extended the same courtesy even though her sympathies were clearly with the South. She remarked to an interviewer:

> *When it came to actual conflict, and the lives of people with whom I always lived, and whose ways were my ways, my sympathies were with them; but my sympathies did not involve my principles. I have always belonged, and do now belong to the whole country.*[47]

Tragically, "Polk Place," contrary to Polk's explicit instructions in his will, was razed, a tragedy for all who love, appreciate and learn from the places where great men and women once lived.

Margaret Mackall Smith Taylor

First Lady, 1849–1850

Born: September 21, 1788, Calvert County, Maryland
Died: August 18, 1852, Pascagoula, Mississippi

Margaret "Peggy" Taylor was thoroughly disgusted when the Whig Party nominated husband Zachary for President. "It was a plot," she said, "to deprive me of his society, and shorten his life by unnecessary care and responsibility."[48] Little could she know how prophetic were those words, as President Taylor died in the White House sixteen months into his term of office.

Margaret Smith was born into a prominent plantation family in Maryland. Her education, normal for the times, stressed the practical rather than the intellectual. When visiting her sister in Kentucky in 1809, she met and married young Lieutenant Zachary Taylor, beginning a typical army marriage of moving from one frontier post to another: Fort Howard in Green Bay, Wisconsin; Fort Selden in Natchitoches, Louisiana; Pentagon Barracks in Baton Rouge, Louisiana; Fort Smith, Arkansas; Fort Washita in Madill, Oklahoma; Fort Snelling in Minnesota; Fort Gibson in Muskogee, Oklahoma; and elsewhere. Mrs. Taylor insisted on following her husband wherever he was stationed, and where her presence might brighten the circumstances of the men under his command.

Despite harsh frontier conditions, and although Peggy was seriously ill for long periods of time, the Taylors had six children, four of whom survived infancy. At one point, husband Zachary requested an extended leave to care for her. "This information has nearly unmanned me, for my loss will be an irreparable one," he wrote.[49]

Her independence was apparent in 1848. She had made an earlier bargain with God, promising to make no public appearances if her husband returned safely from the war with Mexico. She not only disapproved of his 1848 presidential campaign but convinced herself that, even if he won the election, she would not assume the duties of First Lady. Thus, when Zachary won and they moved to the capital, she asked daughter Mary Elizabeth Taylor Bliss to assume the social duties of First Lady while she retreated to the upstairs living quarters. She was not a total recluse, however, as her sitting room became the center of family activities and she joined the family for informal dinners. She merely boycotted state dinners and other formal occasions, and left the White House only to attend daily church services at Saint John's Episcopal Church across Pennsylvania Avenue.

More's the pity, for Peggy Taylor was bright, gentle and refined. During Zachary's presidential campaign, the opposition described her as crude; a sort of Western yokel, illiterate and vulgar. Therefore it was a surprise to many who attended Taylor's inauguration to discover "a most kind and thorough-bred Southern lady."[50] Others were shocked at the President's funeral service to find that he'd been married at all, as Peggy's self-chosen confinement had led some people to believe he was widowed.

President Taylor was felled by a stroke shortly after laying the cornerstone of the Washington Monument on July 4, 1850. His death five days later fulfilled Mrs. Taylor's bitter lament of two years before. After the President's funeral, Mrs. Taylor moved to Mississippi where she lived with daughter Betty Bliss and her family until her own death in 1852.

Abigail Powers Fillmore

First Lady, 1850–1853

Born: March 3, 1798, Stillwater, New York
Died: March 30, 1853, Washington, DC

Abigail Powers was born in a tiny hamlet on the western edge of the Adirondack Mountains. When her Baptist minister father died shortly after her birth, the family was forced to move in with relatives in Cayuga County where her mother taught school and educated her own children. Young Abigail herself became a country schoolteacher at sixteen years of age, probably the first First Lady to have worked for a living outside the home.

She was teaching school in the village of Sempronius, New York, when strapping young Millard Fillmore appeared in class. Largely self-taught, he was, himself, teaching school with an ambition to become a lawyer. An academy had just opened in nearby Kelloggsville and the two young teachers attended it together in pursuit of higher learning. Abigail admired his energy and enterprise and, inevitably, the teachers/pupils fell in love. Becoming engaged, they conducted a long-distance romance when he moved to Buffalo to serve his law apprenticeship. In 1826, they married in the home of her brother in Moravia, New York.

The newlyweds moved to the Buffalo suburb of East Aurora, where Fillmore established a law office and hand-built a comfortable home. Abigail tutored students after the birth of a son, making her most likely the first First Lady to have been a working mother. The family soon made an upward move to downtown Buffalo and, although she stopped teaching, Abigail continued to pursue a life-long learning ambition — she studied French, practiced the piano and was extremely well-read.

Never an activist, Abigail began to take an increased interest in Millard's career as he rose higher in the political world. When he became a New York State assemblyman, she accompanied him to Albany for assembly sessions, and became very much at home in Washington when Millard was elected to Congress, especially when he assumed the vice presidency in 1849. When President Zachary Taylor died after sixteen months in office, Millard and Abigail became President and First Lady.

Once ensconced in the White House, she was appalled to find that it lacked a library and persuaded her husband to ask Congress for an appropriation to provide one. An oval room on the second floor became the library which she filled with books, maps, reference volumes, her piano and daughter Mary's harp. The cozy room became the center of family activities.

During the latter part of Millard Fillmore's term of office, Abigail's health began to deteriorate and many of her social duties were assumed by twenty-year-old daughter, Mary. In spite of Abigail's poor health, the Fillmores looked forward to an extended vacation after leaving the White House, and they checked into the Willard Hotel to prepare for the trip. Sadly, Abigail contracted a chill that developed into pneumonia and she passed away only a few weeks later.

Fillmore House Museum

EAST AURORA, NEW YORK

Millard and Abigail Fillmore's life in East Aurora, from the time of their marriage in 1826 until 1830, was an important period in Fillmore's odyssey from log cabin to the White House. He practiced law and became involved with politics, while she taught school and bore their first child in a modest frame house on Main Street, a house he built himself (Figure 23, Plate V).

The house was abandoned sometime after the Fillmores moved to Buffalo, and stood in disrepair until 1930 when it was purchased by a local artist who moved it to Shearer Avenue, converted it into a studio, and added rooms in the rear. In 1975, the Aurora Historical Society bought the house with plans to restore it to the style of 1826 and the Fillmore occupancy. Extensive research uncovered the original floor plans, paint colors and interior details, and these, combined with the placement of period furniture and other

Figure 23. Fillmore House Museum, East Aurora, New York. Photograph by Rix Jennings.

nineteenth-century artifacts, recreated the sense of a typical small dwelling of the period.

The original home is generally intact, although the kitchen is a recreation. The living room and two upstairs bedrooms are original and are furnished with period pieces, including the Fillmores' bed. A chair belonging to Abigail and one of her hand-made quilts are displayed in the bedroom.

A Victorian library was a 1930 addition, furnished with Empire and Victorian furniture from the Fillmores' White House era and the prosperous Buffalo years that followed. Particularly intriguing are daughter Mary's harp and a large bookcase from the first White House library.

DIRECTIONS: East Aurora is 20 miles southeast of Buffalo, New York, on US Route 20A. **From the New York State Thruway, I 90 (Albany to Buffalo):** Take Exit 48A, turn right (southbound) onto Route 77, continuing for approximately 20 miles to US Route 20A, turn right (westbound) and continue to village of East Aurora and follow the historical markers to the Fillmore House. **From I 90 (Erie to Buffalo):** Take Expressway 400 eastbound 15 miles to East Aurora. Exit at Maple Street and proceed to Main Street. Turn right on Main Street for 1 block to Shearer Avenue. Turn right on Shearer; the Fillmore House is the first house on the right (Figure 24).

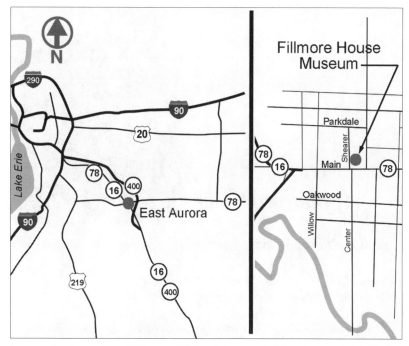

Figure 24. Location of Fillmore House Museum in East Aurora, New York.

PUBLIC USE: Season and hours: June 1-October: Wednesday, Saturday, and Sunday, 1 PM-4 PM. Private and group tours by appointment. **Admission fee:** Yes. Children, free. **For people with disabilities:** No special facilities.

FOR ADDITIONAL INFORMATION: Contact: Aurora Historical Society, PO Box 472, East Aurora, New York 14072, (716) 652-4735. **Web site:** *www.buffaloah.com/a/eastaur/shearer/mus/ext/index.html.* **Read:** Robert J. Rayback. 1959. *Millard Fillmore.*

Jane Means Appleton Pierce

First Lady, 1853–1857

Born: March 12, 1806, Hampton, New Hampshire
Died: December 2, 1863, Andover, Massachusetts

It would be difficult to find any woman less suited for White House occupancy than Jane Pierce. In the first place, she detested politics and, in particular, Washington, DC. Never robust (she was probably tubercular), Jane blamed Washington for much of her poor health and unhappiness, emphasized when after losing two sons in infancy, her only remaining son was killed before her eyes in a train wreck shortly before husband Franklin's presidential inauguration. Deeply religious and consumed by guilt, Jane believed that son Benjamin, only eleven, had been taken by God so as not to be a distraction to her husband as he assumed the presidency. Some historians have observed that the tragedy may also have affected the President's emotional health, thus his inability to properly administer the responsibilities of the high office.

Consumed by grief, Jane Pierce was unable to attend the inauguration, and it was two years before she was strong enough to receive guests in what had become a restrained and gloomy White House. Mrs. Pierce wore black throughout her White House years and, of all the gowns and dresses in the Smithsonian collection of First Ladies' attire, hers is the only black one.

Jane Pierce, sometimes known as "the shadow in the White House," was more fairly described by a close friend, Mrs. Robert E. Lee:

I have known many of the ladies of the White House, none more truly excellent than the afflicted wife of President Pierce. Her health was a bar to any great effort on her part to meet the expectations of the public in her high position but she was a refined, extremely religious and well-educated lady.[51]

When their courtship began, Jane Appleton and Franklin Pierce were considered an odd couple. He was a political animal who enjoyed a drink with the boys at the end of the day; she was the gentle, refined daughter of a Congregational minister who had died when Jane was thirteen. Her mother took Jane and her siblings to Amherst, Massachusetts, to live with Jane's grandmother Means, a formidable aristocrat who made sure Jane was given a thorough education. Jane's family disapproved of the outgoing Pierce as a worthy suitor, but love prevailed and they married in the Means' home in 1834.

Pierce was a congressman at the time, and Jane almost immediately began a campaign to wean him from politics. When the Pierces' first son died in infancy, Jane linked his death to politics and, later, when Pierce served in the United States Senate, she persuaded him to resign and move back home to New Hampshire to practice law. One cannot take politics out of the boy, however, and he did nothing to discourage supporters at the 1852 Democratic Convention where he won the presidential nomination as a compromise candidate. He had kept his ambition from Jane, and one arcane story has it that she fainted upon hearing the news of the nomination. It was also reported that she recovered quickly, even taking pride in the successful result that made her husband President. That is, until the death of their son Benjamin.

The Pierce Manse

CONCORD, NEW HAMPSHIRE

When Franklin Pierce served in the United States Senate, Jane Pierce, who remained home in Hillsborough, New Hampshire, was unhappy, and persuaded her husband to resign his seat, move the family to a home in Concord, New Hampshire, and practice law there. They remained in Concord for many years, his stay broken only when he volunteered for service in the war with Mexico. The new surroundings in Concord brought no peace, however, as their second son, four-year-old Frank Robert, died of typhus in 1843.

The Pierce Manse in Concord (Figure 25) is similar to dozens through-out New England, a two-story white Greek Revival with multiple chimneys. The kitchen, parlor and dining room are on the first floor with four bedrooms above. In 1966, the house was saved from destruction by a group of citizens interested in preserving Pierce's heritage. Calling themselves the Pierce Brigade in honor of his Mexican War service, they kept the house from being lost in a process of urban renewal by moving it from downtown Concord to a city park one mile north of its original location. Refurbished to represent the time of Pierce family occupancy, the furnishings are a combination of original pieces and others brought back to Concord from the White House. A sofa from Jane's dowry and a writing table used by Franklin are part of that collection. Jane's letter portfolio, portraits of the Pierces and their sons, Jane's silver folding fruit knife and many other family artifacts are displayed in the home. The guest room is furnished as it might have been for guests who would have had their breakfast served by the fireplace. In 1993, a carriage house that matched the dimensions and age of the original house was relocated to the property and joined to the historic home.

In 2004, the Pierce Brigade merged with the New Hampshire Political Library and the two organizations now jointly operate the Pierce Manse. The home and carriage house underwent extensive renovation in 2008, including the addition of an Exhibit Gallery about Franklin Pierce and a Political Gallery

Figure 25. The Pierce Manse, Concord, New Hampshire. Photograph by the author.

displaying political memorabilia, papers and photos from the New Hampshire Political Library's collection.

DIRECTIONS: Concord, New Hampshire's capital, is 75 miles northwest of Boston, Massachusetts. From I 93 northbound or southbound, take Exit 15W to I 393 West towards downtown Concord. Turn right on North Main Street. At the end of North Main Street (where it intersects with Penacook Street) the Pierce Manse is visible. Go around the concrete median and look for the driveway entrance on the right (Figure 26).

PUBLIC USE: Season and hours: Guided tours conducted June 15-September 3, Tuesday-Saturday, 11 AM-3 PM; September 10-October 9, Friday and Saturday, 12 M-3 PM. Closed holidays. Open other times by appointment. **Admission fee:** Yes, with discounts for students and groups. Allow 45 minutes to enjoy the Pierce Manse. **Gift shop. For people with disabilities:** A wheelchair ramp provides entry to the house through the carriage house.

FOR ADDITIONAL INFORMATION: Contact: The Pierce Manse, 14 Horseshoe Pond Lane, Box 425, Concord, New Hampshire 03301-0425, (603) 225-4555. **Web site:** *www.piercemanse.org.* **Read:** (1) Roy F. Nichols. 1958. *Franklin Pierce: Young Hickory of the Granite Hills.* (2) Larry Gara. 1991. *The Presidency of Franklin Pierce.*

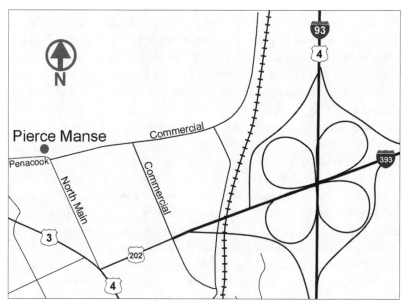

Figure 26. Location of The Pierce Manse in Concord, New Hampshire.

Harriet Lane

White House Hostess, 1857–1861

Born: May 9, 1830, Mercersburg, Pennsylvania
Died: July 3, 1903, Narragansett Pier, Rhode Island

James Buchanan, the nation's only bachelor president, was fortunate to have his niece and ward, Harriet Lane, serve as his White House hostess. Her youth, beauty, sophistication and charm were a welcome change from the four previous administrations: Sarah Polk had cast a pall with her strict Presbyterianism, Margaret Taylor had disdained politics and remained in the family quarters during official social functions, Abigail Fillmore was shy and withdrawn, and Jane Pierce was grieving from the deaths of her sons. It was an expectant Washington that welcomed a president with long capital experience, a wealthy epicurean from Lancaster, Pennsylvania, with an enchanting and attractive young woman by his side, both eager to entertain with flair, no matter the political divisiveness in the country.

Buchanan doted on Harriet. He sent her to excellent preparatory schools and she graduated with honors from the Georgetown Visitation Convent. When he was on a diplomatic mission to Europe in 1854, she joined him in England where she charmed Queen Victoria — and most of England's finest young men. Her greatest contribution, however, was as the President's hostess in the White House during his one term where, in addition to her social responsibilities, she became interested in a number of humanitarian causes.

Following Abraham Lincoln's inauguration in 1861, James Buchanan and Harriet returned to Lancaster. In 1867, at thirty-six, she married banker Henry Johnston and moved to Baltimore where tragedy followed. In the early 1880s, her two teen-aged sons both died from rheumatic fever. Heartbroken, the Johnstons provided in their wills for the creation of a hospital for chronically ill children, manifested in 1912 by the opening of the Harriet Lane Home for Invalid Children in Baltimore, precursor of the Johns Hopkins Children's Center.

Mr. Johnston passed away in 1884, and Harriet Lane Johnston became one of America's great philanthropists. She was instrumental in founding and funding Saint Alban's School, a preparatory school associated with the National Cathedral in Washington, DC. She funded a biography of her uncle, willed a valuable art collection to the Smithsonian Institution that became the foundation of the National Gallery of Art, and financed the statue of James Buchanan in Meridian Park in downtown Washington. Until her death in 1903, she continued to use her considerable influence to restore her uncle's reputation which had been tarnished by decisions that failed to stop the runaway train of distrust, political differences and hatred that polarized the nation and brought on the devastating Civil War.

Wheatland

LANCASTER, PENNSYLVANIA

Wheatland, built in 1828 by a wealthy Lancaster banker who named it for the rich wheat fields surrounding the property, was purchased by Secretary of State James Buchanan as a country estate in 1848. Buchanan loved his time at Wheatland and praised "the comforts and tranquility of home as contrasted with the trouble, perplexities and difficulties of public life."[52]

Wheatland (Figure 27, Plate VI) was destined to become a much more public arena as its rooms were the center of political activity during Buchanan's presidential campaigns in 1852 and 1856. It was not until his retirement from public life that tranquility returned to Wheatland which became, once again, "the beau ideal of a statesmen's abode."[53]

Harriet Lane became the mistress of Wheatland and her exquisite taste in furnishings and décor are evident. The combination sitting room/formal dining room is American Empire in style and contains its original table that seats twenty. The President's bedroom, Miss Lane's bedroom and the President's study and library all reflect the lifestyle enjoyed by the fastidious, epicurean President and the niece he nurtured and trained so well.

The house, with four acres of woodlands, was purchased in 1936 by the James Buchanan Foundation for the Preservation of Wheatland, an educational, non-profit organization that has succeeded brilliantly in preserving

Figure 27. Wheatland, Lancaster, Pennsylvania. Photograph courtesy The James Buchanan Foundation for the Preservation of Wheatland.

not only the residence but in recreating the lifestyle of a wealthy country gentleman — a lifestyle that included leisurely dinner for twenty guests, with piano music and lively conversation as entertainment.

The rooms are spacious, a necessity considering Buchanan's social and political activities. Original furnishings include a Chickering piano played by Harriet Lane. In his description of Wheatland, architectural expert and author A. Cranston Jones wrote:

> *The great charm in visiting Wheatland is that so much of the tang and aroma of this pastoral existence can still be sensed. So magnificently are the rooms maintained, with their Lancaster hostesses in period crinolines, that one almost expects to catch sight of Miss Hetty tidying up the parlor, Harriet Lane once again adjusting her skirts before her fingers ripple the first chords on the Chickering grand, or find elegant and reserved President Buchanan himself standing at the head of the table, ceremoniously greeting each guest in turn.*[54]

DIRECTIONS: Wheatland is 1½ miles west of Lancaster city center on Route 23 (Marietta Avenue). **From US Route 30 eastbound:** Take Route 23 eastbound and follow the historical markers. **From US Route 30 westbound:** Take Route 23 westbound through downtown Lancaster. There is ample parking in the rear (Figure 28).

PUBLIC USE: Season and hours: April 1-October 31, Monday-Saturday, 10 AM-4 PM; November-early December, Friday and Saturday, 10 AM-4 PM. Tours available weekdays by appointment. January-March, tours available weekdays by appointment. Closed all major holidays. December Yuletide tour schedule announced annually. **Admission fee:** Yes, with discounts for students, groups of 10 or more and seniors. **Food service:** Beverages and snacks are sold in the Carriage House and there is a picnic area. **Gift shop. For people with disabilities:** There are two steps to the porch. The main floor is accessible, the second is not. A photographic tour of the second floor is available.

FOR ADDITIONAL INFORMATION: Contact: James Buchanan Foundation, 1120 Marietta Avenue, Lancaster, Pennsylvania 17603, (717) 392-8721.**Web site:** *www.wheatland.org*. **Read:** (1) Philip Shriver Klein. 1963. *President James Buchanan.* (2) Sally Smith Cahalan. 1988. *James Buchanan's Wheatland.*

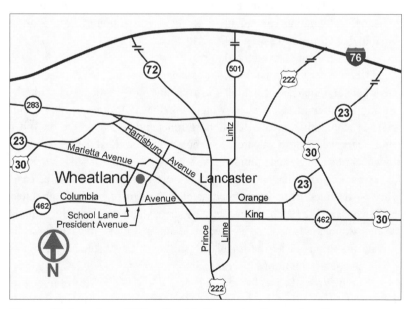

Figure 28. Location of Wheatland in Lancaster, Pennsylvania.

Mary Ann Todd Lincoln

First Lady, 1861–1865

Born: December 13, 1818, Lexington, Kentucky
Died: July 16, 1882, Springfield, Illinois

In the annals of First Ladies, there are few sadder stories than that of Mary Lincoln. During her husband's presidential years, and after, she was subjected to malicious campaigns of personal vilification and humiliation unparalleled in America's long political history.

It was not supposed to be that way.

Her mother died when Mary was six and her father, a well-to-do merchant-banker, remarried soon after — siring nine half-brothers and sisters — causing Mary emotional trauma which, together with a poor relationship with her stepmother, created a stubborn independent streak. On the other hand, Mary was sent to a boarding school which provided her with a superior education and classic training in the social graces. By all accounts, Mary Todd was the proverbial belle of the ball — pretty, charming, well-read and witty — destined to make a "good catch." It surprised and disappointed many when, after a bumpy romance, she married homely, struggling Illinois attorney Abraham Lincoln. They seemed incompatible — the dainty, well-dressed, ambitious society belle and the gangling, clumsy, sometimes forgetful — but equally ambitious — politician.

The newlywed Lincolns rented rooms in the Globe Tavern in downtown Springfield, Illinois, for a year until they purchased a house on Seventh Street that remained their principal residence for seventeen years. Mary was a superior housekeeper, although her attempts to "keep up with the Joneses" contributed to the detriment of the family income and while she was often critical of Abraham's dress and other personal habits, their marriage appeared solid and affectionate. She was certainly supportive of Abraham's career in politics as he served one term in Congress, ran unsuccessfully for the United States Senate twice and aspired to the Republican vice-presidential nomination in 1856. Through success and failure, her confidence in his ability never wavered.

When Abraham was elected President, she looked forward to living in Washington as First Lady. After all, she was an experienced political wife, skilled in the social graces and anxious to stand by her beloved husband as he assumed the reins of the national government. Their welcome in the capital, however, was not what the Lincolns expected. As one biographer wrote:

> *Instead of being welcomed with open arms, she was met with rumors and snubs. The atmosphere was quite unlike that in which any other First Lady has had to operate. Lincoln's prestige was exceedingly low and extremists in his own party were openly antagonistic against him.*[55]

The problem was complex. The Lincolns, from the Middle West, were considered outsiders, and many were suspicious of Mary's loyalty to the Union; after all, she had been raised in Kentucky in a slave-holding household and some family members were sympathetic to, and several were fighting for, the Confederacy. Others considered her overly stingy when White House social affairs were cut back during the Civil War, while others thought her to be unfeeling when she arranged any social entertainment, even if it were designed to boost morale and demonstrate the viability of the federal government. In other words, Mrs. Lincoln could do nothing right. One journalist remarked, "She found herself surrounded on every side by people who were ready to exaggerate her shortcomings, find fault with her deportment on all occasions, and criticize her performance of all her official duties."[56]

If Mary Lincoln had been meek and mild, the problem of social acceptance might have disappeared, but anxious to do everything she could to make the Lincoln administration a success, she was impulsive and short-tempered, a condition that exacerbated whatever problems existed.

The first blow to Mary's emotional state occurred in 1850 — the death of her second-born son, four-year-old Eddie. Infant and child death in those days was not uncommon, yet one tends to forget that the emotional toll on mothers is incurable and everlasting. Then, when the Lincolns had been in the White House for only a year, eleven-year-old Willie succumbed to typhoid fever. Mary was so devastated that she was confined to bed, subject to convulsions and hallucinating visions of Willie. She even attended séances in an attempt to communicate with him and it was clear that she was close to complete mental collapse. One story relates that the President took her to a window in the White House, pointed to a nearby mental hospital and said, "Mother, do you see that large white building? Try to control your grief, or it will drive you mad, and we will have to send you there."[57]

Mary recovered her equilibrium although, incredibly, the personal attacks from the public and the press continued, even as she mourned. The attacks became even more vitriolic during the presidential campaign of 1864, but her spirits improved when Abraham was reelected and the Civil War concluded. What should have been the start of a happier time was shattered at Ford's Theatre on April 14, 1865, when actor and secessionist John Wilkes Booth shot the President as he and Mary sat holding hands while they enjoyed a theatrical performance.

Mary Lincoln was too distraught to attend Abraham's funeral, and it was weeks before she arranged to leave the White House. Even then, she was not allowed to retire in peace as she was again the subject of a vicious hate campaign that fed on her fragile emotional state. For example, William Herndon, Lincoln's old law partner but no friend to Mary, published a scurrilous article about Lincoln's supposed romance with Ann Rutledge years before, claiming that Ann had been the consuming passion of his life. The implication was that Abraham's marriage to Mary was merely one of convenience, designed only to aid his political career.

Bedeviled by such stories and pursued by creditors, Mary obsessed about the poorhouse while at the same time she spent money on clothes and furnishings. She and son Tad traveled to Europe to escape the pressures, but upon their return to America in 1871, eighteen-year-old Tad developed a cold and died. It was the final blow.

> *I feel that there is no life for me, without my idolized Taddie. One by one I have consigned to their resting place my idolized ones, and now, in this world, there is nothing left me, but the deepest anguish and desolation.*[58]

In 1875, surviving son Robert requested a sanity hearing for his mother. Mary Lincoln was declared incompetent and committed to a mental institution, but after a few months she obtained her release and again fled to Europe. She wandered for four years in a desperate and unsuccessful search for peace of mind, returning to Springfield in 1880 where she lived quietly at her sister's home. Two years later, she suffered a stroke, lapsed into a coma and died. At her funeral, the presiding minister's eulogy asked those present to remember her as the woman she'd been before her husband's assassination . . . "The bullet that sped its way and took her husband from earth, took her, too."[59]

Mary Todd Lincoln House

LEXINGTON, KENTUCKY

Mary Todd spent most of her formative years in Lexington, Kentucky, the "Athens of the West." She was unusually well-educated — both an accomplished linguist and well-versed in politics. Her father allowed Mary to join dinner guests such as nationally-known politicians John Crittenden, John C. Breckenridge and neighbor Henry Clay to listen to political discussions. The home of the Todd family from 1832 to 1849 was a fourteen-room, late Georgian with a kitchen, lodging for servants, separate spring house, wash house, smoke house and stables with a carriage house. Due to a discrepancy in Mr. Todd's will, a public auction was held that resulted in the sale of the household furnishings. The auction inventory proved invaluable in the 1970s, however, when the house was purchased and restored by Kentucky Mansions Preservation Foundation, Inc.

Today the house (Figure 29) contains period furniture, family portraits and some original Todd and Lincoln pieces. A tilt-top card table is original and hand-carved laminated rosewood furniture in the front parlor is identical to a set that was commissioned by Mary. The china cabinet in the dining room contains a Tiffany sterling-silver serving pot that Mary purchased in New York. The sideboard is a rare and unusual Federal piece with a lazy susan at each end. Candelabras on the sideboard were owned by Abraham and Mary Lincoln and used in the family quarters in the White House. Each room, whether the twin parlors, dining room, breakfast room, bedrooms or hallways, are filled with precious furniture and paintings. A portrait of Mary painted when she was First Lady dominates the front parlor. Upstairs, Mary's bedroom features an original secretary, and the perfume jars on the dressing table are from her Meissen collection.

Figure 29. Mary Todd Lincoln House, Lexington, Kentucky. Photograph courtesy Mary Todd Lincoln House.

The Mary Todd Lincoln House is a national treasure that represents a period of gracious living in the early-nineteenth century. On the exterior, an historic garden reflects the charm of the original and offers a welcome respite for visitors.

DIRECTIONS: From the south on I 75: Take Winchester Road Exit west to Main Street. Take a right and follow Main Street (US 25, US 421) past Center/Heritage Hall/Rupp Arena. Take a left on Tucker Avenue (between Main Street Baptist Church and Mary Todd Lincoln House). Free parking is down the street on the left, behind the Mary Todd Lincoln House. **From the north on I 64/I 75:** Take Exit 115 (Newtown Pike, Route 922) south to Main Street (US 421). Take a left on Main Street, cross Jefferson Street, turn right on Tucker Avenue (between Main Street Baptist Church and Mary Todd Lincoln House). Free parking is down the street on the left, behind the Mary Todd Lincoln House (Figure 30).

PUBLIC USE: Season and hours: Mid-March-November: Monday-Saturday, 10 AM-4 PM. Guided tours are conducted with the last tour at 3 PM. Group tours available year-round by appointment. **Admission fee:** Yes, with discounts for children and groups. **Gift shop. For people with disabilities:** The

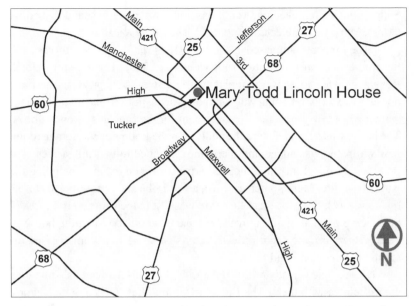

Figure 30. Location of Mary Todd Lincoln House in Lexington, Kentucky.

first floor is accessible. A photo book of the two upper floors is available for those unable to tour the upstairs.

FOR ADDITIONAL INFORMATION: Contact: Mary Todd Lincoln House, 578 West Main Street, Lexington, Kentucky 40407, (859) 233-9999. **Web site:** *www.mtlhouse.org.* **Read:** Justin and Linda Turner, eds. 1972. *Mary Todd Lincoln: Her Life and Letters.*

Lincoln Home National Historic Site

SPRINGFIELD, ILLINOIS

The Lincoln Home at Eighth and Jackson streets (Figure 31, Plate VI) is the centerpiece of a four-square-block restoration project that creates a sense of the nineteenth-century neighborhood where Abraham and Mary Lincoln lived. This is where Lincoln matured, practiced law and gained national recognition as an orator and political thinker, and it was here he learned of his nomination to run for, and subsequent election as, President of the United

States. On election evening, Mary was home when her husband rushed in, "Mary, Mary, we are elected!"[60] Indeed. They were a team.

The Lincolns purchased the house in 1844 for $1,500 ($1,200 cash and the conveyance of a downtown lot valued at $300). The 1½-story Greek Revival wooden house was complete with a cistern, well, privy and carriage house. An exterior retaining wall was constructed in 1850 and major changes were made a few years later to make room for the Lincolns' growing boys. The house was expanded with the addition of bedrooms and a storage room, new wallpaper was added and the home expanded to two full stories. Approximately fifty Lincoln-associated artifacts are on exhibit, including the parlor furniture, Mary's kitchen stove, a wardrobe and candlesticks. Unfortunately, much of the original furniture was lost in the Chicago fire of 1871 after being purchased and moved by tenants who had rented the house in 1861. Otherwise, the décor reflects Mary's personality, a woman of aristocratic breeding and good taste.

Springfield is justly proud of the Lincolns, thus many of its attractions are associated with them. The Lincoln-Herndon Law Office State Historic

Figure 31. Lincoln Home, Springfield, Illinois. Photograph by Richard Frear, National Park Service.

Site, the family pew at the First Presbyterian Church, the Old State Capitol State Historic Site where Abraham served in the state legislature — all have been preserved and are open to the public, as is the relatively new Abraham Lincoln Presidential Library and Museum. Most are within walking distance of the Lincoln Home, including the Great Western Railroad depot where the President-elect made a famous farewell address before he boarded a train for his inauguration journey to Washington — and into history. Just over four years later, another train would stop at Springfield, this one bearing the body of the assassinated President to be placed in an Oak Ridge Cemetery vault. An impressive monument was later constructed to memorialize the site where Abraham and Mary Lincoln lie at rest together with three of their children.

DIRECTIONS: Springfield is in central Illinois at the junction of I 55 and I 72. **From I 55 southbound and I 72 westbound:** Take Exit 98B (Clear Lake Avenue/routes 29/97). Proceed westbound and turn left on 7th Street. The visitor center is 5 blocks south on the left hand side of 7th. **From I 55 northbound and I 72 eastbound:** Take Exit 92A (6th Street/Business I 55) and proceed north on 6th Street 4 miles to Capitol Avenue. Turn right on Capitol, then right again on 7th Street to the visitor center on the left (Figure 32).

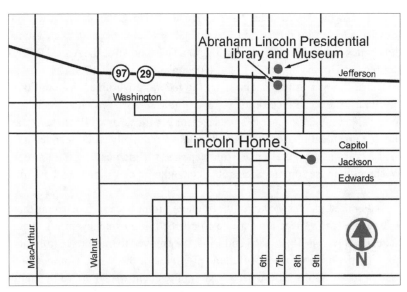

Figure 32. Location of Lincoln Home National Historic Site and Abraham Lincoln Presidential Library and Museum in Springfield, Illinois.

PUBLIC USE: Season and hours: Tours daily, 8:30 AM-5 PM. Closed Thanksgiving Day, Christmas Eve Day, Christmas Day, New Year's Day. Free tickets for tours are available at the visitor center on a first-come, first-served basis. **Fees:** Yes, for parking. **Gift shop. For people with disabilities:** The visitor center and the first floor of the Lincoln Home are accessible to wheelchairs. If assistance is required, advise the staff at the visitor center. Wheelchairs are available.

FOR ADDITIONAL INFORMATION: Contact: Lincoln Home National Historic Site Visitor Center, 426 South 7th Street, Springfield, Illinois 62701-1905, (217) 492-4241 or Write: Superintendent, Lincoln Home National Historic Site, 413 South 8th Street, Springfield, Illinois 62701-1905. **Web site:** *www.nps.gov/ liho.* **Read:** Wayne C. Temple. 1984. *By Square and Compasses: The Building of Lincoln's Home and its Saga.*

President Lincoln's Cottage at the Soldiers' Home

WASHINGTON, DC

Following the Mexican War, a group headed by General Winfield Scott founded a haven for retired and disabled US soldiers on a 250-acre campus three miles north of downtown Washington, DC. Known as the Armed Forces Retirement Home (Figure 33), it was occupied by 1200 retired or disabled veterans. In 1851, it was acquired by the federal government as a military "asylum." The centerpiece is a 2½-story Gothic Revival "cottage," built by a local banker in 1842. Lincoln's predecessor in office, James Buchanan, was the first president invited to occupy the house and likely recommended it to the Lincolns as a retreat, a place to escape the stifling heat and humidity of Washington in the summer as it is 300 feet higher in elevation than the White House.

For the Lincolns, however, the Soldiers' Home became much more than a retreat as they spent almost one-fourth of his presidency in residence there. Each June in 1862, 1863 and 1864, they moved to the cottage to escape not only the heat but the insufferable pressures of the White House. Commuting to the White House each day, the President would arrive by eight, then leave at five o'clock to join his family for dinner. For the President, the home was a place for retreat and for shaping the nation's destiny as it was

Figure 33. Abraham Lincoln's Cottage at the Soldiers' Home, Washington, DC. Photograph by Robert Lautman.

there that he wrote the Emancipation Proclamation. For Mary Lincoln, it was far more; perhaps even life-saving. The first year in the White House had been extremely difficult, culminating with the death of her second son, Willie, to typhoid fever, an event which almost destroyed her already fragile psyche. It was at the cottage that the Lincolns realized some of the privacy and quiet they both required.

After the Lincoln presidency, the cottage was a getaway cottage for presidents Rutherford B. Hayes and Chester A. Arthur, and was used for a variety of other purposes. The historical significance of the cottage faded from public awareness until 2000 when the National Trust for Historic Preservation placed the site on their annual list of the Most Endangered Historic Places, prompting President Bill Clinton to declare the retreat a National Monument. The National Trust, a private, non-profit organization, agreed to steward the restoration and operation of the site for the public benefit. President Lincoln's Cottage officially opened to the public for the first time in 2008 as an important historical treasure.

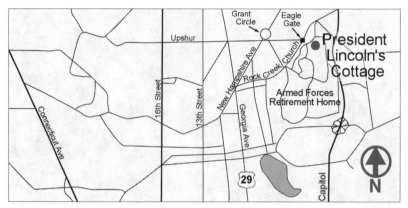

Figure 34. Location of President Lincoln's Cottage at the Soldiers' Home in Washington, DC.

DIRECTIONS: President Lincoln's Cottage is located in northwest Washington at the intersection of Rock Creek Church Road and Upshur Street, NW. From downtown Washington, take 16th Street north to Upshur Street and turn right, crossing the main thoroughfares of 13th Street and Georgia Avenue before reaching the intersection with Rock Creek Church Road (Figure 34).

PUBLIC USE: Season and hours: Open for guided tours year-round, Monday-Saturday, 9:30 AM-4:30 PM. First tour at 10 AM, last at 3 PM. Sunday, open 11:30 AM-5:30 PM, with first tour at 12 M and last at 4 PM. Tour tickets, required, are available at the Visitor Education Center. **For people with disabilities:** The second floor is not accessible.

FOR ADDITIONAL INFORMATION: Contact: President Lincoln's Cottage, AFRH-1315, 3700 N. Capitol Street, NW, Washington, DC 20011-8400, (202) 829-0436. **Web site:** *www.lincolncottage.org*. **Read:** (1) Matthew Pinsker. 2003. *Lincoln's Sanctuary: Abraham Lincoln and the Soldiers' Home*. (2) Elizabeth Brownstein. 2005. *Lincoln's Other White House*.

Abraham Lincoln Presidential Library and Museum

SPRINGFIELD, ILLINOIS

The Abraham Lincoln Presidential Library and Museum comprises two separate buildings situated across the street from one another. The library is archival, containing 12 million documents, books and artifacts relating to Illinois history, including a 50,000-item Lincolniana collection.

The museum section (Figure 35) combines scholarship with showmanship by describing and interpreting the life and times of Abraham and Mary Lincoln in unforgettable ways in which theme galleries, theaters and other facilities are arranged around a central plaza. In *Journey I,* visitors enter the early nineteenth century through a log cabin to visualize Lincoln's early life on the frontier. *Journey II* thrills visitors as they meet the Lincoln family posed on the plaza in front of the White House, then enter the mansion to continue the Lincoln saga. In the Blue Room, Mary Lincoln is seen being fitted for a ball gown (Plate VII) while around the room there are reproductions of the gowns of Mary's social rivals, all younger and more popular. Each woman has something nasty and cruel to say about Mary, resulting in empathy for her.

Figure 35. The museum component of the Abraham Lincoln Presidential Library and Museum, Springfield, Illinois. Photograph by Patricia L. Newcomb.

The Whispering Gallery is a slightly surreal hall containing printed cartoons and hissed insults about Abraham and Mary by their opponents. *The Death of Willie* is an immersive scene showing the Lincolns standing vigil at the bedside of the terminally ill son who passed away in the White House on February 5, 1862, which is followed by *The Hall of Sorrows*, an alcove with a figure of Mary grieving her son's death. Subsequent scenes feature the Civil War, ending with *Ford's Theater, The Funeral Train, Lying in State* and *Remembering Lincoln.*

A family favorite is *Mrs. Lincoln's Attic*, where children can try on period clothing, build a cabin with Lincoln Logs and indulge in other interactive pursuits that engage the children's imagination and allow them to personally project themselves into the Lincoln story through fantasy play that can come only through physical engagement.

DIRECTIONS: From I 55 southbound and I 72 westbound: Take Exit 98B (Clear Lake Avenue/ routes 29/97). Proceed westbound on 29/97, which becomes Jefferson Street (a one-way street westbound), to 6th Street. The museum is located on the northeast corner of this intersection and the library is on the southeast corner. **From I 55 northbound and I 72 eastbound:** Use Exit 92A (6th Street/Business I 55) and proceed north on 6th Street to Jefferson Street (Figure 32).

PUBLIC USE: Season and hours: *Museum:* Daily, 9 AM-5 PM. Closed New Year's Day, Thanksgiving Day, Christmas Day. *Library:* Monday-Friday, 9 AM-5 PM. Closed on most national and state holidays. **Admission fee:** Museum only. **Museum store. Food service:** Full service restaurant in museum. **For people with disabilities:** Accessible.

FOR ADDITIONAL INFORMATION: Contact: The Abraham Lincoln Presidential Library and Museum, 212 North Sixth Street, Springfield, Illinois 62701, (217) 558-8844. **Web site:** *www.alplm.org.* **Read:** Jean H. Baker. 1987. *Mary Lincoln.*

Eliza McCardle Johnson

First Lady, 1865–1869

Born: October 4, 1810, Leesburg, Tennessee
Died: January 15, 1876, Greene County, Tennessee

Eliza McCardle, daughter of a widowed dress and sandal maker, had a basic grammar school education and while she lacked worldly goods, possessed an independent mind and a heart filled with goodness and dignity. A charming and enduring story about Eliza, perhaps apocryphal, is that in the early days of her marriage to Andrew Johnson, she sat with him while he worked in his tailor shop, teaching her almost-illiterate young husband how to read and write. Some historians believe that he was literate, although there is no question that she assisted in the furtherance of Andrew's education. In any event, Andrew always depended on Eliza's patient counsel.

Life was not easy during the Civil War. Eastern Tennessee was a military and political battleground where friends, neighbors and families were often on opposite sides of the conflict. At the onset of the war, Eliza was in Greeneville, Tennessee, while Andrew was in Washington, DC, serving as a United States Senator. President Lincoln appointed Johnson as Military Governor of Tennessee with headquarters in Nashville, but Greeneville, in the eastern part of the state, was controlled by the Confederates. Eliza found herself a refugee. She attempted to keep her family together, but it was not until September, 1862, that she was permitted to cross Confederate lines to join her husband. It was a grueling trip that involved cold, hunger, deprivation and intimidation. She arrived in Nashville weary and seriously ill, probably with pulmonary tuberculosis, an ailment that would cause great suffering through her life.

In March, 1865, Eliza remained in Nashville when Andrew traveled to Washington to take the oath of office as Lincoln's second-term Vice President. When the President was assassinated only six weeks later, Eliza's concern was for her husband's safety. Daughter Martha wrote to her father, "Are you safe and do you feel SECURE? . . . Poor Mother, she is almost deranged fearing you will be assassinated."[61]

A train full of Johnson family members from Tennessee occupied the White House — two sons, daughter Martha Patterson with her husband and their two children, and widowed daughter Mary Stover and her three children. Mrs. Johnson, frail and ailing, remained in a second-floor bedroom and ventured downstairs infrequently. After one such appearance, a correspondent described Eliza as:

> *A lady of benign countenance and sweet and winning manners . . . Perhaps it is well to recall that it was this woman who taught the President to read after she became his wife, and that in all their earlier years she was his counselor, assistant and guide. None but a wise and good mother could have reared such daughters as Mrs. Patterson and Mrs. Stover.*[62]

It fell on daughter Martha Patterson to assume the duties of White House hostess, a task she performed with consummate skill and modesty. "We are called here for a short time by a national calamity. I trust too much will not be expected of us."[63] The entire Johnson family, simple and unassuming, fulfilled their historic destiny with dignity and common sense.

In his attempts to carry out Abraham Lincoln's policies of reconstruction and reconciliation, Johnson came into bitter conflict with radical Republicans and was impeached by the House of Representatives in 1868. His trial concentrated on strict constitutional questions and he was acquitted — by one vote. During the trial Johnson visited his wife every morning to seek her aid and counsel. If he followed his conscience, she advised, he had nothing to fear. Her support was always moral, not political. Following the trial verdict, Johnson's bodyguard, Colonel Crook, rushed to the White House to tell Johnson and his friends the good news, then hurried upstairs to Mrs. Johnson's room.

> *'He's acquitted! The President is acquitted!' The President's frail little wife at once got up from her chair, grasped Crook's right*

hand warmly with both hands, and with tears in her eyes, exclaimed, 'Crook, I knew he'd be acquitted; I knew it . . . Thank you for coming to tell me. [64]

The Democrat party denied Johnson the presidential nomination in 1868 and the couple returned to Greeneville. Andrew, anxious to restore his reputation following the controversial impeachment, ran unsuccessfully for the United States Senate in 1871 and for the House of Representatives in 1872, but in 1875, he was elected to the Senate and returned to Washington in triumph only to die of a stroke within a few months. Eliza died six months later and was buried beside her husband in the Andrew Johnson National Cemetery in Greeneville.

Andrew Johnson National Historic Site

GREENEVILLE, TENNESSEE

Proud of its Johnson heritage, modern Greeneville contains a number of homes, churches and other sites that date to the time of the Johnson residency. One is the Andrew Johnson National Historic Site that encompasses several attractions, including the tiny tailor shop where he worked and took lessons from wife Eliza and hired readers. The shop, protected from the elements, is housed within the walls of a National Park Service Visitor Center that also contains Johnson correspondence and displays that trace the career of one of America's most unusual presidents and his remarkable wife.

Across the street from the visitor center is a small, unfurnished two-story brick house where the Johnsons lived during the early days of their marriage. As their financial situation brightened, they purchased a larger home a few blocks away that became their primary residence (Figure 36, Plate VIII). It houses artifacts and mementos of the Johnson presidential years, including a handsome tilt-top table inlaid with 500 pieces of wood, a gift from the people of Ireland. A guided tour of the 2½-story house includes a view of each room wherein most of the furniture and furnishings are original.

The Andrew Johnson National Cemetery, one mile out of town, is the final resting place for President and Mrs. Johnson, their gravesite marked by a tall marble shaft topped by an American eagle. On one side is a scroll depicting the Constitution of the United States that Johnson defended so valiantly. His epitaph reads, "His faith in the people never wavered."

Figure 36. Johnson Home, Andrew Johnson National Historic Site, Greeneville, Tennessee. Photograph courtesy National Park Service.

Perhaps that of Eliza should read, "Her faith in her husband never wavered."

DIRECTIONS: From I 81 southbound: Take Exit 36 to Route 172 southbound to Greeneville. **From I 81 northbound:** Take Exit 23 to US Route 11E northbound to Greeneville. Historical markers leading to the visitor center and related sites are prominently displayed throughout Greeneville (Figure 37).

PUBLIC USE: Season and hours: Daily, 9 AM-5 PM. Reservations, required for tours of the Homestead, are conducted in groups of 12 at every hour on the half-hour on a first-come, first-served basis. Closed Thanksgiving, Christmas Day, New Year's Day. **Book store. For people with disabilities:** The visitor center and early home are accessible. The Homestead is not. There is a video tour of the Homestead available for the disabled in the visitor center.

FOR ADDITIONAL INFORMATION: Contact: Andrew Johnson National Historic Site, 121 Monument Avenue, Greeneville, Tennessee 37743-5552, (423) 638-3551. **Web site:** *www.nps.gov/anjo.* **Read:** Thomas Lately. 1968. *The First President Johnson.*

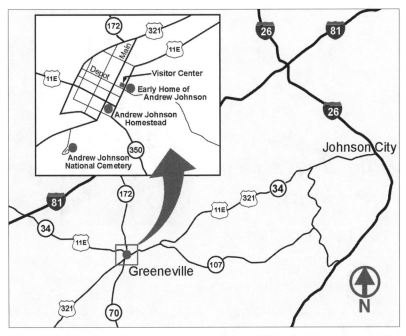

Figure 37. Location of Andrew Johnson National Historic Site in Greeneville, Tennessee.

Julia Boggs Dent Grant

First Lady, 1869–1877

Born: January 26, 1826, Saint Louis, Missouri
Died: December 14, 1902, Washington, DC

The patriarch of the socially prominent Dent family of Saint Louis was not pleased when a West Point classmate of son Frederick visited, and love blossomed between his daughter Julia and young Lieutenant Ulysses S. Grant. The couple would not be denied, however, and they married in the Dent home when Ulysses returned from service in the Mexican War in 1848.

The marriage experienced challenges, especially when Grant was assigned to military duty on the West Coast. Unhappy and depressed by separation from Julia and their two sons, he left the Army in 1854 and returned to Missouri where civilian life also proved difficult. He tried farming and several other jobs to earn a living for his family, which by 1858 included two more children. Grant moved the family to Galena, Illinois, where he worked in a leather goods store owned by his father. Through the most difficult times, he was sustained by Julia's love and confidence.

When the Civil War began, Grant volunteered his services to the Army. The right man had met the right war at the right time — Ulysses S. Grant had found his destiny. Throughout the turbulent years of war, Julia visited her husband at camp as much as possible, to refresh and sustain him. Their devotion was palpable. One aide wrote:

> *When she visited headquarters, they would seek a quiet corner of his quarters of an evening, and sit with her hand in his,*

manifesting the most ardent devotion; and if a staff officer came
accidentally upon them they would look as bashful as two young
lovers spied upon in the scenes of their courtship.[65]

Julia had one eye that turned inward and she was sensitive about it, to
the extent of discouraging full-front photographs. During Grant's presidency,
she arranged for corrective surgery — until her husband learned about it.

I don't want your eyes fooled with. They are all right as they
are. They look just as they did the very first time I ever saw them —
the same eyes I looked into when I fell in love with you — the same
eyes that looked into mine and told me that my love was returned
. . . This operation might make you look better to other people; but
to me you are prettier as you are — as you were when I first saw you.[66]

Julia canceled the surgery.

Julia Grant loved her days in the White House and became a popular
First Lady. The war was over, the nation was prosperous and official social
functions were grandiose and elegant. Julia was disappointed when Grant
decided not to run for a third term, and especially annoyed that he did not
share his decision with her. He sent a letter of declination to the Republican
Convention without her knowledge and when reproached, he replied, "Oh, I
know you too well. It would never have gone out if you had read it."[67]

After eight years in the White House, the Grants embarked on a trium-
phant two-year journey around the world. They visited dozens of countries,
met heads of state and other dignitaries and were received everywhere with
great fanfare. Their globe-trotting adventure came to an end in 1879, a year
before the next presidential-nominating convention where Grant's name was
put forward with his reluctance — and Julia's enthusiastic approval — but
the nomination went instead to James A. Garfield. The Grants retired to a
busy life in New York City, to be closer to their children.

Grant had invested in a brokerage firm that declared bankruptcy in
1884, and the Grants lost almost everything, including the White Haven farm
they had purchased from Julia's family. In an effort to support his family, the
former President wrote magazine articles about the Civil War and, at the
suggestion of legendary author and wit Mark Twain, who secured a lucrative
book contract for him, began to write his memoirs.

Tragically, Grant learned that he had developed inoperable throat cancer. The iron-willed General wrote furiously in an attempt to complete the

memoirs which he hoped would mean financial independence for Julia and their children. Mrs. Grant supervised his medication and cheered him as much as possible. With the end near, the family moved to a small vacation cottage in the mountains above Saratoga Springs, New York, in a search for some relief for the ailing General. Ulysses S. Grant died there on July 23, 1885, only one week after completing the memoirs. Julia, as through life, was by his side.

Ulysses S. Grant National Historic Site and Grant's Farm

SAINT LOUIS, MISSOURI

In 1820, Saint Louis businessman Frederick Dent, in an effort to escape the summer heat of the city, purchased a two-story frame house and an 850-acre farm in the country. He named the place White Haven (Figure 38A). Dent's son Fred was a classmate of Ulysses Grant at West Point, and when Grant was stationed in Saint Louis, he visited the Dents often. It became clear early on, however, that Grant was not calling on the family, but on Fred's sister Julia. The relationship developed into romance, and when Lieutenant Grant's army company was transferred from Saint Louis in 1844, he proposed and Julia accepted. White Haven was a focal point in the lives of the Grants for over forty years. After their wedding, they lived there briefly and their first child was born there in 1850. When Ulysses was assigned to California, Julia waited for him at White Haven, and when he resigned from the Army in 1854, he returned to farm eighty acres of the property that had been presented to Julia by her father. With the help of friends and Dent slaves, Ulysses hand-built a log house that was aptly named "Hardscrabble" (Figure 38B), not only for the land but for the difficulty of the times. The Grants ran both Hardscrabble and Mr. Dent's farm, where they grew potatoes, wheat and vegetables, gathered fruit and corded wood.

Grant worked hard alongside several slaves, but despite their efforts the farm was not profitable and the Grants decided to move to Galena, Illinois, where Ulysses worked in his father's leather-goods store. In 1861, they were living in a small house at 121 High Street when Grant volunteered to again serve in the military and was commissioned Colonel of the 21st Illinois Volunteer Infantry Regiment. The Civil War was to bring opportunity, military success, fame and fortune. The irony of Mrs. Grant's youth, growing up

Figure 38. (**A**) White Haven at the Ulysses S. Grant National Historic Site, Saint Louis, Missouri. Photograph courtesy National Park Service. (**B**) Grant's Farm, Saint Louis, Missouri. Photograph copyright©Anheuser-Busch Cos., Inc. Used with permission of Anheuser-Busch Cos., Inc. All rights reserved.

accustomed to the comforts of a slave-holding family, while her husband fought to save the Union and abolish the institution was not lost on reporters of the period.

During the war the Grants purchased White Haven, with plans to retire where Grant could breed and raise horses. Although that dream was never realized, White Haven remained important to the Grants. When they transferred ownership in 1884, shortly before Grant's death, Julia was heartbroken to give up "the dear old homestead."[68]

Acquisition of the ten-acre core of the White Haven property was authorized by Congress in 1989 and is now maintained as the Ulysses S. Grant National Historic Site for the purpose of interpreting Ulysses and Julia's lives and their Saint Louis home. The site, managed by the National Park Service, contains a modern visitor center plus five historic structures — the original White Haven house, a chicken house, icehouse, stone building and a stable converted to a museum.

Hardscrabble Cabin, restored and furnished in period, is part of Grant's Farm, a 281-acre entertainment and educational complex conceived, owned and operated by the Anheuser-Busch Company. Trams transport visitors through manicured grounds, stopping for elephant and bird shows and passing through Deer Park, home to 30 exotic species of deer, bison, elk and antelope living in a natural habitat. The trams also stop at Hardscrabble Cabin, a carefully preserved symbol of part of our national heritage. Fronting Hardscrabble is a dramatic reminder of the Civil War — a fence built from 2,563 rifle barrels used during the great conflict.

DIRECTIONS: From Saint Louis, take I 44 westbound to I 270 southbound to Exit 3 (Route 30, Gravois Road). Proceed northbound on Gravois Road and follow the historical markers to Grant Road and the National Historic Site and Grant's Farm, which are located across the road from one another (Figure 39).

PUBLIC USE: *Ulysses S. Grant National Historic Site:* **Season and hours:** Daily, 9 AM-5 PM, with guided house tours conducted on the half-hour beginning at 9:30 AM. The last tour is at 4 PM. Closed Thanksgiving, Christmas Day, New Year's Day. **For people with disabilities:** Visitor center, all buildings and restrooms are fully accessible and wheelchairs are available. *Grant's Farm:* The following schedule is for the 2010 season but changes yearly. Spring (April 17-May 2), Saturday 9 AM-3:30 PM, Sunday 9:30 AM-3:30 PM; Summer (May 4-August 15), Tuesday-Friday 9 AM-3:30 PM, Saturday, 9 AM-4 PM, Sunday, 9:30 AM-4 PM. Closed Mondays except Memorial Day and Labor Day, 9 AM-4 PM. Fall (August 20-October 31), Friday 9:30 AM-2:30 PM, Saturday and

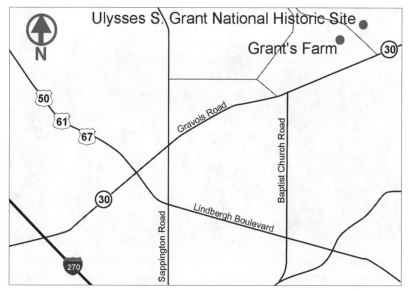

Figure 39. Location of Ulysses S. Grant National Historic Site and Grant's Farm, Saint Louis, Missouri.

Sunday 9:30 AM-3:30 PM. **Admission fee:** There is a parking charge only. **Food service:** The full service Bauernhof restaurant is on site and there are snack kiosks throughout the park. **Gift shop. For people with disabilities:** Fully accessible.

FOR ADDITIONAL INFORMATION: Contact: *Ulysses S. Grant National Historic Site*, 7400 Grant Road, Saint Louis, Missouri 63123, (314) 842-3298 and *Grant's Farm,* 10501 Gravois Road, Saint Louis, Missouri 63123, (314) 843-1700. **Web sites:** *www.nps.gov/ulsg* and *www.grantsfarm.com.* **Read:** John Y. Simon, ed. 1975. *The Personal Memoirs of Julia Dent Grant.*

Ulysses S. Grant Home State Historic Site

GALENA, ILLINOIS

The Grants returned to Galena after the Civil War, with Ulysses heralded as a conquering hero. Following a jubilant civic parade and patriotic speeches, the proud citizens of Galena presented General and Mrs. Grant with a handsome, fully furnished house (Figure 40, Plate VIII) as a symbol of

Figure 40. Ulysses S. Grant Home State Historic Site, Galena, Illinois. Photograph courtesy Illinois Historic Preservation Agency, Galena State Historic Sites.

their pride, respect and gratitude. Julia Grant recalled, ". . . after a glorious triumphal ride around the hills and valleys, so brilliant with smiles and flowers, we were conducted to a lovely villa exquisitely furnished with everything good taste could desire."[69]

The Grants were not destined to enjoy Galena for long as Ulysses was called to further national responsibility in 1868 when he was elected President of the United States. They returned to Galena briefly after his second term before embarking on a two-year trip around the world. Upon their return to Galena, they enjoyed another welcome-home celebration before settling into permanent residency in New York City.

The Galena house remained in the Grant family until 1904 when the Grant children presented it to the City of Galena "with the understanding that the property is to be kept as a memorial to the late General Ulysses S. Grant, and for no other purpose."[70] In 1931, the city deeded the house to the State of Illinois which maintains it under the management of the Illinois Historic Preservation Agency.

Restoration and modernization activities have continued with no destruction to the charm and ambience of the period. The Grant home is imposing, a two-story Italianate brick structure set on a hill and surrounded by lush greenery. Most of the furnishings are original Grant pieces that make the house an excellent example of mid-nineteenth-century taste in exterior design and interior décor. The interior is rich, with oil lamps, woven carpets and tall wooden cabinets. The dining room is set with Havilland china that was made for daughter Nellie's wedding in the White House in 1874. On the sideboard lies a glass bell jar that contains fruits preserved in wax by Mrs. Grant herself. President Grant's favorite stuffed chair in the library went with him to the White House and then was brought back to Galena.

"First Ladies Park" lies just west of the Grant Home, its centerpiece a striking eight-foot bronze statue of Julia Dent Grant. Although women constitute over 50% of our nation's population, less than 2% of its statuary recognizes women's achievements. As Julia Grant was ahead of her time in ideas and actions, believing in women's suffrage and being actively involved in her husband's presidency, Galena citizens organized a movement to honor Julia who found Galena "charming and bustling"[71] and proudly called it home. She joins Martha Washington, Abigail Adams, Dolley Madison, Mary Lincoln, Eleanor Roosevelt and Pat Nixon as the only First Ladies to be honored with statuary. So far.

DIRECTIONS: Galena is in the northwestern corner of Illinois on US Route 20 and Route 84. There are historical site markers leading visitors to the Grant House (Figure 41).

PUBLIC USE: Season and hours: April-October, Wednesday-Sunday, 9 AM-4:45 PM; November-March, Wednesday-Sunday, 9 AM-4 PM. Closed Thanksgiving Day, Christmas Day, New Year's Day, Martin Luther King, Jr. Day, Presidents' Day, Veterans' Day, Election Day. Access to the Grant Home is by guided tours only. **Admission fee:** Donation suggested. **For people with disabilities:** Accessibility is limited to the first floor but photographs of the second floor are displayed for those unable to reach the upstairs.

FOR ADDITIONAL INFORMATION: Contact: Ulysses S. Grant Home State Historic Site, 500 Bouthillier Street, PO Box 333, Galena, Illinois 61036, (815) 777-3310. **Web site:** *www.granthome.com.* **Read:** Thomas A. Campbell, Jr. 1979. "The U.S. Grant Home State Historic Site." *Historic Illinois* 1(February): 1–4.

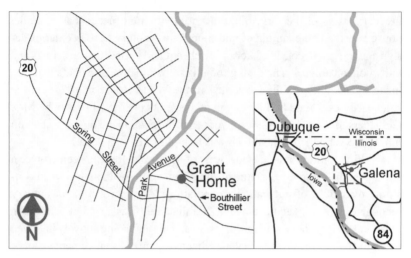

Figure 41. Location of Ulysses S. Grant Home State Historic Site in Galena, Illinois.

Grant Cottage State Historic Site

MOUNT MCGREGOR, NEW YORK

In June 1885, General and Mrs. Grant journeyed to a simple vacation cottage (Figure 42) on the slope of Mount McGregor near Saratoga Springs, New York. Grant, painfully afflicted with terminal throat cancer, hoped that the fresh air, healthy climate and relaxing atmosphere that included Julia's tender solicitude, would ease his suffering. On occasion, he was carried a few hundred yards to a scenic overlook above the Hudson Valley, but he dared not spend much time enjoying the view as he was racing desperately to complete the memoirs of his military and political careers that he hoped would replenish a fortune lost in a bad investment.

He completed the task only one week before his struggle with the cancer ended. Julia, as ever, was by his side. At the moment of death, the clock in the living room was stopped, a spontaneous and symbolic act that prompted a decision to freeze the moment in time — to preserve the cottage, its furnishings, decorations and other effects just as they were — a dramatic tribute to one of the nation's great military and political heroes.

Figure 42. Grant Cottage State Historic Site, Mount McGregor, Saratoga Springs, New York. Photograph courtesy The Friends of the Ulysses S. Grant Cottage.

DIRECTIONS: Mount McGregor is 40 miles north of Albany, New York. From Albany, take I 87 northbound to Exit 16 and proceed westbound on Ballard Road. At the intersection with US Route 9, there are historical markers directing visitors to the cottage located on the grounds of the Mount McGregor Correctional Facility. Visitors will be stopped briefly for identification before driving to the cottage (Figure 43).

PUBLIC USE: Season and hours: Memorial Day-Labor Day, Wednesday-Sunday, 10 AM-4 PM; Labor Day-Columbus Day, Saturdays and Sundays, 10 AM-4 PM. **Admission fee:** Yes, with discounts for children, seniors and groups with advance reservations. **Gift shop. Food service:** Picnics are allowed on Grant's Overlook. **For people with disabilities:** Fully accessible.

FOR ADDITIONAL INFORMATION: Contact: The Friends of the Ulysses S. Grant Cottage State Historic Site, Box 22924, Wilton, New York 12831, (518) 587-8277. **Web site:** *www.nysparks.state.ny.us*. (Click on "Historic Preservation"). **Read:** (1) Thomas M. Pitkin. 1973. *The Captain Departs: Ulysses S. Grant's Last Campaign*. (2) Leonard Poggiali. 1993. "Conditional Surrender: The Death of U. S. Grant, and the Cottage on Mount McGregor." *Blue and Gray Magazine*. February: 60–65.

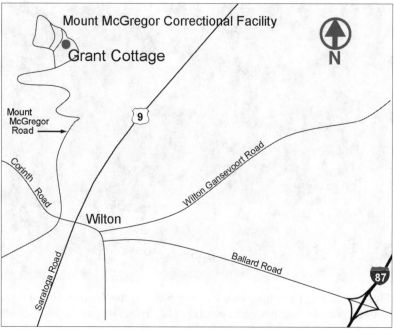

Figure 43. Location of Grant Cottage State Historic Site at Mount McGregor, near Saratoga Springs, New York.

Lucy Ware Webb Hayes

First Lady, 1877–1881

Born: August 18, 1831, Chillicothe, Ohio
Died: June 25, 1889, Fremont, Ohio

Lucy Hayes was considered by some historians to be "representative of the New Woman Era,"[72] perhaps the first "modern" First Lady. Educated at the Ohio Wesleyan University Preparatory School in Delaware, Ohio, before matriculating at Ohio Wesleyan Female College in Cincinnati, she was the first First Lady to graduate from college.

She married young attorney Rutherford B. Hayes in 1852, then bore him eight children, five of whom survived infancy. When Hayes volunteered for the Union Army at the outbreak of the Civil War, she joined her officer husband at military camps where, recognized for her kindness and generosity, she was called "Mother Lucy" by the troops. Hayes, later a general, was elected, in absentia, to Congress during the last year of the war but refused to leave for Washington until the conflict was over. In 1867, he was elected Governor of Ohio, ran unsuccessfully as a candidate for Congress in 1872, and was reelected governor in 1875. From that lofty political position, he was nominated as the 1876 Republican presidential standard-bearer, and inaugurated as President of the United States in 1877.

It was fitting that the country turned to a temperate President and First Lady following what many considered the social extravagance and corruption of the Grant White House and administration. Hayes' election had been controversial, but there was nothing controversial about the couple who assumed White House responsibility. Caring and compassionate, Lucy was a popular First Lady who brought intelligence, political acumen, experience and gracious behavior to the White House. Devoutly religious, the Hayeses began each day with a prayer service, and Lucy instituted hymn singing as regular Sunday-night entertainment. After a state dinner for the Crown Duke of Russia at which alcohol was served and behavior became less than dignified, President Hayes decreed that wine would no longer be served at White House social functions. One wag remarked that at state dinners "the water flowed like champagne."[73] And Lucy was forever, and mistakenly, branded with the nickname of "Lemonade Lucy."

One contemporary writer said that Lucy was of medium height, squarely built and had large features.

> *Her hair is a particularly noticeable feature, partly from the manner in which it is worn (always parted in the middle and combed plainly straight back), and mainly for its abundance and beauty of color and texture. Her brow is low and broad, and is unmarked by care. The mouth is large and adorned with beautiful teeth. Her eyes are large and expressive, and deepen in color from gray to black as the feelings are wrought upon — she is as solid a specimen of physical womanhood as the country can boast, and her presence is a tonic to weaker women.*[74]

What women particularly liked about Lucy was her identification with Rutherford's public life, especially her activities as a temperance leader and activist in women's causes and charities. Talk of women's suffrage and equal rights was in the political air and many hoped that Lucy's presence as First Lady signaled a breakthrough. She disappointed the reformers as there is no evidence that she contributed her opinion in any political decision-making, remaining, in many respects, a proper eighteenth-century woman — active, but not too active. It was reported that her husband admonished her about her activities.

On December 30, 1877, the President and Mrs. Hayes renewed their wedding vows in the Blue Room of the White House. Lucy, attended by the same bridesmaids, and in the wedding gown she had worn twenty-five years earlier, stood with Rutherford before the same minister who had conducted their original wedding ceremony.

Shortly before his death, Rutherford referred to his forty years of marriage to Lucy as "the most interesting fact of my life," explaining that the "crowning felicity" of his life had been "to dwell" with Lucy as she delighted in shedding "happiness on all around her" and tried to treat others as she would have wished to be treated.[75]

Lucy Hayes Heritage Center

CHILLICOTHE, OHIO

Lucy Ware Webb was born in a Federal-style home (Figure 44, Plate IX) built in 1825. Her physician father passed away when Lucy was two, her mother left in straitened circumstances. The most influential male figures in her life were Grandfather Isaac Cook and Uncle Matthew Cook, but she remained close to her mother. Lucy attended Miss Baskerville's School for Young Ladies and Chillicothe Female Seminary until 1844 when the family moved to Delaware, Ohio, to enroll her brothers Joseph and James at newly chartered Ohio Wesleyan College. It was there, as a student herself, that Lucy met Rutherford B. Hayes.

Figure 44. Lucy Hayes Heritage Center, Chillicothe, Ohio. Photograph by Jerry N. McDonald.

In 1883, the birth house in Chillicothe was moved from East 4th Street to its present location at 90 West 6th Street. Condemned in 1968, it was saved through the efforts of the Chillicothe Restoration Foundation which restored the house, a task complete in 1985. For many years it served as headquarters for a local arts council and was also rented out as a meeting house and site for other community activities. It was not until 1996 that an official organization was formed as the non-profit Friends of the Lucy Hayes Heritage Center which became its caretakers by forming and registering the "Birthplace of Lucy Webb Hayes" as a house-museum. The interior woodwork is original, but the Empire-style furniture only represents the period of the Webb residency. In the late 1990s, the Friends added second-floor displays featuring five cases of Webb and Hayes memorabilia and the first floor features a scale model showing the original house decorated with miniature representations of the period furnishings. Exterior landscaping includes a kitchen herb garden, a large lawn emphasizing the simplicity and grace of the birthplace, and Lilies of the Valley from the Hayes White House which continue blooming to welcome visitors.

A not-to-be-forgotten part of one's visit to the Lucy Hayes Birthplace is the serving of lemonade to each visitor, a charming tribute to "Lemonade Lucy," the gracious lady born there.

DIRECTIONS: Chillicothe is 45 miles south of Columbus, Ohio. From Columbus, take US Route 23 southbound to Main Street in Chillicothe (US 50) and proceed westbound to Walnut Street. Turn left on Walnut Street and drive southbound until reaching the Lucy Hayes Heritage Center on the southeast corner of Walnut Street and West 6th Street. Parking is just past the house on the left (Figure 45).

PUBLIC USE: Season and hours: Open for tours April-September, Monday 10 AM-2 PM, Saturday 1 PM-4 PM. Other times by appointment. **Admission fee. For people with disabilities:** Only the first floor is accessible. The first-floor model shows the second-floor for those unable to go upstairs.

FOR ADDITIONAL INFORMATION: Contact: Lucy Hayes Heritage Center, 90 West Sixth Street, Box 1790, Chillicothe, Ohio 45601, (740) 775-5829. **Web site:** *www.lucyhayes.com.* **Read:** Emily Apt Geer. 1984. *First Lady: The Life of Lucy Webb Hayes.*

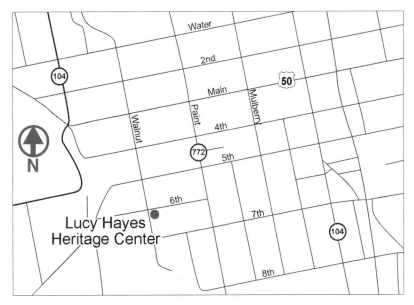

Figure 45. Location of the Lucy Hayes Heritage Center in Chillicothe, Ohio.

Rutherford B. Hayes Presidential Center

FREMONT, OHIO

A pleasant, twenty-five-acre wooded estate in the small town of Fremont is crowned by a stately red brick house filled with precious antiques and memories of the distinguished presidential couple who lived there.

Rutherford Hayes' uncle, Sardis Birchard, built the basic structure around 1860, and subsequent additions enlarged the Victorian home to its present dimensions of three stories and thirty-one rooms. Birchard named the estate Spiegel Grove (Figure 46), using the German word for "mirror" to describe the reflection of pools of water sparkling after a rain. When Birchard died in 1874, he bequeathed the estate to his nephew. The Hayeses loved the serene beauty of Spiegel Grove and made it their permanent home in the period between his second and third terms as Governor of Ohio, and they returned often during his presidency. The imposing family residence represents the glory days of Victorian architecture and interior décor. The formal dining room, the drawing room, the library, the master bedroom and others are furnished in Victorian splendor, all preserved and maintained for the enjoyment of modern visitors.

In the early part of the twentieth century, the Hayes' descendants presented Spiegel Grove to the State of Ohio under the condition that the state construct a separate library/museum to house the President's books and family memorabilia. Thus, in 1916, the nation's first presidential library came into existence in a classic building of Ohio sandstone.

The museum section (Plate IX) contains two floors filled with exhibits that chronicle the life and career of our nation's nineteenth president. Among the more popular items are a presidential carriage, two doll houses owned by daughter Fanny, Lucy Hayes' wedding gown and a display of the Hayes' White House china. As a major research collection for the post-Civil War period, the library contains 75,000 volumes and 4,500 linear feet of manuscript and photographic material, including the President's and Lucy's personal papers.

The flower- and tree-filled estate is enclosed by a decorative wrought-iron fence that features six gates brought from the White House grounds. Winding paths enable visitors to enjoy and appreciate the quiet grandeur of

Figure 46. "Spiegel Grove" at Rutherford B. Hayes Presidential Center, Fremont, Ohio. Photograph courtesy Rutherford B. Hayes Presidential Center.

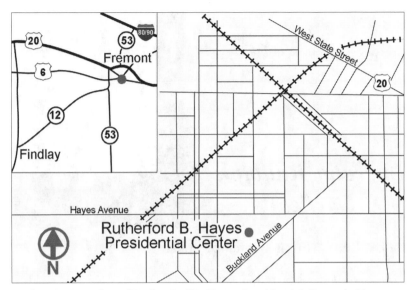

Figure 47. Location of Rutherford B. Hayes Presidential Center in Fremont, Ohio.

a particularly restful and relaxing presidential home and retreat. President and Mrs. Hayes are buried on a wooded knoll near an old Indian trail that winds through the serenity of Spiegel Grove.

DIRECTIONS: Fremont is just off the Ohio Turnpike (I 80/I 90). From I 80/I 90, take Exit 91 (Route 53/Fremont) and follow historical markers to the Hayes Center (Figure 47).

PUBLIC USE: Season and hours: Tuesday-Saturday, 9 AM-5 PM; Sundays and holidays, 12 M-5 PM. Guided tours of the house are conducted every thirty minutes. Museum tours are self-guided. The research library is closed Sundays and all holidays and all attractions are closed Thanksgiving Day, Christmas Day, New Year's Day, Easter Sunday. **Admission fee:** Yes, with discounts for groups, students and seniors. Admission includes access to the house and the museum. The library is open without charge. **Museum shop. For people with disabilities:** The museum is accessible. The first floor of the mansion is accessible and a videotape tour of the second floor is available.

FOR ADDITIONAL INFORMATION: Contact: Rutherford B. Hayes Presidential Center, Spiegel Grove, Fremont, Ohio 43420-2796, (419) 332-2081. **Web site:** *www.rbhayes.org.* **Read:** Ari Hoogenboom. 1995. *Rutherford B. Hayes: Warrior and President.*

Lucretia Rudolph Garfield

First Lady, March–September 1881

Born: April 19, 1832, Garrettsville, Ohio
Died: March 14, 1918, South Pasadena, California

Lucretia Rudolph attended the Western Reserve Eclectic Institute (later Hiram College), where she met her future husband, James Garfield. Upon graduation, she worked as a teacher in Ohio while he attended advanced classes at Williams College in Massachusetts. He graduated in 1856 and returned to Hiram where he was named president of the institute the following year. The two married in 1859 and, two years later, he left for the Civil War as Lieutenant Colonel of the 42nd Regiment, Ohio Volunteer Infantry. In 1862, he was elected to Congress, but it was not until December of the following year that he resigned his commission, by then a Major General, to serve his congressional term.

The first few years of the Garfield marriage were deeply troubled. James was gregarious and outgoing while Lucretia was shy and withdrawn. James was once quoted as feeling the marriage had been a mistake and Lucretia was certainly unhappy with James' extended absences. She gave birth to one child during one absence and another while he was in the army. Faced with yet another separation when he left for Washington, she prepared a note showing that in less than five years of marriage, they'd lived together for only twenty weeks. Garfield, shocked and surprised, vowed that he would never again go to Washington without her.

Lucretia, although shy, performed her duties as First Lady with tact and grace. Her philosophy was that if one had a job to do, it only made sense to learn to like it. She was naturally hospitable and the White House social calendar was filled with delightful events that included, incidentally, state dinners where wines and spirits were served.

The Garfields brought five active children, ranging in age from eight to seventeen, to the White House along with James' mother, eighty-year-old Eliza Garfield, who was the first mother to see her son inaugurated as President. The family was close, and their private activities revolved around education, as one might expect from a former teacher married to a former college president.

In May, 1881, Lucretia became seriously ill with malaria. James was devastated and remained at her bedside, attended to her needs, and even carried her from room to room. By the end of the month, Lucretia was out of danger and traveled to a summer house in Long Branch, New Jersey, to continue her convalescence. On July 2nd, the President was at Washington's Baltimore and Potomac Railroad Station en route to join her when he was shot by Charles Guiteau, a disgruntled office-seeker. Badly wounded, he was carried back to the White House. "Whatever happens, I want you to look after Crete," the President told those in attendance. To Mrs. James G. Blaine, wife of the Secretary of State, he said, "Don't leave me until Crete comes."[76] Lucretia rushed to his side and when her husband began to tell her how to bring up the children in his absence, she cut him short. "Well, my dear, you are not going to die as I am here to nurse you back to life; so please do not speak again of death."[77]

It was thought at first that Garfield's wound was mortal, then that he might fully recover. During the President's incapacity, Lucretia performed heroically, confidently and with optimism, although it could not have been easy. In the pre-air-conditioning atmosphere of mid-summer Washington, and before modern medicine, the days must have seemed endless. By early autumn the President, in agony but philosophical, insisted on a move to the cool breezes of the New Jersey shore. Once there, his condition worsened and he passed away on September 19, 1881. Lucretia, as ever, was by his side.

Lucretia Garfield moved back to Ohio to educate her children according to the plans she and James had made years before. She divided her remaining years between Ohio and a home in California where she passed away in 1918.

James A. Garfield National Historic Site

Mentor, Ohio

In 1876, Congressman and Mrs. James A. Garfield, who were spending summers back in Ohio, bought a run-down farm and 1½-story farmhouse in Mentor, the nucleus of which would evolve into a twenty-nine-room Victorian mansion with gables and bay windows. The property was named "Lawnfield" by reporters who camped there during the 1880 presidential campaign, although the Garfield family preferred to simply call it their "Mentor Farm" (Figure 48).

President Garfield enjoyed the home all too briefly. A great national grief followed his assassination, and thousands of citizens, concerned for Mrs. Garfield's welfare, sent donations. Moved by their generosity, and a desire for a suitable place to house the President's papers and books, she decided that the addition of a library to Lawnfield would be a most appropriate tribute to her late husband. The library, completed in 1886, was filled with the President's books as well as mementos, souvenirs, gifts and other remembrances, including Garfield's congressional desk, a (preserved) funeral

Figure 48. "Lawnfield" at James A. Garfield National Historic Site, Mentor, Ohio. Photograph courtesy National Park Service.

wreath sent by Queen Victoria and the President's Wooton desk with 110 filing compartments.

Visitors to Lawnfield enjoy seeing daughter Mollie's piano in the parlor and a fire screen in her mother's bedroom that features a picture of the President. The dining room features examples of Lucretia's artwork, as well as the Garfield's White House china. The interior museum includes Indian clubs that Garfield used for exercise and a white cradle first used when Lucretia was a baby and through the years by many of her grandchildren and great-grandchildren. Mrs. Garfield's decorating tastes are seen throughout, including a Japanese temple bell, stained glass windows and a finely appointed reception hall.

Lawnfield remained in the family until the 1930s when family members donated the house and its furnishings to the Western Reserve Historical Society, although the National Park Service now owns and manages the property. In 1998, an extensive restoration project was completed that involved structural repair and refurbishing.

A visitor center in an 1893 carriage house features exhibits that include the hat Garfield was wearing when he was shot, the original manuscript of his inaugural address and the Bible upon which he took the oath of office. There is also a bookstore and availability of an eighteen-minute video presentation covering President Garfield's life. Outbuildings on the eight-acre property consist of the campaign office, horse barn, chicken coop and a restored 1894 windmill.

DIRECTIONS: Mentor is east of Cleveland, just off I 90. From I 90 eastbound or westbound, take the Route 615/Center Street Exit and proceed northbound for 2 miles to US Route 20 (Mentor Avenue) then go west on Mentor Avenue 2 miles to Lawnfield on the right (Figure 49).

PUBLIC USE: Season and hours: May 1-October 31, Monday-Saturday 10 AM-5 PM, Sunday 12 M-5 PM. November 1-April 30, Saturday and Sunday only, 12 M-5 PM. Closed New Year's Day, Thanksgiving Day, Christmas Eve Day, Christmas Day. There is a special schedule during the Christmas holiday. Call for information. **Admission fee:** Yes. Children under 15, free. **Gift shop. For people with disabilities:** The Historic Site is largely accessible. The exception is a small section of the house which may be viewed by video.

FOR ADDITIONAL INFORMATION: Contact: James A. Garfield National Historic Site, 8095 Mentor Avenue, Mentor, Ohio 44606, (440) 255-8722. **Web site:** *www.nps.gov/jaga.* **Read:** Allen Peskin. 1978. *Garfield.*

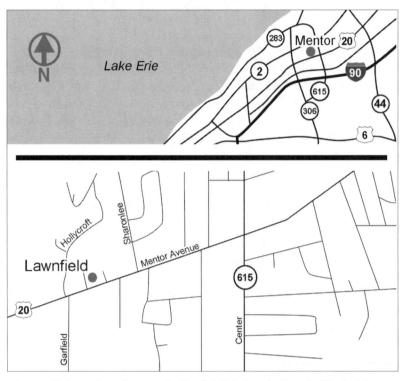

Figure 49. Location of James A. Garfield National Historic Site in Mentor, Ohio.

Ellen Herndon Arthur

Born: August 30, 1837, Culpeper County, Virginia
Died: January 12, 1880, New York, New York

Twenty months before her Vice-President husband succeeded to the presidency following the death of President Garfield, Ellen Arthur, only forty-two, died of pneumonia. Little is known of the Arthurs' married life, as President Arthur destroyed his personal papers shortly after leaving the White House, but there are indications that Ellen Arthur would have been an exemplary First Lady. According to one observer, she was "one of the best specimens of the Southern woman."[78]

Ellen Herndon, well-educated, graceful and interesting, came from a distinguished Virginia family. She moved easily in Washington society and it was a surprise to many that she and Chester Arthur, northern son of a Baptist minister, would fall in love. The couple appeared happy, although the Civil War created considerable domestic tension as Ellen's family had been slave owners.

The upwardly mobile couple lived well. They resided in a lavish apartment in New York, employed servants, sent their children to the best schools and traveled widely. Ellen's unexpected and premature death, however, struck her husband an emotional blow from which he never fully recovered. Politics had kept him away from home far too often, and he was filled with anguish for his feelings of guilt and neglect. When he succeeded to the presidency, he donated a stained glass window to Saint John's Church in Ellen's memory. It was placed on the south side of the building where he could see it from the White House.

Arthur did not remarry and asked his youngest sister, Mrs. Mary McElroy, to serve as White House hostess. She spent several months each year in Washington where her cheerful presence and inherent grace provided a woman's touch to the social necessities of the administration. At large parties, she had the good sense to invite other ladies — Julia Gardiner Tyler, widow of President John Tyler, and Harriet Lane Johnston, niece of President James Buchanan, former White House occupants — to receive with her.

Frances Folsom Cleveland

First Lady, 1886–1889, 1893–1897

Born: July 21, 1864, Buffalo, New York
Died: October 29, 1947, Baltimore, Maryland

Frances Folsom literally grew into the job of First Lady. Her father, who died when she was eleven, was Grover Cleveland's Buffalo law partner and Cleveland became administrator of the Folsom estate and acted as sort of guardian/honorary uncle for young "Frankie." By the time Cleveland entered the New York Governor's Mansion in 1883, Frankie had matured into an attractive, gracious young lady with whom he fell in love. His affection was reciprocated and following his inauguration as President and her coincident graduation from Wells College, they became secretly engaged.

Amazingly, the secret remained just that. Frances and her mother visited the White House one time and the rumor mill prophesized that the bachelor President would soon marry the widowed Mrs. Folsom, never suspecting that the future bride was her young and vivacious daughter. To everyone's shocked surprise, Cleveland announced the glad news the following year, and the wedding was held in the Blue Room, the first presidential marriage ceremony held in the White House.

At twenty-two, Mrs. Cleveland became the youngest First Lady. She was, nonetheless, socially mature and her soirees, teas and other events were carried off with aplomb and great success. Chief Usher "Ike" Hoover wrote, "No more brilliant and affable lady than Mrs. Cleveland has ever graced the portals of this old mansion. Her very presence threw an air of beauty on the entire surroundings, whatever the occasion or the company."[79]

There is no indication that Frances Cleveland developed an interest in politics; her influence was restricted to domestic household matters. She was content to be the "sensible, domestic wife"[80] her husband wanted, although her calming influence helped tone down his temper, polish his manners and smooth many personal relationships. She even persuaded the workaholic Cleveland to relax and take an occasional vacation.

At the end of the first Cleveland administration, defeated by Benjamin Harrison, she instructed the White House staff to keep the house in good order as she predicted that she and Grover would return four years later, which they did. After his second term, the Clevelands retired to Princeton, New Jersey, where they purchased a fine estate home, "Westland," and settled into a quiet life. The President passed away in Princeton in 1908.

Mrs. Cleveland, only forty-four, remained in "Westland" and became friendly with Thomas Preston, a professor of archaeology at Princeton University. Their marriage in 1913 made her the first presidential widow to remarry. She entertained frequently, engaged in charitable work and became involved in the affairs of Princeton University and fund raising for her alma mater, Wells College. Mrs. Preston died in 1947 at eighty-three.

Caroline Lavinia Scott Harrison

First Lady, 1889–1892

Born: October 10, 1832, Oxford, Ohio
Died: October 25, 1892, Washington, DC

Caroline ("Carrie") Scott and Benjamin Harrison met when he was a freshman at Farmers' College in Cincinnati, where her Presbyterian-minister father taught mathematics and science. Reverend Scott later established a school for girls in Cincinnati that moved to Oxford, Ohio, and was renamed Oxford Female Institute. Anxious to be near Carrie, Benjamin transferred to Miami University in Oxford and they began a serious courtship. Upon his graduation in 1852, they became engaged but he left shortly to study law in Cincinnati. She graduated from the Female Institute the following year and began to teach music in Oxford. They married on October 20, 1853, saving money by residing at his father's farm near North Bend, Ohio.

The following summer, they moved to Indianapolis to experience the hardships of many young couples — establishment of a law practice, childbirth and the embarrassment of having to borrow money from family and friends to pay for food and lodgings. By dint of hard work and long hours, Benjamin's law practice improved and they gradually moved upward to better homes and a more comfortable lifestyle.

In 1862, Harrison entered the Union Army; he joined as a captain and was a brevet brigadier general by the end of the conflict. The long wartime separations from Carrie, however, produced loneliness and a sense of self-reproach, a time of reflection in which he realized how much he loved and depended on her. A man of deep reticence, he once wrote, "I now see so many faults in my domestic life that I long for an opportunity to correct. I know I could make your life so much happier than ever before."[81] He was true to his word. After the war he appeared to be as busy as ever, yet when he entered the maelstrom of politics, he always found time for Carrie and their two children. More importantly, he encouraged her efforts at self-expression, especially in watercolor painting. She also became active in civic affairs, served as president of the local women's club and kept busy with china painting and playing the organ in church, where she also taught Sunday school.

When Benjamin and Caroline Harrison moved into the White House in 1889, they brought her ninety-year-old father; her young widowed niece, Mary Dimmick; and their daughter Mary Harrison McKee along with her husband and two lively children. Son Russell with his wife and young child were also around much of the time, so not only was it the first four-generation White House, it was crowded!

The White House, not built to accommodate so many residents, was badly in need of repairs. Congress talked of constructing a new White House somewhere else in Washington, or perhaps separating the executive offices from the family living quarters. Traditionalists prevailed, however, when Congress appropriated $35,000 for renovations to the existing building. It became Mrs. Harrison's responsibility to supervise and accomplish a daunting task that involved, for starters, the eradication of insects and rodents from the basement.

Caroline Harrison was up to the task. By then a fifty-six-year-old grandmother, she was experienced in politics, society and the arts. Animated, peppy and outgoing, she was the antithesis of her more formal and socially uncomfortable husband and became an extremely active First Lady. Paul Boller wrote:

> *While giving the White House a facelift, Mrs. Harrison continued to pursue one of her favorite hobbies, needlework, and donated most of her handiwork to church bazaars and charities. She did a lot of painting, too, decorating White House candlesticks, milk pitchers, flower-pot saucers and cracker boxes with her favorite designs: flowers, leaves, shepherdesses, milkmaids and, of course, four-leafed clovers. She even painted her favorite decorations onto porcelain dishes for Washington ladies looking for White House souvenirs. 'Many a baby whose parents have named him for*

the president,' noted one reporter, 'has received a milk set painted by Mrs. Harrison with cunning Kate Greenaway children.' In 1890, the First Lady helped organize the Daughters of the American Revolution, served as the organization's first president-general and, in an address to the DAR's First Continental Congress, declared, 'We have within ourselves the only element of destruction; our foes are from within, not from without. Our hope is in unity and self-sacrifice.'[82]

Mrs. Harrison enjoyed the White House and more than made up for her husband's iciness in personal relations. Unfortunately, she was not well physically and became seriously ill early in 1892. During the presidential campaign that year, she was bedridden, and the President reduced his public appearances to remain at her side. His opponent, former President Grover Cleveland, out of respect for the ailing First Lady, also cut down on his campaign appearances. Just two weeks before Election Day, Caroline Harrison died of tuberculosis, the second First Lady to die in the White House.

President Harrison was defeated by Grover Cleveland. For the remaining months of Harrison's term, daughter Mary McKee acted as White House hostess.

President Benjamin Harrison Home

INDIANAPOLIS, INDIANA

After distinguished military service in the Civil War, General Benjamin Harrison returned to Indianapolis to join his family in their pre-war home; subsequently they constructed a sixteen-room mansion (Figure 50) in the brick Italianate style where Caroline Harrison, a talented professional artist, filled the house with her colorful work.

Following Caroline's death and the conclusion of his presidency, President Harrison moved back to the family home to which was added a spacious porch reflecting the Colonial Revival style popular in the 1890s. In 1896, Harrison married his late wife's niece, Mary Dimmick, and the couple lived in the home until his death in 1901. Mrs. Mary Harrison remained there until 1913 when she leased the house to private tenants and moved to New York. In 1937, the home was sold to the Arthur Jordan Foundation as a student dormitory and, in 1965, the President Benjamin Harrison Foundation assumed

Figure 50. President Benjamin Harrison Home, Indianapolis, Indiana. Photograph courtesy President Benjamin Harrison Home.

control and converted it to represent the time of its residency by Benjamin, Caroline and Mary Dimmick Harrison; family members contributed papers, furniture and memorabilia to the memorial effort. The house contains approximately 10,000 artifacts, eighty-five percent of which belonged to the Harrison family. Just inside the home's handsome dark walnut double doors is a portrait of Caroline Harrison and a full-length picture of her hangs in the master bedroom suite.

Ten rooms on two floors have been fully restored. The third floor serves as a museum gallery for the Harrisons' personal artifacts and exhibits delineating the President's life and political career. The most striking display is the White House china designed by Caroline Harrison — corn tassels on the border, forty-four stars symbolizing the states of the Union and an American eagle representing strength and unity. Many of her watercolors are hung throughout the house and an oil painting of peaches, attributed to Caroline, is a feature of the dining room.

DIRECTIONS: The Harrison Home is 1 block north of I 65. **Southbound on I 65:** Take the Meridian Street Exit to 11th Street and continue straight on 11th to Delaware Street. Turn left for one block to the home. **From I 65 northbound:** Exit at Pennsylvania Street, immediately turning left for 1 block to 11th, left again for one block to Delaware and left to the home. Parking is in the rear (Figure 51).

PUBLIC USE: Season and hours: Monday-Saturday, 10 AM-3:30 PM; Sundays in June and July, 12:30 PM-3:30 PM. Guided tours are conducted every 30 minutes, the first at 10 AM, the last at 3:30 PM. Closed Memorial Day weekend, Labor Day, Thanksgiving Day, December 24–26, New Year's Eve, and the first three weeks in January. **Admission fee:** Yes, with discounts for groups, students and AAA members. **Gift shop. For people with disabilities:** There is a ramp to the first floor and all floors are accessible by elevator.

FOR ADDITIONAL INFORMATION: Contact: President Benjamin Harrison Home, 1230 North Delaware Street, Indianapolis, Indiana 46202-2531, (317) 631-1888. **Web site:** *www.pbhh.org.* **Read:** (1) Harry J. Sievers, S.J. 1960. *Benjamin Harrison, Hoosier Warrior.* (2) Harry J. Sievers, S.J. 1959. *Benjamin Harrison, Hoosier Statesman. From the Civil War to the White House, 1865–1888.* (3) Harry J. Sievers, S.J. 1997. *Benjamin Harrison, Hoosier President.* (4) Charles W. Calhoun. 2005. *Benjamin Harrison.*

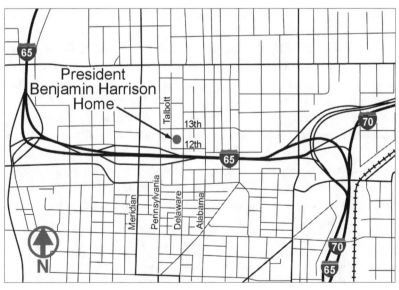

Figure 51. Location of President Benjamin Harrison Home in Indianapolis, Indiana.

Ida Saxton McKinley

First Lady, 1897–1901

Born: June 8, 1847, Canton, Ohio
Died: May 26, 1907, Canton, Ohio

While attending the Pan-American Exposition in Buffalo, New York, on September 6, 1901, President William McKinley was shot by anarchist Leon Czolgosz. Assisted to a chair, the President whispered to his secretary, "My wife . . . Be careful how you tell her . . . Oh, be careful."[83]

William McKinley was considered a saint among husbands, as he lavished attention, consideration and love on his wife Ida through their marriage of 30 years, 28 of which she spent as a semi-invalid. Phlebitis, a circulatory disease, had left her crippled, unable to stand or walk without difficulty. Then, after the deaths of her mother and two children in rapid succession, Ida became subject to epilepsy, manifested in sudden rigidity and memory loss. If McKinley resented the years of care devoted to Ida, there was never an indication. Some politicians expressed dissatisfaction that McKinley's solicitude took too much of his time and attention, but the general public loved and appreciated his sincere devotion to his frail, delicate wife. Journalist Charles Willis Thompson observed:

> *There is nothing more beautiful than his long devotion to his invalid wife, whose invalidism was not of the body alone. The terrible illness which ruined her health permanently impaired her spirit, but this only made her man her knight: it made him more unselfishly devoted, more tender.*[84]

Ida's illness had ups and downs, and when McKinley was President, the First Lady presided at occasional receptions and state dinners, although accommodations were made for her frailty. She remained seated at receptions, with a bouquet of flowers in her hands so people might understand there would be no handshake. At state dinners, normal protocol was revised so that she, rather than the wife of the guest of honor, sat next to the President so he might tend to her in case of a mild seizure. Mrs. McKinley's brave performance as First Lady was "an inspiration to all women who for one reason or another are hindered from playing a brilliant individual role in life," read an article in *Harper's Bazaar*.[85]

Ida Saxton had been the "belle of the ball" — bright, witty, vivacious. And headstrong. She attended Brooke Hall Academy in Philadelphia and toured Europe before she took a job in her father's bank. She "set her cap" for handsome young attorney William McKinley, and they were soon deeply in love; their mutual admiration was extreme. He catered to her every wish, and she idolized him. The birth of first daughter Katherine added to their happiness but lasted only two years before death, illness and misfortune marred their lives. Ida's mother died a few months before the birth of the McKinley's second child, who lived only five months. Mrs. McKinley became obsessed with surviving daughter Katherine's well-being and, when the youngster died of typhoid fever in 1876, only three years-old, Ida McKinley became totally dependent on her husband. Through the calamities, William McKinley persevered. His love and devotion remained constant.

First Ladies National Historic Site

CANTON, OHIO

The Saxton McKinley House (Figure 52, Plate X), the family home of Ida Saxton McKinley, served as the McKinleys' official residence when William served in Congress from 1878 to 1891.

In 1998, the Saxton McKinley House was dedicated as the home of the National First Ladies' Library — the first facility dedicated to the commemoration of the lives and accomplishments of America's First Ladies and other influential American women. As such, "the Library will fulfill this mission by serving as both a physical education facility and an electronic virtual library, in an effort to educate people in the United States and around the world."[86]

Figure 52. Saxton McKinley House. Photograph courtesy National First Ladies' Library.

In October, 2000, the house was acquired by the National Park Service and was designated First Ladies National Historic Site. The site is operated by the National First Ladies' Library under a cooperative agreement with the park service.

Visitors to this site learn about the contributions of our First Ladies through permanent and changing exhibits. The only complete collection of portraits of all the First Ladies and other women serving as White House hostesses is on permanent display in the third-floor ballroom where, more than a century ago, many parties had been held, as the Saxtons were among the most prominent families in Canton. On the exterior, the massive wrap-around porch was recreated by studying early photographs of the house.

The public rooms have been restored to their original splendor, complete with ornate historical wallpaper and period furniture typical of the era. The few existing early photographs of the interior were carefully studied for design elements so that the furnishings and wallpaper in President McKinley's study and those in Ida McKinley's sitting room and bedroom might be duplicated.

The front entry and stair hall are particular favorites, as they feature a recreated wallpaper of a dense fruit, flower and foliage design while the library and parlor are decorated in the more opulent Italianate style that became popular after the Civil War. That area features twenty-three different wallpaper patterns in subtle shades of tan, grayish green, rose and warm beige. The Wilton carpet with a chrysanthemum pattern was loomed in the same mill that Dolley Madison used when she ordered some of the carpet for the White House during her tenure as First Lady. According to Dr. Sheila Fisher who is in charge of the restoration, "We are a work in progress, and are always looking for historic items from the First Ladies."[87]

The National First Ladies' Library began to run out of space almost immediately after its creation, but in the late 1990s, the Marsh Belden, Sr. family donated the entire City National Bank Building to the library. Renovations necessary to adapt the building from a banking establishment to a library began immediately and in September, 2003, First Lady Laura Bush inaugurated the National First Ladies' Library Education and Research Center. The Library — a seven-story, 20,000 square-foot building containing an archive of writings, artifacts and resources associated with First Ladies and other famous women — is only one block from the Saxton McKinley House. In addition, the Center provides K-12 educational programs, curricular enrichment materials and a constantly expanding electronic bibliography of more than 45,000 entries, manuscripts and publications about some of the most influential women in history, available to students, educators and scholars from any internet-accessible personal computer.

Each of its seven floors is named after a First Lady from Ohio — Florence Harding, Nellie Taft, Ida McKinley, Caroline Harrison, Lucretia Garfield, Lucy Hayes and Anna Harrison. The Florence Harding Floor on the lower level, for example, contains a 91-seat Victorian Theatre featuring film, live presentations and lectures. The Nellie Taft Floor contains the main exhibit room and a library with current releases, rare books and a collection replicating the first White House library, founded by First Lady Abigail Fillmore. Other floors contain conference rooms, a research library, archival storage rooms and offices.

The building dates to 1895 and every effort has been made to retain its Victorian ambience. A large skylight over the main banking room on the first floor has been fully restored and a monumental staircase of cast iron railings, a wood handrail and slate steps leads to the upper floors. According to Mary A. Regula, president and founding chair of the National First Ladies' Library:

This project is really about creating a living library for future
generations that will serve as a tool for learning and exploring

the historic contributions of influential American women. Our main goal is education, education, education and education at all levels to make history come alive.[88]

DIRECTIONS: The First Ladies National Historic Site/Saxton McKinley House and the National First Ladies' Library Education and Research Center are located in Canton. From I 77, take Exit 105 (Tuscarawas Street/ Route 172) and proceed eastbound to Market Avenue. Turn right (south) to the corner of 4th Street SE, and the Saxton McKinley House on the right at 331 Market Street South. The Education and Research Center, one block north, is at 205 Market Avenue South (Figure 53).

PUBLIC USE: Season and hours: Both the Saxton McKinley House and Education and Research Center are open by guided tour only. Tours are conducted Tuesday-Saturday, 9:30 AM-2:30 PM, beginning on the half-hour except 11:30 AM. During June, July and August, tours are also conducted on Sundays at 12:30 PM, 1:30 PM and 2:30 PM. Tours, which take 1½-hours, begin at the Education and Research Center, then continue at the Saxton McKinley House. Reservations are required for groups of six or more and recommended for all others. Closed New Year's Eve and Day, Presidents' Day, Memorial Day, July 4, Labor Day, Thanksgiving Day and day after, Christmas Eve Day and Christmas Day. **Admission fee:** Yes, with discounts for students and seniors. **Gift shop. For people with disabilities:** Accessible.

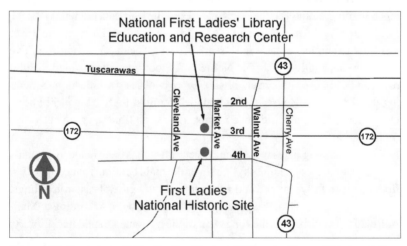

Figure 53. Location of First Ladies National Historic Site and National First Ladies' Library Education and Research Center in Canton, Ohio.

FOR ADDITIONAL INFORMATION: Contact: National First Ladies' Library, 205 Market Avenue South, Canton, Ohio 44702, (330) 452-0876. **Web site:** *www.firstladies.org*. **Read:** (1) Edward T. Heald. 1992. *The Condensed Biography of William McKinley*. (2) Carl Sferrazza Anthony, ed. 2003. *"This Elevated Position . . ." A Catalogue and Guide to the National First Ladies' Library and the Importance of First Lady History.*

William McKinley Presidential Library & Museum

CANTON, OHIO

The William McKinley Presidential Library & Museum (Figure 54) is a living memorial serving the cultural needs of Stark County and the City of Canton, Ohio. One gallery is devoted exclusively to the largest collection of McKinley memorabilia in the world — clothing, furniture, photographs and personal mementos that represent the public and private life of William and Ida McKinley. Several of Ida McKinley's dresses and items of her jewelry are displayed and the gallery is dramatized by a tableau of the fully decorated

Figure 54. William McKinley Presidential Library & Museum. Canton, Ohio. Photograph courtesy William McKinley Presidential Library & Museum.

McKinley parlor, with animatronic figures of the McKinleys in full evening dress, welcoming good friends to their cheery home. Portions of the McKinley bedroom and a section of his office are also represented in the tableau.

The McKinley Monument which overlooks the Library and Museum, is one of the most impressive and imposing presidential resting places. One hundred and eight broad granite steps lead up to a magnificent mausoleum high above the city McKinley served with devotion and love. President and Mrs. McKinley and their two daughters, both of whom died in early childhood, are entombed in a handsome double-domed building of pink Milford granite, the exterior dome seventy-five feet in diameter and ninety-five feet high.

DIRECTIONS: From I 77 in Canton, take Exit 106 eastbound onto 12th Street, NW. Proceed eastbound on 12th Street to the bottom of the hill and turn right/southbound onto Stadium Park Drive that leads to McKinley Monument Drive and parking areas for the museum and monument (Figure 55).

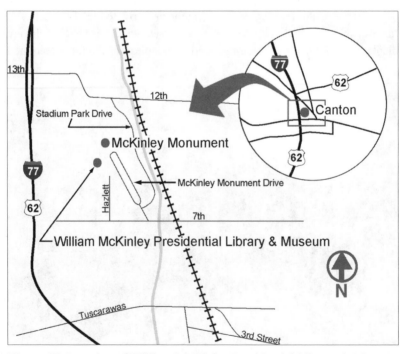

Figure 55. Location of William McKinley Presidential Library & Museum and the McKinley Monument in Canton, Ohio.

Plate I

Top: Life-size sculpted figures of George and Martha Washington and two of Martha's grandchildren, Wash and Nelly, shown here overlooking part of their beloved plantation home, welcome visitors to Mount Vernon. **Bottom:** George and Martha Washington with Martha's granddaughters Nelly and Eliza, and a servant, pictured in George's study at Mount Vernon. Painting, oil on canvas, by Thomas Pritchard Rossiter.

Plate II

Top: The long room – the living room – at Peacefield, long-time residence of John and Abigail Adams, in Quincy, Massachusetts. **Bottom:** Life-size sculpted figures of thoughtful and devoted James and Dolley Madison grace the back lawn at Montpelier, the Madison family estate near Orange, Virginia.

Plate III

Top: The drawing room at Ash Lawn-Highland, farm home of James and Elizabeth Monroe in the Piedmont near Charlottesville, Virginia. The panoramic wallpaper in the drawing room was a popular feature of fine homes in the eighteenth century. **Bottom:** The children's room with its king's crown canopy bed was used by James and Elizabeth Monroe's daughters, Eliza and Maria, at Ash Lawn-Highland.

Plate IV

Top: The dramatic entrance hall at The Hermitage, home of Andrew and Rachel Jackson near Nashville, Tennessee, was noted for its panoramic wallpaper and beautiful circular staircase. **Bottom:** A section of *Rachel's Garden* at The Hermitage, a fine example of a southern plantation garden, maintained today as it was designed and tended by Rachel Jackson early in the nineteenth century.

Plate V

Top: One of the ten fireplaces at Grouseland, the grand home of William Henry and Anna Harrison, located at Vincennes, Indiana, on what was the early-nineteenth-century American frontier. **Middle:** The living-room fireplace at the Fillmore House Museum, the hand-built home of Millard and Abigail Fillmore, in East Aurora, New York. **Bottom:** A "tumbling block" quilt sewn by Abigail Fillmore gracing a bedroom of the Fillmore House Museum.

Plate VI

Top: The family parlor at Wheatland, the Lancaster, Pennsylvania, home of James Buchanan and his ward, niece and White House hostess, Harriet Lane. The table in the foreground remains as it was, set for tea for two. **Bottom:** The rear parlor at the home of Abraham and Mary Lincoln, centerpiece of the Lincoln Home National Historic Site in Springfield, Illinois.

Plate VII

Dramatic rendering of Mary Todd Lincoln at the Abraham Lincoln Presidential Library and Museum in Springfield, Illinois. Titled *What Are They Wearing in Washington?*, this exhibit depicts Mary being fitted with a ball gown in the Blue Room of the White House. Surrounding Mary are reproductions of gowns worn by her social rivals, each of whom has something unkind to say about the First Lady.

Plate VIII

Top: One corner of the bedroom of Eliza Johnson in the Johnson home, part of the Andrew Johnson National Historic Site, Greeneville, Tennessee. Mrs. Johnson was tubercular, hence the spittoon. **Bottom:** Statue of First Lady Julia Grant, situated in a garden adjacent to the Grant home at the Ulysses S. Grant Home State Historic Site, Galena, Illinois.

Plate IX

Top: Refurbished bedroom with trundle bed in the childhood home of Lucy Webb Hayes, the centerpiece of the Lucy Hayes Heritage Center, Chillicothe, Ohio. **Bottom:** Part of the Lucy Hayes display at the Rutherford B. Hayes Presidential Center, Fremont, Ohio. The ruby gown is that worn by the First Lady for her official White House portrait.

Plate X

Top: The restored formal parlor in the Saxton McKinley House, Canton, Ohio. The house was First Lady Ida Saxton McKinley's girlhood home and now serves as the First Ladies National Historic Site. **Bottom:** Ida McKinley's restored bedroom and dressing room in the Saxton McKinley house. Note the dressmaker's form at left; wasp-waisted dresses were very stylish during the late part of the nineteenth century.

Plate XI

Top: Edith Roosevelt's private sitting room at Sagamore Hill, Theodore and Edith Roosevelt's retreat near Oyster Bay, New York. **Bottom:** The Lou Hoover gallery at the Herbert Hoover Presidential Library and Museum in West Branch, Iowa, provides overviews of her important contributions as, among other fields, geologist, world traveler, humanitarian, social progressive — and long-time supporter of the Girl Scouts of America.

Plate XII

Top: The Dresden Room at Springwood, ancestral home of Franklin D. Roosevelt, utilized by First Lady Eleanor Roosevelt as a sitting room. **Bottom:** The kitchen at Springwood, part of the Home of Franklin D. Roosevelt National Historic Site in Hyde Park, New York.

Plate XIII

Top: Sitting room at the Campobello cottage, the Franklin Roosevelt family vacation retreat on Campobello Island, New Brunswick. **Bottom:** Sitting room at Val-Kill, First Lady Eleanor Roosevelt's residence on the grounds of the Eleanor Roosevelt National Historic Site in Hyde Park, New York.

Plate XIV

Top: Exterior of Val-Kill cottage, Eleanor Roosevelt's private residence in Hyde Park, New York. **Bottom:** First Lady Eleanor Roosevelt's porch bedroom at Val-Kill, Hyde Park, New York.

Plate XV

Top: The screened porch and view at Truman Home, Harry S Truman National Historic Site, Independence, Missouri. **Middle:** First Lady Mamie Eisenhower's famous "pink bedroom" in the Eisenhower home, Eisenhower National Historic Site, Gettysburg, Pennsylvania. **Bottom:** The formal dining room at the Lyndon and Lady Bird Johnson ranch home, now part of the Lyndon B. Johnson National Historical Park, Stonewall, Texas.

Plate XVI

Top: The First Lady Rosalynn Carter gallery at the Jimmy Carter Library and Museum, Atlanta, Georgia. **Bottom:** Entrance to the gallery at the George Bush Presidential Library and Museum, College Station, Texas, focusing on Barbara Bush's activities as First Lady and thereafter.

PUBLIC USE: Season and hours: Monday-Saturday, 9 AM-4 PM; Sunday, 12 M-4 PM. Closed all major holidays. **Admission fee:** Yes, with discounts for groups, seniors and children. **Picnic Area. Gift Shop. For people with disabilities:** Fully accessible.

FOR ADDITIONAL INFORMATION: Contact: William McKinley Presidential Library & Museum, 800 McKinley Monument Drive, NW, Canton, Ohio 44708, (330) 455-7043. **Web site:** *www.mckinleymuseum.org.* **Read:** (1) Margaret Leech. 1959. *In the Days of McKinley.* (2) Edward T. Heald. 1992. *The Condensed Biography of William McKinley.*

Edith Kermit Carow Roosevelt

First Lady, 1901–1909

Born: August 6, 1861, Norwich, Connecticut
Died: September 30, 1948, Oyster Bay, New York

If patience is a virtue, then Edith Roosevelt was a most virtuous woman. Theodore Roosevelt and Edith Carow grew up in the same New York City Union Square neighborhood and had known one another for years as Edith was a close friend of Theodore's sister Corinne. Edith, a reserved young lady who attended Miss Comstock's fashionable private school, was a voracious reader interested in many subjects and she and Theodore developed an intellectual and personal relationship. There was an assumption that it would develop into romance, and as they grew older there was talk of marriage, but a quarrel during Theodore's second year at Harvard caused an estrangement and in his junior year he fell in love with Alice Lee, whom he married in 1880. There is no record of Edith's feelings, but as a lifelong friend of the Roosevelt family and with impeccable social credentials, she put aside any negative feelings and attended the Roosevelt-Lee wedding. After all, she was brought up to behave properly, no matter how painful the experience might be.

Theodore's marriage to Alice was happy, and the couple looked forward to the birth of their first child in 1884. Theodore was at the state capital in Albany on business when notified of the baby's impending birth, but as he prepared to join Alice at home in New York City, he was further informed that she was experiencing serious complications. He rushed to the city to discover that both his wife and his mother were critically ill. His mother died the next morning of typhoid fever, and Alice, stricken with Bright's Disease, died eleven hours later. The baby survived.

In an attempt to assuage his grief, Roosevelt left the infant, named Alice, with his sister and moved to a ranch in North Dakota to assume the rugged outdoor life of a cowboy. The ranching venture faltered after two years and he moved back to New York.

Theodore Roosevelt, a romantic, felt that he should be true to his wife forever. Years later, his daughter Alice spoke of her father's feelings.

> *I think my father tried to forget he had ever been married to my mother. To blot the whole episode out of his mind. He didn't just never mention her to me, he never mentioned her name to anyone . . . There was that awful sentimentality about the concept that you loved only once and you never loved again.*[89]

He avoided contact with his old sweetheart, Edith Carow, but when they happened to meet one afternoon, the inevitable happened. Edith overcame her early sense of rejection and Theodore overcame his feelings of guilt. The two, made for each other from the beginning, married in London on December 2, 1886.

The marriage was extremely happy, although hindsight tells us that the peripatetic TR (his nickname) was not the easiest man to handle. The family grew to include four boys and two girls, and while Edith was a restraining influence on TR, she was no meek and mild wife. Personable and warm-hearted, she was also forthright, unsentimental and reserved, a perfect foil for her exuberant, brash and often irritating husband. She handled the children, the house, the budget — and her husband. Without question, Edith was the anchor in TR's life.

She was a superb First Lady. Author Paul Boller wrote:

> *Mrs. Roosevelt managed it all with imperturbable effortlessness, imposing discipline on the youngsters but permitting them a great deal of freedom. She also supervised the household with quiet efficiency and won the devotion of the White House staff with her thoughtfulness. As hostess, too, for countless dinners, parties, teas, receptions and 'at homes,' she was always 'dignified and wise,' according to her husband, and took her place beside Dolley Madison in the opinion of Washington social observers with a historical bent.*[90]

The Roosevelt years in the White House were glorious, and they departed the presidency with reluctance.

Retirement was not easy. TR ran for the presidency again in 1912 as a third party candidate, but suffered a humiliating defeat. Then, in 1918, the family was devastated by the tragic news that youngest son, fighter pilot Quentin, had been shot down and killed in aerial combat in France during World War I. Less than a year later, January 6, 1919, TR passed away at home. While Edith continued permanent residence at their Long Island home and traveled extensively through Europe and South America, life was not always kind. Son Kermit took his own life in 1943, and eldest son, Brigadier General Theodore Roosevelt, Jr., died of a heart attack in 1944 while on active duty in France in World War II.

By 1947, Edith Roosevelt was mainly bedridden, but as one of her last actions, she wrote her own epitaph, "Everything she did was for the happiness of others." On September 30, 1948, Edith Kermit Carow Roosevelt passed away at eighty-seven. Biographer Sylvia Morris commented, "It was her second passing from this world. The first had been on January 6, 1919."[91]

Sagamore Hill National Historic Site

OYSTER BAY, NEW YORK

Two months before his marriage to Alice Lee in 1880, Theodore Roosevelt purchased acreage on a promontory overlooking Oyster Bay on the northern shore of Long Island, New York. Plans were drawn for a house to be named Leeholm, but before construction began, Alice passed away in childbirth, leaving a baby girl in Theodore's care.

Persuaded by his sister that he needed a home for his infant daughter, Roosevelt proceeded with the building plans and constructed a rambling Queen Anne house of frame and brick with a wide, sweeping veranda that provided a panoramic view of Oyster Bay and Long Island Sound. He renamed the property Sagamore Hill after Sagamore Mohannis, the Indian chief who had signed away the land two hundred years earlier (Figure 56).

In December, 1886, Roosevelt married childhood sweetheart Edith Carow, and the couple moved into Sagamore Hill the following spring (Plate XI). The house soon filled with the sounds of five more children, a fact Roosevelt acknowledged as a source of delight:

For unflagging interest and enjoyment, a household of children, if things go reasonably well, certainly makes all of the forms of success and achievement lose their importance by comparison.[92]

As Roosevelt progressed politically, the house resounded, too, with adult talk as it became a Mecca for innumerable public figures — potentates, prizefighters, politicians and professors — all associates of the gregarious, inquisitive Roosevelt.

While Sagamore Hill provided an escape for Theodore Roosevelt, it may not have been so relaxing for Edith, burdened with six children, and Roosevelt himself. One famous story is that, when Edith was preparing to leave Washington for Sagamore Hill with the children, a friend asked whether Theodore was also going. "For Heaven's Sake!" Edith replied, "Don't put it into Theodore's head to go, too. I should have another child to think of!"[93] At Sagamore Hill and elsewhere, she provided a steadying influence on his boyish enthusiasm and exuberance, not only running the household and handling the family finances, but overseeing the farm operation — the manager reported to her, not to TR. Of course, she supervised the children with firmness and tact.

Figure 56. Sagamore Hill National Historic Site, Oyster Bay, New York. Photograph courtesy National Park Service.

With the exception of the North Room filled with TR's hunting trophies, Sagamore Hill reflects the exquisite taste of Edith Roosevelt, from the second-floor bedrooms to the dining room with opalescent glass sconces lighting the Florentine table, sideboard and Dante chairs. Edith's sanctuary, the blue and white drawing room, is the only totally feminine room in the house, furnished with Edith's personal family pieces. Apparently no one could enter the room uninvited, with the exception of family pets that were allowed to drop by and drink water from a Delft bowl kept under Mrs. Roosevelt's writing table. The bowl is still there. Sagamore Hill truly represents the spirit and ebullience of a special family.

After Edith Roosevelt passed away at Sagamore Hill, the Theodore Roosevelt Association, a non-profit organization which owned Theodore Roosevelt's Birthplace in New York City, purchased the estate from the Roosevelt children and opened it to the public in 1953. In 1963, the association donated both places to the federal government for the enjoyment and edification of the American people.

DIRECTIONS: By train from New York City: Take the Long Island Railroad from Penn Station in New York City to Oyster Bay. Taxis meet all trains. **By car from New York City:** Take the Long Island Expressway (I 495) to Exit 41N, or the Northern State Parkway to Exit 35N and proceed northbound on Route 106 for 4 miles. Turn right (eastbound) on Route 25A and travel 2.5 miles. At the third traffic light, turn left and proceed on Cove Road for 1.7 miles. Turn right (northbound) and take Cove Neck Road 1.5 miles to Sagamore Hill (Figure 57).

PUBLIC USE: Season and hours: *Grounds:* Dawn to dusk. *The Home*: Memorial Day-Labor Day, 9 AM-5 PM with guided tours conducted 10 AM-4 PM; rest of year, Wednesday-Sunday, 9 AM-5 PM with tours from 10 AM-4 PM. Closed Thanksgiving Day, Christmas Day, New Year's Day. **Admission fee:** For the house tour only. **Picnic area. Book store. For people with disabilities:** The Roosevelt Home is not accessible. A video description is available for those unable to tour the house.

FOR ADDITIONAL INFORMATION: Contact: Sagamore Hill National Historic Site, 20 Sagamore Hill Road, Oyster Bay, New York 11771, (516) 922-4447. **Web site:** *www.nps.gov/sahi.* **Read:** (1) Hermann Hagedorn and Gary Roth. 1977. *Sagamore Hill: A Historic Guide.* (2) Sylvia Jukes Morris. 1980. *Edith Kermit Roosevelt: Portrait of a First Lady.*

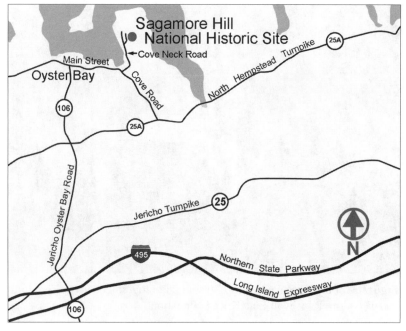

Figure 57. Location of Sagamore Hill National Historic Site near Oyster Bay. New York.

Pine Knot

KEENE, VIRGINIA

Shortly after Theodore Roosevelt began his first term, wife Edith looked for a place where she and the President might occasionally escape the strains of the presidency — or perhaps the summer humidity of the capital. In 1905, she secretly purchased fifteen acres in the deep woods of Albemarle County, Virginia, that contained a small farm-worker's cabin with no electricity, indoor plumbing or other modern facilities. She named it "Pine Knot" (Figure 58), reflecting the surrounding trees. She was confident that the rustic retreat fit the style and character of the President who relished strenuous living and close contact with nature. Pine Knot's curator Paula Beazley said, "Pine Knot very much provided a window into their souls."[94] The Roosevelts made eight visits to Pine Knot, visits that lasted from two to four days during

157

Figure 58. Pine Knot near Keene, Virginia. Photograph courtesy The Edith and Theodore Roosevelt Pine Knot Foundation.

holidays or other times, such as in May, the peak of the birding season. At dusk, they relaxed on the piazza to watch the sun disappear behind the foothills of the Blue Ridge where "it was lovely to sit there in the rocking chairs and hear all the birds by daytime and at night the whippoorwills and little forest folk."[95] In the fall or winter, they passed long evenings reading or doing needle work by lamplight beside a log fire.

The tiny (12x32-foot) cabin on two floors (Mrs. Roosevelt added only an outdoor piazza) is owned by the Theodore Roosevelt Association which is implementing long-term plans for development of the area as an historic site. Pine Knot is without question the most unusual presidential retreat, but one that accurately reflects the character and interests of its "ecologically proper" residents.

DIRECTIONS: From the intersection of SR 20 and SR 712 in Keene, Virginia, follow SR 712 southeast for about 2 miles. Pine Knot is on the southwest/ right side of the road; the entrance is identified by a 4-board black wooden fence with the address "Pine Knot 711 Coles Rolling Road" located on the second board from the top (Figure 59).

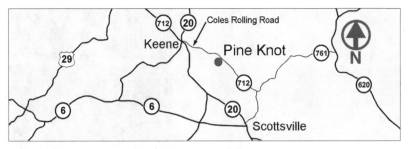

Figure 59. Location of Pine Knot near Keene, Virginia.

PUBLIC USE: Season and hours: Pine Knot is open year-round by appointment only. **Admission fee:** Contribution suggested. **For people with disabilities:** Accessible.

FOR ADDITIONAL INFORMATION: Contact: Pine Knot, PO Box 213, Keene, Virginia 22946. Telephone, (434) 286-6106. **Web site:** *www.pineknot.org.* **Read:** William H. Harbaugh. 1993. *The Theodore Roosevelts' Retreat in Southern Albemarle: Pine Knot 1905–1908.*

Helen Herron Taft

First Lady, 1909–1913

Born: January 2, 1861, Cincinnati, Ohio
Died: May 22, 1943, Washington, DC

Seventeen-year-old Helen Herron visited the White House as a guest of her father's old friend and law partner, President Rutherford B. Hayes, and announced, upon her return home, that she liked the White House so much she had decided to marry a man destined to be President of the United States. As apocryphal as that story might be, she fulfilled her girlhood dream in 1901 when she moved into the White House as Mrs. William Howard Taft.

The Taft presidency got off to a bad start. Inauguration Day was the worst day, weather-wise, in Washington, DC, history. A freezing blizzard tied up transportation and left thousands of visitors stranded all over the East. The capital was so affected that the inaugural ceremony was moved indoors to the Senate chamber, but Mrs. Taft nonetheless considered it a complete success. When retiring President Roosevelt decided to leave the inauguration ceremony and travel directly to the railroad station rather than travel back to the White House with the new President, Helen Taft set her first precedent as First Lady; she rode from the capitol building to the White House seated by her husband's side.

Helen Herron and Will Taft had much in common. Born and raised in Cincinnati, their fathers were attorneys and the families moved in comfortable social circles. Their personalities, however, differed. Will was placid and easy-going while Helen was intense and outspoken. She graduated from Miss Nourse's School and attended classes at Miami University in Ohio before becoming a schoolteacher. She also studied music and became a competent pianist. Will Taft, impressed by her ambition, once remarked to his father, "Her eagerness for knowledge of all kinds puts me to shame. Her capacity for work is wonderful." They found mutual understanding of "topics intellectual and economic" and married in 1886.[96]

A year later, only thirty years of age, Will was appointed a judge of the Ohio Superior Court, an astonishing promotion for such a young attorney. Helen, on the other hand, was concerned that a seat on the court would deter his chances for political advancement, so when he was appointed Solicitor General of the United States in 1890, she was pleased as that position necessitated a move to Washington, DC, a place where she was convinced she was destined to thrive.

She was dismayed a year later, however, when Will was appointed to the Federal Circuit Court of Appeals, necessitating a return to Ohio. In 1900, Judge Taft, with Helen's approval, accepted an appointment to head a federal commission mandated to govern the recently annexed Philippines and he was subsequently named the first civil governor of the Philippines. The Tafts loved the Philippines and left there with reluctance in 1904 when Will accepted the prestigious post of Secretary of War in the cabinet of Theodore Roosevelt.

President Roosevelt offered Taft an appointment to the Supreme Court in 1906, but Helen was vigorously opposed. She — and President Roosevelt — felt Will had a solid chance to receive the Republican nomination for President in 1908 as Roosevelt's chosen successor, and the presidency, after all, was what she wanted. Taft himself was reluctant as his lifelong ambition and passion was centered on the law, but Helen, ever since her impressionable visit to the Hayes White House as a young girl, had her eye on the White House.

Taft won the presidential election. Once in the White House, Mrs. Taft became extremely active. She put her stamp on every facet of its management, to considerable criticism from a White House staff used to the timidity of Ida McKinley and the informality of the Roosevelts. They found Helen Taft to be demanding, feeling that she brought Malacanan regality from the Philippines to replace American democratic simplicity. While that may or may not have been true, she did bring one idea from the Philippines that lives on. Inspired by the beauty of Luneta Park in the Philippine capital of Manila, Mrs. Taft arranged that Potomac Drive in Washington be converted to a promenade, beautified by a reproduction of the Tokyo cherry-blossom festival. She accepted a gift of 3,000 trees from the Mayor of Tokyo, thus initiating what has become one of the most popular tourist attractions in the nation's capital, the annual blossoming of the cherry trees around the Tidal Basin and East Potomac Park.

It's not known what effect, if any, Helen Taft had on her husband politically, although it may have been considerable as she kept track of his appointments and attended White House conferences at times.

The Taft presidency was only a few months old when Mrs. Taft suffered a stroke that left her partially paralyzed and barely able to speak. She recovered, although her convalescence was slow and she never regained a full measure of her former vigor and vitality. Illness aside, Helen Taft supported her husband's decision to run for reelection in 1912, but the sharply divided Republicans were no match for Woodrow Wilson and the Democrats who won the presidency.

The Tafts left Washington for New Haven, Connecticut, where Taft had accepted a professorship at Yale Law School, but when President Warren G. Harding appointed the former President to be Chief Justice of the Supreme Court in 1921, the Tafts were happy to return to Washington where they discovered that life outside the White House wasn't so bad. They owned a fine home, reveled in the success of their children and did not miss the world of politics. William Howard Taft died in 1930. Helen followed in 1943 and is buried beside her husband in Arlington National Cemetery. Her obituary in the *New York Times* credited Helen with "having played an important part in planning the career of her distinguished husband."[97] Some might have added, "in spite of himself."

Ellen Louise Axson Wilson

First Lady, 1913–1914

Born: May 15, 1860, Savannah, Georgia
Died: August 6, 1914, Washington, DC

Ellen Axson Wilson, like husband Woodrow, was the child of a Southern Presbyterian minister, and it was in her father's manse in Rome, Georgia, that they met, love at first sight, at least on the part of Woodrow, then completing graduate work at Johns Hopkins University. He conducted an intense long-distance courtship with Ellen, a graduate of the Female Seminary in Rome, then studying at the Art Students League in New York, an effort she happily put aside for the man she described as "the greatest man in the world and the best."[98] She believed that he was destined for greatness and she, in turn, became the center of his existence. They were married in the manse of her grandfather's church in Savannah in 1885.

During their marriage, Ellen assumed all of the household responsibilities — supervision of family finances, preparation of menus, cooking, sewing and caring for their three daughters. And always, but always, she tended to the physical and emotional needs of her husband, assisting Woodrow as his counselor, editor and advisor. Wilson was well aware of her importance to his success.

My love for you released my real personality, and I can never express it perfectly in either act or word away from you and your immediate inspiration . . . Love unlocks everything within me that is a pleasure for me to use. I never used my mind, even, with satis-faction till I had you.[99]

Ellen Wilson's term as First Lady was all too short as she died of Bright's Disease after only seventeen months in the White House. In that short period, however, she assisted her husband and hosted obligatory social functions, all the while reaching out with personal interest in the arts and, in particular, caring for and assisting those in the capital living in poverty. She was especially effective in pressuring Congress to provide decent housing for slum dwellers; her efforts resulted in legislation called "Mrs. Wilson's Bill," passed shortly before her death.

Ellen Wilson's life philosophy may be summed up in her quotation, "I wonder how anyone who reaches middle age can bear it if she cannot feel on looking back that, whatever mistakes she may have made, she has on the whole lived for others and not for herself."[100] To the very end, her thoughts were of her husband. Her final words to her physician were, "Doctor, if I go away, promise me that you will take good care of Woodrow."[101]

Edith Bolling Galt Wilson

First Lady, 1915–1921

Born: October 15, 1872, Wytheville, Virginia
Died: December 28, 1961, Washington, DC

His wife's death was a crushing emotional blow to Woodrow Wilson as Ellen was an integral part of his life — companion, lover, counselor and friend for twenty-nine years. When she died, he fell into a period of deep depression that worried his family, colleagues and doctors. While the mourning period was difficult, there was to be closure. In March, 1915, Woodrow Wilson was introduced to Mrs. Edith Bolling Galt, an attractive widow in her forties. Mrs. Galt was from a once-prosperous Virginia plantation family whose lifestyle had been unalterably changed by the Civil War. Their plantation lost, the family was forced to move to a modest second-floor apartment in Wytheville, Virginia, where Edith, the seventh of eleven children, was born in a second-floor bedroom. Wytheville was the county seat, and Edith's father was appointed a Circuit Court Judge. Judge Bolling made sure that his children were well-educated, and his stern but positive influence was important in Edith's maturation, as was that of her invalid grandmother. Indomitable in spirit, Grandmother Bolling's room became the center of family activity. Edith was especially receptive to her grandmother, and became the elderly lady's eyes and ears. Her grandmother gave her special lessons in reading, writing, the Bible, French, dressmaking and crocheting. She also taught Edith that the past was to be revered and treasured (in Grandmother's heart, the South won the war); that to have strong likes and dislikes was natural, religion was essential for life and that a person was either among the chosen or not — and there wasn't much one could do about it.

At twenty-four, Edith married Norman Galt, a Washington, DC, jeweler. When Mr. Galt passed away in 1908, she was bequeathed the family's jewelry store and proved to be a capable businesswoman — she supported herself, her mother and other family members, traveled extensively and was a popular dinner guest in Washington society, known for her grace and convivial conversation.

Her romance with Woodrow Wilson was passionate and controversial, as the marriage came barely a year after Ellen Wilson's death. The similarities between the two women are interesting — both Southern-bred, each was utterly and passionately devoted to Woodrow Wilson's physical and emotional health. Each was a rock. Wilson, though a strong, thoughtful political leader, had an absolute need for such a helpmeet. First wife Ellen bore his children and served as primary counselor, editor and advisor up through the first year of his presidency. Edith's tenure was no less important as she helped ease the President's burdens through the devastating years of World War I and beyond. She traveled with him to Europe during difficult peace negotiations and stood by him through agonizing domestic political battles when he attempted to establish a League of Nations.

Edith's influence on her husband became controversial when the President suffered a stroke in October 1919 that incapacitated him physically. In those days, before full disclosure of presidential illnesses, neither the nation nor the Congress was informed of Wilson's condition. His body was wracked, but his mind was clear, and attending physicians recommended that work would be useful therapy. They suggested, however, that he be isolated from outside influences — that Mrs. Wilson should act as a liaison between the President and Congress; that only she have access to him; that he see papers that she, and only she, would decide were important enough for his review. That bizarre procedure went on for seven months, until the President was strong enough to resume normal activities. Public and political response to the months of secrecy, however, led to speculation and suspicion as well as virulent attacks on Mrs. Wilson as "The Presidentress."

History has been a bit kinder to Edith Wilson. Her unwavering devotion to Woodrow, her belief in her husband's policies and the need to promulgate them, placed on her shoulders massive and unusual responsibilities unknown in American presidential affairs. Edith survived Woodrow Wilson by thirty-seven years, passing away the day before the 105th anniversary of his birth. She never remarried and, to the end, continued to promote his legacy.

Edith Bolling Wilson Birthplace Museum

WYTHEVILLE, VIRGINIA

In 2005, William J. and Farron Smith of the small town of Wytheville, Virginia, formed the Edith Bolling Wilson Birthplace Foundation, designed to honor Wytheville's famous daughter — one of the most influential and politically significant women in our nation's history. As President Woodrow Wilson's second wife, her tenure as First Lady was one of the most dramatic and controversial in America's political history.

Edith Bolling was born on the second floor residence of a downtown Wytheville commercial building (Figure 60) and is now part of a museum that recognizes Edith's singular life — its purpose to show how her humble beginnings served her well as First Lady and to engender public awareness of her contributions to the nation, the institution of the presidency and the example she set for women then and now.

Visitors enter a modern ground floor museum which contains photographs, displays and artifacts associated with the life of this remarkable person — not only did she become First Lady, but most visitors are surprised to discover that she was a direct descendant of the American Indian legend Pocahontas and that Mrs. Wilson's great-great-grandmother was a sister of Thomas Jefferson. In all respects, Edith Bolling Wilson was fascinating.

The Bolling Home includes the the bedroom where Edith was born and other rooms that made up the living quarters; the family living there consisted of her parents, her ten siblings, two grandmothers, two aunts, a cousin, several dogs and 26 canaries! The actual Bolling Home is in a pre-renovated state and can be explored during guided tours.

With the dedication of the museum in 2008, Edith Bolling Wilson joins an exclusive list of First Ladies having publicly accessible interpretive homes or libraries of their own — Abigail Adams, Dolley Madison, Mary Lincoln, Lucy Hayes, Grace Coolidge, and Mamie Eisenhower. An outstanding "modern" woman — she was the first in Washington, DC, to own and drive her own electric car! — Edith Bolling Wilson's life of caring contributions to America is a shining example to people everywhere.

Directions: **Southbound on I 77:** Take Exit 41 right onto Peppers Ferry to 11th Street, turn left onto 11th and go one block, then go right onto Main Street to 145 East Main Street. Northbound on I 81, take Exit 70 onto 4th Street, turn

Figure 60. Edith Bolling Wilson Birthplace Museum, Wytheville, Virginia. Photograph courtesy Edith Bolling Wilson Foundation.

left onto Main Street to 145 East Main Street. **Southbound on I 81:** Take Exit 73 onto Main Street and proceed to 145 East Main Street (Figure 61).

Public Use: Season and hours: The museum is open to the public Tuesday-Saturday, 10 AM-5 PM. Closed Thanksgiving, Christmas. Pre-renovated Bolling Home tours conducted April-October, Friday, 1:30 PM; Saturday, 10 AM. **Admission fee**: Museum is free. There is a fee for pre-renovated Bolling Home tours. **For people with disabilities:** The Bolling Home is not accessible.

For Additional Information: Contact: Edith Bolling Wilson Foundation, 145 East Main Street, Wytheville, Virginia 24382. **Telephone** (276) 223-3484. **Web site**: *www.edithbollingwilson.org.* **Read**: Edith Bolling Wilson. 1939. *My Memoirs.*

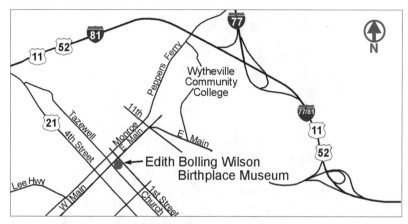

Figure 61. Location of the Edith Bolling Wilson Birthplace Museum in Wytheville, Virginia.

Woodrow Wilson House Museum

WASHINGTON, DC

Woodrow and Edith Wilson moved from the White House to a handsome, four-story red-brick townhouse (Figure 62) in an exclusive Washington neighborhood where he passed away in 1924. Mrs. Wilson carefully preserved the home's ambience and furnishings and, upon her death, the house was bequeathed to the National Trust for Historic Preservation which converted it to a house museum dedicated to the life and career of one of America's great leaders and first internationalists.

Each room, from the fully-stocked kitchen to the cheery solarium overlooking a formal walled garden, reflects the variety of the Wilsons' lives and the honesty and simplicity of their values. Large and light, the rooms are rich with souvenirs, gifts and other possessions highlighting Wilson's career as professor, administrator, governor, president and international statesman. Visitors may be intrigued by a collection of presidential memorabilia — his inaugural Bible, typewriter, a framed mosaic presented by the Pope and a copy of Edith Wilson's White House portrait that hangs in the stair hall.

In the elegant dining room, the Wilsons entertained family, friends and world leaders. Food was prepared in a kitchen that documents the changes in

Figure 62. Woodrow Wilson House Museum, Washington, D. C. Photograph by Todd A. Smith, use courtesy Woodrow Wilson House Museum.

domestic design during and after World War I. On the third floor, two principal bedrooms were on either side of an open loggia from which President Wilson could enjoy a view of the garden. Visitors may be touched when they view the closet where the President's clothes still hang, or the bed in which the ailing President spent so much time, tended by his ever-attentive wife. In this house, one gains an intimate understanding of how difficult Wilson's last days were, both on him and those who loved and cared for him.

Yet the house is not unhappy. It is pleasant, cheerful and friendly, testimony to the indomitable spirit of the man who led his nation through a great world war and into the modern era of international responsibility. The nation owes a debt of gratitude to his wife, Edith Wilson, who cared for him deeply, tended him lovingly and generously presented their home to the nation.

DIRECTIONS: From downtown Washington, DC, take the Metro Red Line subway to Dupont Circle and use the Q Street exit. Follow Q Street to Massachusetts Avenue, then Massachusetts for 4 blocks to 24th Street. Turn right on 24th, then right on S Street to #2340 (Figure 63).

PUBLIC USE: Season and hours: Tuesday-Sunday, 10 AM-4 PM. Closed major holidays. **Admission fee:** Yes, with discounts for groups, students, seniors and children. Guided tours that begin with a short orientation film take about 1 hour. **For people with disabilities:** The first floor is fully accessible and there is a small elevator that can accommodate most disabled visitors.

FOR ADDITIONAL INFORMATION: Contact: Woodrow Wilson House Museum, 2340 S Street, NW, Washington, DC 20008, (202) 387-4062. **Web site:** *www.woodrowwilsonhouse.org*. **Read:** (1) Frances Wright Saunders. 1985. *First Lady Between Two Worlds: Ellen Axson Wilson.* (2) Tom Schactman. 1981. *Edith and Woodrow: A Presidential Romance.*

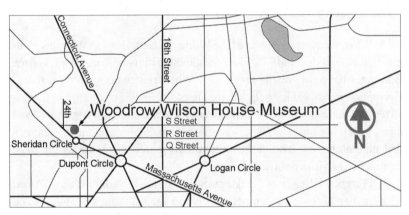

Figure 63. Location of Woodrow Wilson House Museum in Washington, DC.

Florence Kling DeWolfe Harding

First Lady, 1921–1923

Born: August 15, 1860, Marion, Ohio
Died: November 21, 1924, Marion, Ohio

When the Hardings entered the White House following Warren's inauguration as President in 1921, Florence turned to him and said, "Well, Warren Harding, I have got you the presidency. What are you going to do with it?" His reply was, "May God help me, for I need it."[102] The story may be fictionalized, yet there is little doubt that Florence was more ambitious, focused and intense than her husband, who was trusting, malleable and naïve, qualities that ultimately sent his administration sliding into disrepute as the most corrupt in American political history.

Florence Kling was the daughter of Marion's leading citizen, Amos Kling, a man of ferocious temper and enmity against those who might stand in his way. Unfortunately, one of them was Florence herself who rebelled against her father's iron rule. At twenty, she eloped with Peter deWolfe, a likeable but lazy young man with a bent for the bottle. This was a relationship — there are no existing records proving the marriage was even legalized — destined to fail, and when Florence returned to Marion without her "husband" — but with a baby — her father refused to allow her back home. She lived with friends and became a piano teacher to support herself and infant son, Marshall. It was not until a "divorce" was finalized in 1886 that she moved back into the Kling home, although her father exacted a terrible price. He assumed custody of the child.

A grass widow at thirty, Florence was intrigued by newcomer Warren Harding, the 25-year-old editor of the *Marion Star,* the town's daily newspaper. She succeeded in her romantic quest and they married, to the further displeasure of her father who boycotted the wedding and predicted a gloomy future for the couple. Florence, however, persevered. Early in the marriage, she went to the *Star* to help out on a temporary basis and remained for fourteen years, proving to be a shrewd businesswoman, managing the circulation and advertising departments while Warren concentrated on the editorial department and acted as a goodwill ambassador. His forte as a backslapping, gregarious and entertaining man-about-town placed him in demand as a public speaker and he began to travel extensively throughout the state. Florence tagged along to handle the nitty-gritty of travel expenses and, not incidentally, to temper Warren's wandering eye.

Team Harding entered politics in 1894 when Warren ran unsuccessfully for Marion County Auditor, an office he won the next year. In 1899 he was elected to the Ohio Senate, and in 1904 became lieutenant governor of the state. In 1910 he was defeated for the governorship and retired from politics briefly, but won election to the United States Senate in 1914. The Hardings left for Washington, DC, with high expectations and were not disappointed. They loved the city and the excitement of national politics, but it was with some trepidation that Warren considered a run for the presidency in 1920.

Warren's campaign manager, Harry Daugherty, persuaded him that there was a good chance of victory, but Warren was hesitant. Florence was another matter. She did not want her husband to run at all. She enjoyed being the wife of a senator and the thought of the responsibility and pressure of higher office had no appeal. Once Warren was convinced by Daugherty and others, however, Florence gave the campaign her full attention and support. The idea of a morally secure leader with strong midwestern values was popular, and a "front porch" campaign swept him into the presidency. Florence also enjoyed a positive reputation as her honest, forthright manner and good works, especially her association and work with returning World War I veterans, made her highly popular.

Behind the façade of popularity, things were quite different. Neither Warren nor Florence was physically healthy. Warren had heart problems and Florence suffered from kidney disease. In addition, Warren Harding was an irrepressible philanderer whose extramarital affairs prior to the presidential years soured their marriage, and his weakness as an administrator led to the great scandal known as Teapot Dome.

Florence Harding returned to Ohio briefly following the President's death in 1923; she survived him by just over a year. Through an agonizing time, both physically and emotionally, especially as the Teapot Dome scandal unfolded, Florence Harding continued to uphold her husband's image and proclaim his goodness.

The Harding Home

Marion, Ohio

On July 8, 1891, the Hardings were married in a newly completed Victorian house — a wedding present to Florence from Warren — a typically midwestern and contemporary home reflecting popular architecture and styling of the day: 2½ stories, originally painted red with dark red trim, then painted green and white in 1903, with pots of petunias and geraniums on the porch (Figure 64). The couple had planned every facet of the house together, but Florence's influence is most apparent in the interior décor — furniture, wallpaper, paint colors, china, silver and wall hangings.

Figure 64. The Harding Home, Marion, Ohio. Photograph courtesy The Harding Home.

The Hardings lived in Marion until leaving for Washington in 1915 to serve Harding's Senate term. They returned home to conduct the famous "front porch" presidential campaign in 1920 wherein an estimated 600,000 people visited Marion to see and hear the candidate.

They left for the White House in 1921, although Mrs. Harding did not return to the house following her husband's death due to illness and respect for the folks who were renting the house. Upon her death in 1924, the house and furnishings were bequeathed to the Harding Memorial Association which opened four rooms to the public in 1926. In 1965, the Association renovated the house to appear as at the time of the Hardings' residency. Ceiling light fixtures were replaced by the original gas fixtures, some Harding wallpaper was duplicated and furniture was returned to its original arrangement. Personal effects were left as they were found, and the house now feels as if Warren Harding stepped out for a stroll, leaving his straw hat and cane in the hall. Another favorite piece is Florence's piano upon which she banged out her favorite tune, "End of a Perfect Day."

A separate press house used during the 1920 campaign currently serves as a museum dedicated to President and Mrs. Harding, who are entombed under a monument of white marble situated in the center of ten acres of landscaped parkland about a mile from the house.

DIRECTIONS: Marion is 50 miles north of Columbus, Ohio, just off US Route 23. From US Route 23, take the Route 95 Exit and proceed westbound on Route 95 that becomes Mount Vernon Avenue in Marion. Follow the historical markers to the Harding Home (Figure 65).

PUBLIC USE: Season and hours: Guided tours are conducted Memorial Day to Labor Day, Wednesday-Sunday, 12 M-5 PM; also July 4, 12 M-5 PM. September and October, Saturday and Sunday, 12 M-5 PM. Open year-round by appointment. **Admission fee:** Yes, with discounts for groups, students and seniors. **Gift shop. For people with disabilities:** Not accessible.

FOR ADDITIONAL INFORMATION: Contact: The Harding Home, 380 Mount Vernon Avenue, Marion, Ohio 43302, (740) 387-9630. For tour reservations and appointments, (800) 600-6894. **Web site:** *www.ohiohistory.org/places/harding*. **Read:** Carl Sferrazza Anthony. 1998. *Florence Harding.*

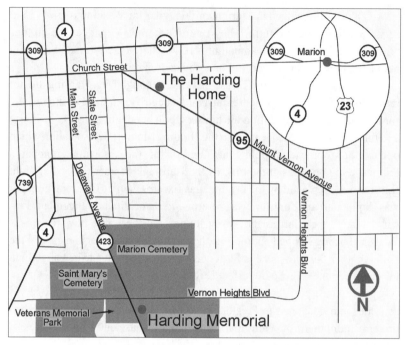

Figure 65. Location of The Harding Home in Marion, Ohio.

Grace Anna Goodhue Coolidge

First Lady, 1923–1929

Born: January 3, 1879, Burlington, Vermont
Died: July 8, 1957, Northampton, Massachusetts

If, as they say, opposites attract, Grace and Calvin Coolidge are prime examples. She — warm, friendly, gregarious and cheerful. He — quiet, dour and uncommunicative, never one to suffer fools gladly. Yet theirs was a marriage that survived twenty-eight years of trials and moments of joy, perhaps because Grace and Calvin shared Vermont's rock-like values — to strive and succeed, sink or swim, work and win, with pluck not luck.

After graduating from the University of Vermont, Grace Goodhue became a teacher at the Clarke School for the Deaf in Northampton, Massachusetts, where she met young attorney Calvin Coolidge. He may have been reticent in nature, but he recognized a good thing and began a fervent courtship. Although they had different personalities, the two Vermonters did agree on the two-sphere theory of sexual relations — a man's domain was that of the provider while a woman's was that of the homemaker. Modern observers might feel that Calvin and Grace carried it to extremes as she rarely attended his political speeches and when he was Lieutenant Governor of Massachusetts, she remained in Northampton while he lived in a small suite at the Adams Hotel in Boston. When he became governor of the Commonwealth, he merely rented a larger space when Grace visited Boston for special state events.

The victory of the Warren Harding-Calvin Coolidge Republican national ticket in 1920 necessitated a major life-style change for the Coolidges as he assumed the vice presidency with its high political recognition. Grace became a visible public person, but she found herself enjoying it. For the first time in her married life, she shared her husband's work, accompanying him to dinners, dedications and other official functions. They lived in comfortable quarters at the New Willard Hotel, and even Calvin began to loosen up. Washington insiders initially thought of the Coolidges as rural bumpkins, but Grace's native intelligence, charm, wit and conversational gifts melted even the most critical observer. One hostess remarked:

> *Everybody liked her, and because she went everywhere and did everything, she became a familiar as well as a popular figure. She is the one woman in official life of whom I have never heard a single disparaging remark in the course of nearly twenty years.*[103]

Following the death of President Harding in 1923, Calvin Coolidge assumed the presidency. Grace remained aloof from politics and sometimes chafed under her husband's restrictions, but by and large she enjoyed the White House experience. Their contentment was tragically shattered when sixteen-year-old son, Calvin Jr., contracted blood poisoning from an infected foot and died in July 1924. Their lives would never be the same again.

In the summer of 1927, taciturn Calvin Coolidge issued a brief statement to the press, "I do not choose to run for President in 1928,"[104] the first inkling that Grace had of his intentions. After his term ended, she dutifully, and with no idea of the President's future plans, returned with him to their old duplex at 21 Massasoit Street in Northampton where Calvin resumed his law practice and worked on his memoirs.

The small duplex did not provide privacy they sought, so they purchased a larger home, "The Beeches," where President Coolidge passed away in 1933. Mrs. Coolidge was uncomfortable in the large house without him, and had a smaller house built which she filled for her remaining years with knitting, listening to her beloved Boston Red Sox games broadcast on the radio and visiting surviving son John and his family. She passed away in 1957 at seventy-eight.

Figure 66. Goodhue Home, Burlington, Vermont. Photograph courtesy Champlain College.

Goodhue Home

BURLINGTON, VERMONT

A frame house at 312 Maple Street was the family home of Grace Goodhue who married Calvin Coolidge in the parlor on October 4, 1905. Today the house (Figure 66) is situated on the campus of Champlain College, which renovated it and utilizes it for administrative offices. The college is committed to the preservation of the house as a historically significant structure, and the front parlor features a small exhibit of memorabilia from the Coolidge era. At the time of its purchase by the College in 1988, President Robert Skiff said, "We will make every reasonable effort to ensure that the important features and living room are retained in a historically accurate fashion."[105] There is no official tour of this house, but visitors are welcome to drop by during regular business hours.

DIRECTIONS: Burlington is in north central Vermont, on the eastern shore of Lake Champlain. From I 89, northbound or southbound, take the "Burlington West" exit (Main Street) and proceed westbound to Willard Street (US Route 7). Turn left on Willard Street to Maple Street, turn right on Maple Street, and proceed to #312 (Figure 67).

PUBLIC USE: Season and hours: The Goodhue Home, an administrative office for Champlain College, is open Monday-Friday, 9 AM-5 PM. Closed all federal and college holidays.

FOR ADDITIONAL INFORMATION: Contact: Champlain College, Burlington, Vermont 05402-0670, (802) 860-2700.

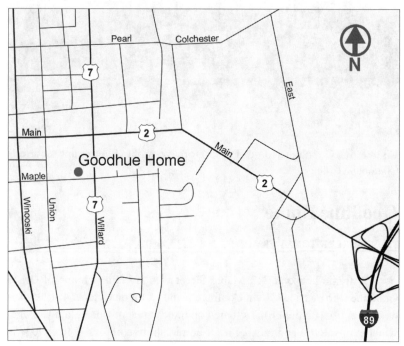

Figure 67. Location of the Goodhue Home in Burlington, Vermont.

Lou Henry Hoover

First Lady, 1929–1933

Born: March 29, 1874, Waterloo, Iowa
Died: January 7, 1944, New York, New York

If ever there was a couple with total commonality of interests, it was Lou and Herbert Hoover. Born less than a year apart, both in Iowa, each moved to California as a youngster and graduated from Stanford University with degrees in geology. Lou's family had moved to California in 1874; first to Whittier, then to Monterey where her father established a bank. She graduated from San Jose Normal School with a degree in biology and geology and transferred to Stanford to continue her studies in those subjects that were, at that time, of rare interest to women. At Stanford, she met and was courted by fellow student Herbert Hoover, who accepted a mining job in Australia following his graduation. When he was transferred to a similar post in China, he wired a marriage proposal to Lou, then employed as a schoolteacher in Monterey. The couple married in 1899 and immediately embarked for China, where they experienced the bloody Boxer Rebellion first hand. Their house was transformed into a fortress under siege, one result of which was that Mrs. Hoover became known as the American lady who could cook horse meat better than anyone else!

Herbert Hoover's success as a mining engineer entailed world travel, bringing the family three addresses in London, seven in California, one in New York City, one in Virginia, one in Paris and five in Washington, DC, including, not incidentally, 1600 Pennsylvania Avenue. Lou became proficient in the establishment of each as a home, sometimes under trying circumstances. A Hoover friend once said:

Wherever she went, she made a home for her husband and her children. She had a great skill in making domestic things simple, in welcoming and entertaining guests, and in providing a background of comfort for the household, particularly for her husband. His friends and associates became at once her friends and associates.[106]

In 1914, at the outbreak of World War I, the Hoover family, which by then included two small boys, was residing in London. The American Ambassador asked Herbert Hoover to organize and supervise a group to care for over 100,000 American travelers stranded in Europe. He was later named to head Belgian relief efforts, the success of which led to post-war appointment as War Food Administrator, a job necessitating a move to Washington, DC. There he was appointed Secretary of Commerce by President Harding, and was retained by President Coolidge. The Hoovers purchased a large home at 2300 S Street, entertained extensively and rarely dined alone.

Lou Henry Hoover's abilities as a gracious hostess continued when she became First Lady. She had a special knack with strangers and made her guests feel at ease with her charm and conversational brilliance. Levi Pennington, president of Pacific College and a longtime friend, once remarked:

I have said many times that Mrs. Hoover was as near to being a perfect hostess as any woman I have ever known. I believe that she would have had the Queen of England, an Irish washerwoman and a Negro 'mammy' as guests together and all three of them feeling at home and having a happy time as guests of the President's wife.[107]

Following Herbert's one-term presidency, the Hoovers returned to their home on the campus of Stanford University. Hoover fished, organized Boys' Clubs and enjoyed their grandchildren. Mrs. Hoover continued her Girl Scout work which had begun during their time in Washington; she had accepted the national presidency of the Girl Scouts and helped build that organization from a membership of 100,000 to over a million.

As the couple became more and more involved in charitable works, the Hoovers found it convenient to live in New York City, although they retained their Stanford house. They were both devoted to public service, and as Herbert Hoover was known as "The Great Humanitarian," Lou Henry Hoover deserved equal honor. Herbert, always appreciative of Lou's talent and wisdom, knew it.

On January 7, 1944, Lou Henry Hoover died of a heart attack in New York City. A gracious woman who spoke several languages and built households and relationships in many parts of the world, she was remembered for her dignity, sincerity, warmth and devotion to her family.

Herbert Hoover Presidential Library and Museum

West Branch, Iowa

The Herbert Hoover Presidential Library and Museum (Figure 68, Plate XI) shares an area of almost two hundred acres with the Herbert Hoover National Historic Site, a National Park Service facility that comprises a restored portion of mid-nineteenth century West Branch that includes Herbert Hoover's birthplace cottage, the town's first schoolhouse, a Quaker meeting house and a blacksmith shop similar to the one owned by Hoover's father.

The Herbert Hoover Presidential Library, like all presidential libraries managed by the National Archives, is committed to preserving and making

Figure 68. Herbert Hoover Presidential Library and Museum, West Branch, Iowa. Photograph courtesy Herbert Hoover Presidential Library and Museum.

archival materials available to researchers and is generally reserved for those efforts. A separate museum section open to the public tells the extraordinary life story of Herbert Hoover — that of an orphan boy who lived the American dream by becoming a multi-millionaire engineer, world-wide humanitarian and the 31st President of the United States. There are galleries containing exhibits, displays, memorabilia, documents and photographs covering Hoover's ninety years of life and the decades he and Mrs. Hoover spent in public service. Visitors may be charmed by a reproduction of the President's retirement office in New York City's Waldorf Towers, amused by an exhibit of Roaring 20s souvenirs and moved by a display chronicling the Hoovers' monumental work in feeding Europe after World War I, the effort that earned him the sobriquet "The Great Humanitarian" — which Mrs. Hoover should surely share.

One gallery dedicated to Lou Henry Hoover is called "An Uncommon Woman," and she was that: geologist, architect, linguist, Girl Scout leader, mother and First Lady. She reminded her sons at one time of the importance of doing something worthwhile with their lives:

> *The ambition to do, to accomplish irrespective of its measure in money or fame, is what should be inculcated. The desire to make the things that are, better, in a little way with what is at hand — in a big way if the opportunity comes.*[108]

The graves of President and Mrs. Hoover, marked by simple marble slabs, lie within a memorial on a grassy knoll overlooking the town of West Branch.

DIRECTIONS: West Branch is 10 miles east of Iowa City, Iowa, just off I 80. From I 80 eastbound or westbound, take Exit 254 and follow the historical markers 0.5 mile northbound to the site (Figure 69).

PUBLIC USE: Season and hours: Daily, 9 AM-5 PM. Closed Thanksgiving Day, Christmas Day, New Year's Day. **Admission fee:** Yes, with discounts for students and seniors. **Museum shop. For people with disabilities:** Fully accessible with the exception of the schoolhouse in the village.

FOR ADDITIONAL INFORMATION: Contact: Herbert Hoover Presidential Library and Museum, 210 Parkside Drive, PO Box 488, West Branch, Iowa 52358, (319) 643-5301. **Web site:** *www.hoover.archives.gov.* **Read:** Nancy A. Colbert. 1998. *Lou Henry Hoover: The Duty to Serve.*

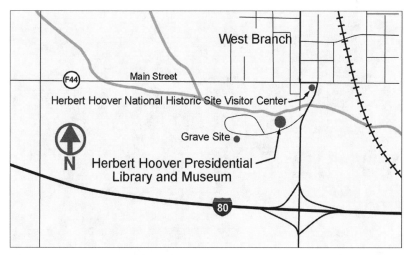

Figure 69. Location of Herbert Hoover Presidential Library and Museum in West Branch, Iowa.

Rapidan Camp

SHENANDOAH NATIONAL PARK, VIRGINIA

Before Shangri-La, Key West, the Cape or Camp David, there was an expressed need for some kind of isolated retreat where a president might find relaxation, refreshment and recreation, far from the crushing responsibilities of Washington, DC.

Recognizing that need, President and Mrs. Hoover purchased 164 acres of secluded woodlands on the eastern slope of the Blue Ridge Mountains of Virginia, where two small streams merged to form the Rapidan River. Their intention was to construct a summer and weekend retreat that would provide the President with isolation — and the availability of good fishing!

The multi-millionaire Hoovers purchased building supplies, hired an architect and Mrs. Hoover personally supervised the design and construction of a complex of 13 buildings connected by a network of paths of stone or wooden bridges designed to blend with the natural landscape. There were sleeping cabins for guests and servants, public spaces and workspaces. The centerpiece was "The Brown House" — facetiously compared with "The White House" — which became "The President's House" (Figure 70). Construction

Figure 70. Rapidan Camp within Shenandoah National Park, Virginia. Photograph courtesy National Park Service, Shenandoah National Park.

was performed by US Marines under the guise of a "training exercise." Some of the furniture was brought from the former presidential yacht and augmented by the Hoovers' personal purchases. The rustic décor reflected Mrs. Hoover's excellent taste.

Named Rapidan Camp, the complex also served as a meeting site for President Hoover and his cabinet and on occasion hosted foreign statesmen. The Hoovers donated Rapidan Camp to the Commonwealth of Virginia in 1932 as a summer retreat for subsequent presidents and in 1935 it became part of Shenandoah National Park. The camp was used sparingly, however, and the National Park Service tore down most of the buildings in 1959.

Two important buildings remain — "The Brown House" and "The Prime Minister's Cabin" where England's Ramsay MacDonald stayed in 1929. The Park Service restored the exteriors to reflect their 1932 appearance and the restored interior of "The Brown House" and a museum inside "The Prime Minister's" cabin are open for ranger-led tours.

Many of the trails, bridges, fountains, trout pools and other landscape features survive, with markers provided to show the location of buildings that no longer exist. Rapidan Camp is not easy to reach as it involves a long walk into the woods from the visitor center. Its isolation, however, is its charm and a true reflection of the personality of the "outdoor" President and his life partner who were responsible for building it and generously donating it to the American people.

DIRECTIONS: Rapidan Camp lies within Shenandoah National Park, whose Skyline Drive follows the crest of the Blue Ridge Mountains for 105 miles between Front Royal and Rockfish Gap. Take Skyline Drive either north-bound or southbound to the Harry F. Byrd, Sr. Visitor Center at Mile Marker 51 (Figure 71).

PUBLIC USE: Season and hours: Ranger-led tours, conducted Memorial Day to Labor Day, begin at the Byrd Visitor Center. Advance reservations are required as visitors are transported two miles to the camp by bus on an irregular schedule.

FOR ADDITIONAL INFORMATION: Contact: National Park Service, Shenandoah National Park, 3655 U. S. Highway 311 East, Luray, Virginia, (540) 999-3283. **Web site:** *www.nps.gov/shen.* **Read:** Darwin Lambert. 1971. *Herbert Hoover's Hideaway: The Story of Camp Hoover on the Rapidan River in Shenandoah National Park.*

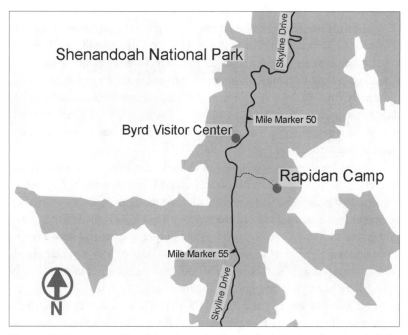

Figure 71. Location of Rapidan Camp in Shenandoah National Park, Virginia.

Anna Eleanor Roosevelt

First Lady, 1933–1945

Born: October 11, 1884, New York, New York
Died: November 11, 1962, New York, New York

Eleanor Roosevelt was unquestionably the most progressive, peripatetic and phenomenal First Lady in our nation's political and social history — at least until Rosalynn Carter and Hillary Clinton came along. Mrs. Roosevelt's list of accomplishments is impossible to exaggerate. She was more active in political and governmental affairs, both domestic and foreign, than all the previous First Ladies combined. She traveled thousands of miles, met people great and small all over the world, and was recognized as "First Lady of the World."

Anna Eleanor Roosevelt was an unlikely candidate for such activism and fame. Her parents, Anna Rebecca Hall and Elliot Roosevelt, Theodore's brother, died before she was ten years old. In the summer, she was raised by her grandmother in a palatial but gloomy mansion on the Hudson River above Poughkeepsie, New York, and in her grandmother's equally gloomy brownstone on West 37th Street in New York City the rest of the year. Her grandmother, a strict disciplinarian, made life difficult for the shy, plain and lonely young lady searching desperately for love and attention. As a teenager, however, Eleanor was sent to a London boarding school where headmistress Mademoiselle Souvestre recognized and cultivated the intelligence and latent charm of her young charge.

At eighteen, young ladies of social standing "came out" into New York society, and Eleanor was no exception. She returned from England with reluctance, and thereafter was required to participate in an endless round of parties, teas, dances and receptions. It was difficult for Eleanor — a plain, awkward and diffident girl — yet one young man recognized the intelligence, grace and steel behind her exterior shyness. He was distant cousin Franklin D. Roosevelt, and he pursued her vigorously. They married in a formal New York wedding in which she was given away by her Uncle Theodore, President of the United States. One story about the wedding was that the guests, smitten with the flamboyant President, ignored the bride and groom who were literally left alone at their own reception.

Recognition for Eleanor as a person would never be easy, especially as the newlyweds lived under the thumb of Franklin's domineering mother, Sara, who ran family affairs with an iron hand. Her wedding present of a New York City brownstone was tempered by the fact that she bought the adjoining building for herself and had a connecting door put in! Eleanor was dominated by her mother-in-law for many years; it was not until Franklin was appointed to a government post in Washington, DC, that Eleanor escaped Sara's intimidation, and then only temporarily.

A defining moment in Franklin and Eleanor's marital relationship occurred in 1918, when Eleanor inadvertently discovered letters indicating that Franklin was involved romantically with Lucy Mercer, her own social secretary. Hurt and humiliated, Eleanor offered Franklin his freedom, but when he — and his mother — considered the effects of divorce on their five children and, not coincidentally, on his own political ambitions, he rejected the notion, promising instead to terminate the extramarital relationship. The Roosevelts reconciled, and while they remained seemingly devoted partners, Eleanor was never the same. She began to rethink her life and priorities, vowing to throw off the mantle of dependency — to strike off on her own path, defined by her own interests.

A second defining moment was when Franklin became disabled by polio in 1921. Mother-in-law Sara argued that Franklin should succumb to the disease, forget politics and retire to the family estate in Hyde Park, New York. Eleanor, on the contrary, was determined that he remain active. While neutral about his activities in the past, she involved herself in politics and became a knowledgeable, effective campaign worker.

By 1928, when Franklin was elected Governor of New York, Eleanor had built her own hideaway on the Hyde Park estate, started a thriving furniture business, edited the weekly *Women's Democratic News*, taught at Todhunter School — of which she was part-owner and vice principal — and served on the boards of several civic and charitable enterprises. As the governor's wife, she moved the family to the capital in Albany, but commuted to New York City regularly to continue her work, all the while performing the social responsibilities expected as New York's First Lady. Most important to her self-confidence was the trust Franklin showed in her judgment. She became her disabled husband's eyes, ears and legs, touring the state on various inspection trips he was unable to make.

When she became First Lady of the United States in 1931, Eleanor actually increased her pace and involvement with various causes. She traveled, lectured and wrote magazine articles and while she often disagreed with her husband, it is not recorded that he ever tried to curtail her activities. On the contrary, he found her to be a useful sounding board. After his death, she remarked:

> *He might have been happier with a wife who was completely uncritical. That I was never able to be, and he had to find it in other people. Nevertheless, I think I sometimes acted as a spur, even though the spurring was not always wanted or welcome. I was one of those who served his purposes.*[109]

Part way through Roosevelt's first term, she began to write a daily syndicated newspaper column titled *My Day,* appeared on a regular radio program and contributed articles to magazines. Her constant traveling made her famous, especially for showing up in unlikely spots. A contemporary *New Yorker* cartoon showed two grubby coal miners deep in the bowels of the earth, one looking up to exclaim, "For gosh sakes! Here comes Mrs. Roosevelt." In 1942, she flew to England to visit American servicemen and women and in 1943 she made a dangerous mission to the South Pacific, a trip not welcomed initially by Area Commander Admiral Halsey, who fretted about her safety. He followed her activities closely as she made her rounds, and later remarked:

> *I marveled at her hardihood, both physical and mental. She walked for miles, and she saw patients who were grievously and gruesomely wounded. But I marveled most at their expressions as she leaned over them. It was a sight I will never forget. She alone had accomplished more good than any other person, or any group of civilians, who had passed through my area.*[110]

After President Roosevelt's death in 1945, Mrs. Roosevelt remained active. President Truman named her to the United Nations Commission on Human Rights. She resigned during the Eisenhower administration but was re-appointed by President Kennedy and continued her UN work until her death in 1962.

Mrs. Roosevelt, like her husband, was the subject of severe and sometimes unfair criticism, she primarily as a meddlesome do-gooder. She was reviled by some for what was perceived as radical positions on race relations, social change and economic affairs. She was lampooned for excessive traveling and caricatures of her physical appearance were often cruel. Yet she plodded on, patient with her critics, ever concerned for the have-nots throughout the world. Always modest, she once summed up her life:

> *About the only value the story of my life may be, is to show that one can, even without any particular gifts, overcome obstacles that seem insurmountable if one is willing to face the fact they must be overcome.*[111]

She, of course, possessed "particular gifts" in abundance and her life story shall always remain inspirational.

Home of Franklin D. Roosevelt National Historic Site and Franklin D. Roosevelt Presidential Library and Museum

HYDE PARK, NEW YORK

> *This is the house in which my husband was born and brought up . . . He always felt that this was his home and he loved the house and the view, the woods, special trees.*

— Eleanor Roosevelt[112]

Franklin D. Roosevelt was born and raised in a seventeen-room clapboard house named Springwood (Figure 72A, Plate XII), built in the early part of the nineteenth century. Here he was shaped into a man, here he brought his bride and here is where he attempted to recuperate from the psychological, physical and emotional trauma of infantile paralysis (polio). Unable to walk after acquiring the disease in 1921, he was to spend the rest of his life in a wheelchair.

Following his marriage to Eleanor in 1905, Franklin and his mother, Sara, initiated extensive alterations and renovations to Springwood. By 1916, Franklin and Eleanor had five children and another had died in infancy. The interior improvements included the addition of a floor of bedrooms, nurseries and maids' quarters. Seven additional bathrooms were installed, and the addition of a paneled living room and library lent a dignity to the house it had not previously enjoyed. On the exterior, clapboard siding was covered by stucco, two native blue fieldstone wings were added and the exterior blossomed with a classic columned portico. The house thus assumed its present exterior form, although the heavy Victorian interior was not changed.

Today, the library at Springwood features Roosevelt's governor's chair and beloved books, as well as two massive fireplaces and a Gilbert Stuart portrait of Roosevelt's great-great-grandfather. The library opens to a screened porch overlooking a sweeping lawn and a dramatic view of the Hudson Valley. In her book, *The Roosevelt I Knew*, Secretary of Labor Frances Perkins described the scene:

> *Many times in summer, when I would be told that "the family was on the lawn," I approached through the library and saw through the open door an unforgettable picture: Mrs. Sara Roosevelt, in a soft, light summery dress with ruffles, her hair charmingly curled, sitting in a wicker chair and reading; Mrs. Roosevelt, in a white dress and white tennis shoes with a velvet band around her head to keep the hair from blowing, sitting with her long-legged, graceful posture in a low chair and knitting, always knitting; Roosevelt looking off down the river at the view he admired, with a book, often unopened, in one hand, and a walking stick in the other; dogs playing near by, and children romping a little farther down the lawn. The scene was like a Currier and Ives print of Life along the Hudson.*[113]

The Franklin D. Roosevelt Presidential Library and Museum (Figure 72B) is located a short distance north of Springwood. Until 1939, presidential papers were considered private property to be retained by the President after leaving office — sometimes to be saved, but often lost forever. Franklin Roosevelt arranged to perpetuate his place in history by constructing a presidential library paid for with private funds, then turning the building over to the National Archives for maintenance, thus ensuring that his records would become the property of the people.

Figure 72. (A) Springwood Mansion, Home of Franklin D. Roosevelt National Historic Site, Hyde Park, New York. Photograph by W. D. Urbin, use courtesy National Park Service. **(B)** Franklin D. Roosevelt Presidential Library and Museum, Hyde Park, New York. Photograph courtesy FDR Presidential Library.

A museum section of the library opened in 1941 and the library itself opened to scholars in 1946. The library is a repository of President Roosevelt's papers, dealing with his entire political career, plus Mrs. Roosevelt's papers that cover her distinguished career as "First Lady of the World." The arrangement of displays in the museum, personally supervised by the President, provide an intimate glimpse into his life and the historical period he dominated. A special gallery devoted to the life of Eleanor Roosevelt features a biographical film, numerous photographs and many mementoes and artifacts associated with the life of a very special First Lady.

The year 2003 marked the opening of the Henry A. Wallace Visitor and Education Center, a public-private project designed to serve students, teachers and all visitors to the library and museum and the sites administered by the National Park Service in Hyde Park — Springwood, Eleanor Roosevelt's cottage Val-Kill, FDR's retirement retreat Top Cottage and the nearby Vanderbilt Mansion. The center's magnificent architecture, first-class visitor's facilities, bold exhibits and a state-of-the-art orientation video provide a totally refreshed experience for visitors.

In late 2011, a three-year renovation project will begin in the library and museum. The work will be performed in stages and the facility will remain open to the public while the renovation takes place. When completed, new permanent exhibits will increase the emphasis on Eleanor Roosevelt as her husband's full political collaborator.

The Hyde Park estate — the presidential library and museum, Springwood mansion, the Wallace visitor center and the spacious grounds — creates an atmosphere of relaxation and nostalgia. Visitors may contemplate Franklin and Eleanor Roosevelt's historical contributions in the museum — a truly evocative experience, culminated by admiring the exquisite Rose Garden where President and Mrs. Roosevelt now lie at rest, their graves as simple as the President had specified: "a plain white monument — no carving or decoration . . ."[114] These markers may be simple, but they are adorned forever with the love and respect of all Americans.

DIRECTIONS: The Village of Hyde Park is on US Route 9, 8 miles north of Poughkeepsie, New York. Historical markers guide visitors to the national historic site and presidential library (Figure 73).

PUBLIC USE: Season and hours: *Springwood*: Daily, 9 AM-5 PM. Closed Thanksgiving Day, Christmas Day, New Year's Day. Tours of the mansion are guided. Groups of ten or more must have reservations. *Museum:* November-March, 9 AM-5 PM; April-October, 9 AM-6 PM. Closed Thanksgiving Day, Christmas Day, New Year's Day. *Library*: The library, reserved for research, is open Monday-Friday, 8:45 AM-5 PM. *Grounds*: Open 7 AM-sunset. **Admission fee:** Yes. Ages 16 and under and seniors over 62, free. **Museum shops. For people with disabilities:** The library/museum and home are fully accessible.

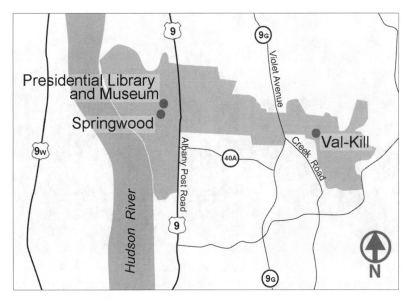

Figure 73. Location of Springwood, Home of Franklin D. Roosevelt; the Franklin D. Roosevelt Presidential Library and Museum; and Val-Kill, Eleanor Roosevelt National Historic Site — all in or near Hyde Park, New York.

FOR ADDITIONAL INFORMATION: Contact: Home of Franklin D. Roosevelt National Historic Site, 4079 Albany Post Road, Hyde Park, New York 12538, (845) 229-9115 (Home) *or* Franklin D. Roosevelt Presidential Library and Museum, 4097 Albany Post Road, Hyde Park, New York 12538, (800) FDR-VISIT (Library/Museum). **Web sites:** *Home*: *www.nps.gov/hofr*. *Museum/Library: www.fdrlibrary.marist.edu*. **Read:** Joseph P. Lash. 1971. *Eleanor and Franklin.*

Roosevelt Campobello International Park

Welshpool, New Brunswick, Canada

In the late-nineteenth century, a group of investors purchased property on Canada's Campobello Island lying off the coast of northern Maine, and promoted it as a summer resort for the wealthy. Franklin D. Roosevelt's father bought four acres and a partially-built house that was completed in 1885. Franklin spent most of his summers on the rugged, beautiful island and,

Figure 74. Campobello Cottage, Campobello Island, New Brunswick, Canada. Photograph courtesy Roosevelt Campobello International Park Commission.

after their marriage, Eleanor, too, fell in love with the informal atmosphere wherein the entire family enjoyed sailing, hiking, swimming and picnicking. When the Roosevelt children were young, they had lessons in the mornings and spent their afternoons playing games, riding horses and boating. Evenings were more relaxed; FDR spent time with his stamp collection while Eleanor knitted, wrote letters and read.

In 1909, Franklin's mother Sara purchased a furnished Dutch Colonial cottage near the main house for the use of Franklin and Eleanor and their growing family (Figure 74, Plate XIII). The interior of the cottage was comfortable, but the house had neither electricity nor telephone. Running water was gravity-fed from a storage tank on the third floor. Outside, either a windmill or single-cylinder gas engine pumped water from the well to the tanks. The Roosevelts loved it — the peace and quiet, the salt air, the fog. Eleanor once wrote, "Fog is nice if you know a place and are with someone you like. It is like a winter storm. It shuts you in and gives you a close and intimate feeling and adds to the joy of your fire."[115]

It was in that cottage that Franklin D. Roosevelt, after a cold swim, was stricken with infantile paralysis in 1921. After that, Franklin rarely visited Campobello, but Eleanor returned several times, notably in 1935 when she began to write a volume of memoirs which were later published as the first volume of her autobiography.

The Roosevelt Campobello International Park was jointly established by the governments of the United States and Canada in 1964, opening the cottage to the public and maintaining it as it was during the President's last visit. It is furnished with original Roosevelt possessions and reminders of the vigorous personalities who vacationed there: a family telescope, Eleanor's Wedgewood tea set, the President's cabinet-room chair from the White House, even a megaphone used to hail boats — or perhaps to call the children to dinner. The cottage (of 34 rooms!) is a unique reminder of the opulence of the Victorian period.

The Campobello Park contains landscaped gardens that include plants that would have been found in Roosevelt-era gardens where manicured paths lead to woods, fields and glorious views of the islands and shores of Passamaquoddy and Cobscook bays in Canada and Maine.

DIRECTIONS: Take US Route 1 northbound to Route 189 that crosses the Roosevelt Memorial Bridge at Lubec, Maine, and becomes Canada Route 774. The park is 1.5 miles past Canadian Customs (Figure 75).

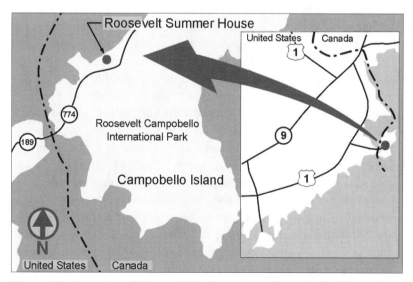

Figure 75. Location of Campobello Cottage on Campobello Island, New Brunswick.

PUBLIC USE: Season and hours: From the Saturday preceding Memorial Day through Columbus Day, daily 10 AM-6 PM, ADT (9 AM-5 PM Eastern Daylight Time).The visitor center is also open Canadian Thanksgiving (US Columbus Day) through October 31, 9 AM-4 PM EDT. **Picnic areas. Gift shop. For people with disabilities:** The first floor of the cottage is accessible, a filmed presentation of the second floor is available.

FOR ADDITIONAL INFORMATION: Contact: Roosevelt Campobello International Park Commission, PO Box 129, Lubec, Maine 04652, (506) 752-2922. **Web site:** *www.fdr.net.* **Read:** August Hecksher, 1985. "Historic Houses: Campobello."

Eleanor Roosevelt National Historic Site

HYDE PARK, NEW YORK

Eleanor Roosevelt was not comfortable at Springwood. Her mother-in-law Sara was domineering and their relationship was not close. Springwood, after all, was Sara's home; she, and sometimes Franklin, made all the decisions, leaving Eleanor with little role. Then, as Franklin rose higher in the political world, Springwood became a hotbed of male-dominated political activity that left Eleanor isolated, prompting her to wish for more privacy.

When Eleanor lamented the fact that Springwood was to be closed for the winter of 1924, Franklin suggested that she and some friends build a year-round getaway cottage at the far end of the estate, an area that was a favorite spot for family picnics and activities. Franklin even aided in the design of a small Dutch Colonial fieldstone house named Val-Kill (Figure 76) after a stream running through the property. Eleanor's close friends, Nancy Cook and Marion Dickerman, moved in immediately and Eleanor joined them on weekends.

Val-Kill was initially a refuge and hideaway for Eleanor, but gradually became a more vibrant place. In 1926, she and her friends had a larger building constructed to house an experimental furniture business wherein local farmers facing difficult economic times might learn manufacturing skills. The venture failed during the Great Depression, so Eleanor, by then First Lady, converted the building into apartments for herself and a secretary. Val-Kill (plates XIII and XIV) was a place where she could rest after her whirlwind trips around the nation and also a hotbed of activity; family and friends came and went and she continually met with political associates, social reformers, UN associates, student activists, disadvantaged children — it became a place

Figure 76. Stone Cottage at Val-Kill, Eleanor Roosevelt National Historic Site, Hyde Park, New York. Photograph by W. D. Urbin, use courtesy National Park Service.

where she could practice a personal sort of diplomacy. It was at Val-Kill that she conducted massive correspondence and wrote her syndicated newspaper column *My Day,* magazine articles and numerous books. When Franklin could not accompany her to Hyde Park, she invariably spent her time at Val-Kill rather than the Springwood mansion.

Val-Kill, which became Mrs. Roosevelt's permanent home from 1945 until her death in 1962, is furnished with some original pieces and includes the dining room, set for a family gathering, including jelly glasses for the children. Other points of interest are the Stone Cottage (the original building on-site), a playhouse, swimming pool, tennis court and huge outdoor fireplace used for barbeques cooked for the famous, and not-so-famous, by the gracious hostess. During the Roosevelt presidential administration, foreign heads of state visiting Hyde Park often dined at Val-Kill beside the fireplace, and Eleanor continued that tradition long after the President's death.

As specified in Franklin Roosevelt's will, Springwood was to be turned over to the federal government, but Eleanor remained in residence at Val-Kill for another seventeen years. After her death, the house was made into four rental units, but in 1970 the property was sold to private developers who planned to build additional units. Concerned citizens organized a drive to preserve Val-Kill as a home of historical interest and, in May 1977, President Jimmy Carter signed a bill creating the Eleanor Roosevelt National Historic Site, "in order to commemorate for the education, inspiration, and benefit of present and future generations the life and work of an outstanding woman in American history."[116]

DIRECTIONS: From US Route 9 in the village of Hyde Park, turn right onto Route 40A/Saint Andrews Road. Proceed to Route 9G and turn left. Val-Kill is 0.25 mile farther on the right (Figure 73).

PUBLIC USE: Season and hours: May-October, daily, 9 AM-5 PM; November-April, Thursday-Monday, 9 AM-5 PM. Closed Thanksgiving Day, Christmas Day, New Year's Day. The grounds are open year-round until sunset. **Admission fee:** Visits to the grounds are free. There is a charge for tours of the house. Children under 17, free. **For people with disabilities:** Accessible.

FOR ADDITIONAL INFORMATION: Contact: Eleanor Roosevelt National Historic Site, 4097 Albany Post Road, Hyde Park, New York 12538-1997, (845) 229-9115. **Web site:** *www.nps.gov/elro*. **Read:** Eleanor Roosevelt. 1978. *Autobiography of Eleanor Roosevelt.*

Elizabeth Virginia Wallace Truman

First Lady, 1945–1953

Born: February 13, 1885, Independence, Missouri
Died: October 18, 1982, Independence, Missouri

On April 12, 1945, Vice President Harry Truman was called to the White House where he was informed by First Lady Eleanor Roosevelt that the President had passed away. Truman asked what he might do to help her, and she gently replied, "What can we do to help you? You have the burden now."[117]

Truman immediately called home where daughter Margaret answered the phone and began to josh with him when he asked for her mother. She was startled when her father, in a voice she'd seldom heard, exclaimed, "Margaret! I want to speak to your mother!"[118] Within moments she, her mother and her grandmother, tears streaming down their faces, opened the door to find the Secret Service already on guard and, within the hour, Margaret and Bess were on their way to the White House for Harry Truman's swearing-in as President of the United States.

Their lives had been changed forever. Harry Truman was thrust into a job many thought was impossible, and the idea of Bess stepping into the shoes of Eleanor Roosevelt was daunting. Well, Bess Truman didn't even try. She and Harry remained themselves, which turned out to be quite enough.

Harry Truman met Independence neighbor Bess Wallace in Sunday school when he was six, she five, and his written history has told us that he knew, even then, that she was the only girl in the world for him. Their courtship was prolonged by his World-War-I service in France as an artillery captain. When they married in 1919, Harry moved into the house that Bess and her widowed mother occupied, the house that would become their permanent home.

The Trumans spent many years in Washington when Harry served as a United States Senator and President, yet neither lost their rock-solid, midwestern values of hard work and honesty. They survived difficult financial and emotional times in the early days of their marriage, yet never forgot their roots, remaining unassuming Missourians who found the pomposity and pretentiousness of Washington society often wearing, yet accepting it with grace and good humor. If Harry ever showed signs of pomposity, Bess brought him back down to earth quickly. That was her forte — not necessarily to prick the balloon of self-importance, but to point out a human failing. Daughter Margaret wrote, "If ever she found a man she could trust . . . Bess vowed she would share his whole life, no matter how much pain it caused her. She rejected absolutely and totally the idea of a woman's sphere and a man's sphere."[119] Bess herself was quoted as saying of politics, "A woman's place in public is to sit beside her husband, be silent, and be sure her hat is on straight."[120] Quite different from Eleanor Roosevelt's attitude!

In a way that was unfortunate, for Bess Truman was a gifted, charming woman who performed the duties of First Lady with character and grace. It was her choice to remain a private person, eschewing press conferences and interviews. Once, in answer to an interviewer's written question, she wrote back that the most necessary qualities for a First Lady were "Good health and a strong sense of humor."[121]

Daughter Margaret, in *My Own Story*, noted her mother's reticence:

> *Mother is perhaps the least understood member of our family — a woman of tremendous character, a warm-hearted, kind lady with a robust sense of humor, a merry twinkling wit and a tremendous capacity for enjoying life. From all I can gather, although not from her, as her modesty is so deep-seated, nothing can be done about it, she was an Independence belle.*[122]

Harry Truman lived for Bess, and she for him. Their love and commitment was constant through fifty-three years of marriage, and it is inconceivable to think that Harry Truman, beset with the monumental problems faced by any president, could have sustained, governed and performed as he did without Bess as his guiding star. Follow in Eleanor Roosevelt's footsteps? Of course not. One lady was flamboyant and active, the next reticent and modest. Their personal needs and those of their husbands were quite different and distinct. Each lady performed brilliantly. Each was right for her time. And her man.

Harry S Truman National Historic Site

INDEPENDENCE, MISSOURI

Harry and Bess Truman embodied the basic and honest values nurtured in the small towns, neighborhoods and farms of Middle America. One example is the Truman home at 219 North Delaware Street in Independence (Figure 77, Plate XV), where the neighborhood has a distinctive assortment of architectural styles that represent every decade since the mid-nineteenth century — a neighborhood where President Truman took his famous constitutionals — a neighborhood of solid citizens proud of, but not intimidated by, their famous neighbors.

Harry and Bess Truman returned from their honeymoon to live with Bess' widowed mother. Except for their time in Washington, the house would be their home until Bess's death in 1982. A fourteen-room Victorian built by

Figure 77. Truman Home at Harry S Truman National Historic Site, Independence, Missouri. Photograph courtesy National Park Service.

Mrs. Truman's grandfather in 1885, the house has six bedrooms, a high-ceilinged parlor, a music room and a large dining room. The interior reflects prosperity — tiled fireplaces, heavy mahogany and walnut furniture, windows with colored glass borders and a pleasant screened porch that leads to a small, shrubbery-bordered rear yard and a two-car garage. The exterior is decorated with the exaggerated jigsaw trim typical of the late-nineteenth century.

The Trumans were not a couple for change, and the house received minimal modernization over the years — only central heating, electricity, telephone and radio. Thus the house has remained, as one visitor remarked, "Harry and Bess Truman-comfortable,"[123] a home in the best sense — warm and charming, a true reflection of the ordinary folks who lived within its walls.

After Mrs. Truman bequeathed the home to the nation, it was declared a National Historic Site to be maintained by the National Park Service. A visitor center is located on Main Street, five blocks away, where tickets are available for guided tours of the house.

DIRECTIONS: From I 435 west of Independence: Take Exit 60 (Route 12/ Truman Road) and proceed eastbound for 3 miles on Truman Road to Main Street. The visitor center is on the southeastern corner of the intersection, with adequate parking across the street. **From I 470/Route 291 in Independence:** Exit onto Route 12/Truman Road and proceed westbound for 2.5 miles to Main Street and the visitor center. The Truman home itself, at 219 North Delaware Street, is 5 blocks west of the visitor center (Figure 78).

PUBLIC USE: Season and hours: Visitor center is open daily, 8:30 AM-5 PM. Guided tours of the Truman home in the summer begin at 9 AM, conducted on a first-come, first-served basis. No tours are offered on Mondays, September-May. Closed Thanksgiving Day, Christmas Day, New Year's Day. **Admission fee:** Yes. 16 and under, free. **Book store. For people with disabilities:** Accessible.

FOR ADDITIONAL INFORMATION: Contact: Harry S Truman National Historic Site, 223 North Main Street, Independence, Missouri 64050, (816) 254-9929. **Web site:** *www. nps.gov/hstr*. **Read:** Margaret Truman. 1986. *Bess W. Truman*.

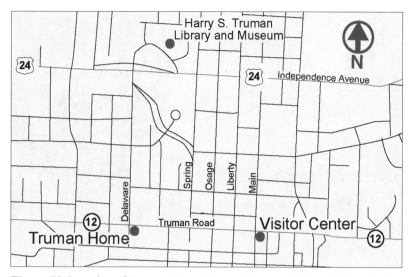

Figure 78. Location of Truman Home, Harry S Truman National Historic Site, in Independence, Missouri.

Mamie Geneva Doud Eisenhower

First Lady, 1953–1961

Born: November 14, 1896, Boone, Iowa
Died: November 1, 1979, Washington, DC

A month after their wedding, nineteen-year-old Mamie Eisenhower was horrified when her Army officer husband was ordered to leave on a three-month military tour. "You're not going to leave me this soon after our wedding day, are you?" she cried. Gently, Second Lieutenant Eisenhower put his arms about her. "Mamie, there's something you must understand. My country comes first and always will. You come second."[124]

Those shocking words would never be forgotten. Army marriage has always meant long separations, loneliness and, worst of all, fear that a spouse was in harm's way in some distant place. It meant moving from post to post, setting up a new home in each one, making new friends and social adjustments all too frequently. In a single year, Mrs. Eisenhower recalled, they lived on seven different Army posts.

It was not easy, as Mamie, before her marriage, was accustomed to a pampered life filled with cotillions, movies, picnics, parties and lots of attention from a string of beaus. Pretty, vivacious and gregarious, her adjustment to Army life was difficult — especially since she couldn't cook! — but love, tenacity and common respect prevailed. Many years later she said:

I knew from the day I married Ike that he would be a great soldier. He was always dedicated, serious and purposeful about

his job. Nothing came before his duty. I was forced to match his
spirit of personal sacrifice as best I could. Being his wife meant I
must leave him free from personal worries to conduct his career as
he saw fit.[125]

Like most couples, the Eisenhower marriage had its ups and downs. At times, Ike's career foundered which caused frustration and tension. Constant moves were physically and emotionally exhausting. There were illnesses, none more traumatic than the loss of their firstborn, infant Doud, to scarlet fever in 1921. Ike and Mamie were tormented with self-reproach and guilt that put a palpable strain on their marriage. Doud's death devastated Mamie and nearly caused Ike to have a nervous breakdown. Only deep commitment and the strength of their love enabled them to weather the storm. The birth of second son John in 1922 was a major factor in the recovery process.

In 1936, Ike was assigned to the staff of General Douglas MacArthur in the Philippines, a post Mamie faced with dread but which became a defining experience, for it was there that Mamie Eisenhower reached maturity as an Army wife and as a person. When they left the islands in 1939, Philippine President Quezon awarded Eisenhower the Distinguished Service Cross of the Philippines, but handed the medal to Mamie. "You put it on him," he said, "for you helped him to earn it."[126]

With their marriage secure, the Eisenhowers faced another challenge. World War II brought General Eisenhower fame and glory, but Mamie was subject to loneliness and anxiety. She called those years "My three years without Eisenhower."[127] While Ike was stationed in Europe, she lived in the Wardman Park Hotel in Washington, often ill with various ailments, some dating from the years she spent on bases in the tropics. She worried about Ike constantly, but finally realized that she was doing herself no good by remaining in isolation. She volunteered at the Stage Door Canteen and spent a good deal of time answering the hundreds of letters she received from mothers and wives of the service personnel serving under Ike's command.

Life after the war was more tranquil, if no less exciting. Ike became president of Columbia University before being named Supreme Commander of NATO forces in Europe. She wanted him to stay out of politics, but pressure was brought for him to run for the presidency so, as usual, she was by his side. "Honey, it's your decision. My job will be the same as always — to take care of you and our home."[128]

In the White House, Mamie was a natural, molded by temperament and experience. Chief White House Usher J. B. West wrote:

> *As wife of a career Army officer, she understood the hierarchy of a large establishment, the division of responsibilities, and how to direct a staff. She knew exactly what she wanted, every moment, and exactly how it should be done.*[129]

Ike agreed.

> *I think that Mamie's biggest contribution was to make the White House livable, comfortable and meaningful for the people who came in. She was always helpful and ready to do anything. She exuded hospitality. She saw that as one of her functions and performed it, no matter how tired she was. In the White House, you need intelligence and charm — to make others glad to be around you. She had that ability.*[130]

The American people who came to adore Mamie for her sprightly personality, wide smile (and bangs) would surely agree with Ike's sentiment.

Mamie Doud Eisenhower Birthplace

Boone, Iowa

Mamie Geneva Doud was born in the family home at 718 Carroll Street in 1896. When she was an infant, the family moved to Cedar Rapids briefly before moving west in 1905 to Colorado — first to Pueblo, then Colorado Springs and, finally, to Denver, where Mamie lived with her parents until her marriage to Dwight Eisenhower. The Denver home is privately owned and not open to the public.

Mamie's Iowa birthplace (Figure 79) passed through several owners including the First Baptist Church which wished to build an addition to the church building in 1970. A Birthplace Restoration Committee was formed, a local philanthropist donated a plot across the street from the church and in 1975 the house was moved to 709 Carroll Street, completely restored to its 1890s appearance and opened to the public.

The completely restored Victorian contains many pieces of furniture from Mamie's family. The parlor has matching chairs donated by Mamie and a brown chair, gold settee, piano, bench and family Bible are from the home of

Figure 79. Mamie Doud Eisenhower Birthplace, Boone, Iowa. Photograph courtesy Boone County Historical Society.

her maternal grandparents. The master bedroom furniture, on loan from the Colorado Historical Society, includes the bed in which Mamie was born and a museum and library on the ground floor contains exhibits that match a chronology of Mamie's life, her baptismal certificate, a baby shoe, wedding announcement, family photographs and gowns and other personal items. A favorite is an original oil painting by President Eisenhower.

The exterior features an 1890s wrought iron fence and a summer kitchen. A carriage house to the rear houses a 1949 Chrysler Windsor sedan presented by the Eisenhowers to Mamie's uncle, and a 1962 Plymouth Valiant Mamie once owned.

DIRECTIONS: Boone is in central Iowa, 15 miles west of Ames, just north of US 30. From US 30 in Boone, go north on Story Street to 8th Street, then west on 8th for 4 blocks to Carroll, turning south for 0.5 block to the birthplace on the west side of the road (Figure 80).

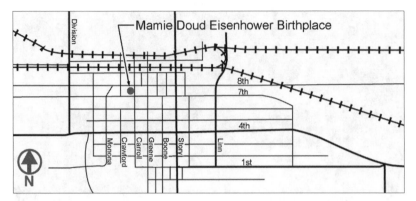

Figure 80. Location of the Mamie Doud Eisenhower Birthplace in Boone, Iowa.

PUBLIC USE: Season and hours: June-October, Monday-Saturday, 10 AM-5 PM. All other times by appointment. **Admission fee:** Yes, with discounts for children. **Gift shop. For people with disabilities:** Not accessible.

FOR ADDITIONAL INFORMATION: Contact: Boone County Historical Society, 602 Story Street, Boone, Iowa 50036, (515) 432-1907. **Web site:** *www.mamiesbirthplace.homestead.com.* **Read:** (1) Susan Eisenhower. 1996. *Mrs. Ike.* (2) Marilyn Irwin Holt. 2007. *Mamie Doud Eisenhower: The General's First Lady.*

Eisenhower National Historic Site

GETTYSBURG, PENNSYLVANIA

Dwight Eisenhower graduated from West Point in 1915 as a second lieutenant. By 1918 he was a captain, then was promoted to Lieutenant Colonel in command of the Army's fledgling tank corps training center in Gettysburg, Pennsylvania. Frustrated by stateside duty while a war was being fought in Europe, he and his wife nonetheless fell in love with Gettysburg, a pretty rural town in the foothills of the Appalachian Mountains.

Thirty-three years later, General of the Armies and Mrs. Dwight D. Eisenhower bought a ramshackle farm and house on the outskirts of Gettysburg, a dream come true for an Army couple who had spent a lifetime moving from one military post to another, one rental to another — twenty-seven homes in thirty-eight years of marriage. At last they had found permanence and pride of ownership, the first property either had ever owned.

The house was partially razed and replaced with "Mamie's Dream House," a twenty-room modified Georgian, completed in 1955 (Figure 81, Plate XV). The house has eight bedrooms, eight baths, living room, dining room, kitchen and porch. With the exception of Ike's private office and "out of bounds" den, the house is a reflection of Mamie's decorating taste in furniture, colors and space. The living room is filled with Mamie's treasures: an accumulation of furniture, family pictures and decorative objects, as well as gifts received from friends and admirers around the world. Several of Ike's paintings are displayed, and visitors may be intrigued by the curio cabinet in the entrance hall that contains Mamie's knickknacks, including a presidential plate she purchased from a nearby Stuckey's souvenir stand and plastic figurines of presidents and First Ladies that were collected from cereal boxes. There is no pretense in this home!

After so many years as an Army wife, Mrs. Eisenhower felt that, when she reached fifty, she was entitled to remain in bed until noon. It was her habit in the White House, and later in Gettysburg, to meet with staff, dictate correspondence and plan the social agenda while propped up in bed. The bedroom, as well as her bathroom, is decorated in pink, her favorite color.

The heart of the house was the sun porch. Mrs. Eisenhower said, "We lived on the porch,"[131] and it is easy to see why as its comfortable furniture and

Figure 81. Eisenhower Home at Eisenhower National Historic Site, Gettysburg, Pennsylvania. Photograph courtesy National Park Service.

casual ambience were perfect for informal entertaining and relaxation. Its view faces east to the Gettysburg Civil War battlefield, and just outside the porch is a putting green and sand trap installed by the Professional Golfer's Association in the late 1950s as a thank-you gift to America's most illustrious duffer.

During the Eisenhower presidency, the Gettysburg farm was an essential retreat from the pressures of Washington, and even served as temporary Executive Office when the President recuperated from his first heart attack in 1955. Thus it hosted many national and world leaders. The Eisenhowers presented the farm to the federal government in 1967, but they remained in residence until their deaths, Ike's in 1969 and Mamie's in 1979. She'd often remarked, "We only had one home — our farm."[132]

DIRECTIONS: Gettysburg is 35 miles southwest of Harrisburg, Pennsylvania, on US Route 30, just west of its junction with US Route 15. The Historic Site is on US Route 15 (Business) southwest of downtown Gettysburg. Follow the historical markers to the National Park Service Visitor Center where visitors are transported by shuttle bus to the Eisenhower farm (Figure 82).

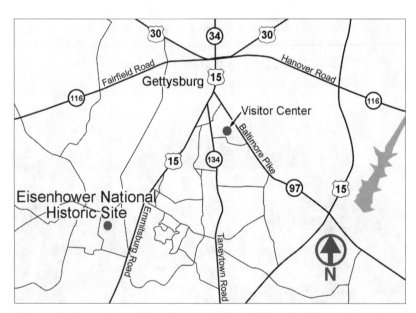

Figure 82. Location of Eisenhower National Historic Site at Gettysburg, Pennsylvania.

PUBLIC USE: Season and hours: Daily, 9 AM-4 PM. Closed Thanksgiving Day, Christmas Day, New Year's Day. Due to the lack of on-site parking and space limitations at the Eisenhower home, visits may be made only by shuttle bus leaving from the Gettysburg National Military Park Visitor Center. The Center opens at 8 AM and tickets may be purchased on a first-come, first-served basis for the next available tour. **Admission fee:** Yes, with discounts for children and educational groups. **Gift shops. For people with disabilities:** Advance arrangements should be made at the visitor center.

FOR ADDITIONAL INFORMATION: Contact: Superintendent, Eisenhower National Historic Site, 250 Eisenhower Farm Lane, Gettysburg, Pennsylvania 17325, (717) 338-9114. **Web site:** *www.nps.gov/eise*. **Read:** Dorothy Brandon. 1954. *Mamie Doud Eisenhower: A Portrait of a First Lady*.

Dwight D. Eisenhower Presidential Library and Museum

ABILENE, KANSAS

Dwight David Eisenhower — General of the Army, President of the United States, world leader — and graduate of Abilene High School, class of 1909. Abilene, Kansas, will never let the memory of Dwight Eisenhower fade, proud as it is of its most famous son. To perpetuate his memory, the city, in association with the Eisenhower Foundation, initiated and built The Eisenhower Center, a twenty-two-acre complex consisting of five buildings, a statue of General Eisenhower, and a group of pylons — all arranged around and within a central mall. The five buildings consist of the Visitors Center, the Eisenhower Boyhood Home, the Dwight D. Eisenhower Presidential Library and Museum and the Place of Meditation.

General information and orientation, including a film reviewing the life of President Eisenhower, is available at the Visitors Center. East of the Visitors Center is the Eisenhower Boyhood Home where Dwight Eisenhower spent much of his childhood and adolescent years.

The most extensive interpretation of Dwight and Mamie Eisenhower's lives is provided at the museum (Figure 83). Four major galleries in the museum contain items associated with President Eisenhower, including childhood artifacts, high school memorabilia, military life and career, the presidency and after and souvenirs and gifts to the president from heads of state and ordinary citizens.

Figure 83. The museum at Dwight D. Eisenhower Presidential Library and Museum, Abilene, Kansas. Photograph courtesy Dwight D. Eisenhower Presidential Library and Museum.

The First Lady's gallery contains several kiosks devoted to Mamie Eisenhower, displaying several of her gowns, personal items and a stunning portrait of the former First Lady. A short biographical movie includes coverage of her early life, marriage, time as First Lady and life after the White House years.

The library, located across the mall from the museum, was established to preserve the President's papers and related historical material. Like other presidential libraries, it is archival, dedicated to scholarly research.

President Eisenhower requested burial in Abilene where he, Mrs. Eisenhower and their three-year-old son Doud are entombed in the Place of Meditation, a steepled sanctuary near the western end of the mall.

DIRECTIONS: From I 70, take Exit 275 and proceed southbound on Route 15 to Abilene. Historical markers guide visitors to the Eisenhower Center (Figure 84).

PUBLIC USE: Season and hours: Daily, 9 AM-4:45 PM, with extended summer hours, 8 AM-5:45 PM. Closed Thanksgiving Day, Christmas Day, New Year's Day. **Admission fee:** For the museum only, with discounts for seniors. Children under fifteen, free. **Gift Shop. For people with disabilities:** Fully accessible.

FOR ADDITIONAL INFORMATION: Contact: The Eisenhower Center, 200 Southeast Fourth Street, Abilene, Kansas 67410, (785) 263-6700. **Web site:** *www.eisenhower.archives.gov.* **Read:** Marilyn Irwin Holt. 2007. *Mamie Doud Eisenhower: The General's First Lady.*

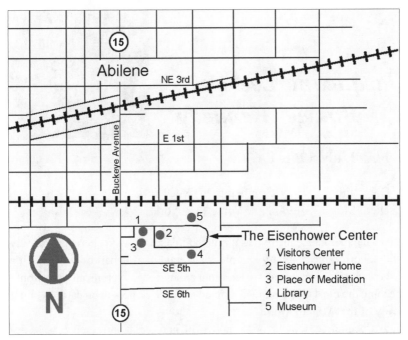

Figure 84. Location of The Eisenhower Center and Dwight D. Eisenhower Presidential Library and Museum in Abilene, Kansas.

Jacqueline Lee Bouvier Kennedy

First Lady, 1961–1963

Born: July 28, 1929, Southampton, New York
Died: May 19, 1994, New York, New York

Jacqueline Kennedy was a reluctant celebrity who cherished privacy and abhorred the publicity and press coverage that is part of politics. "It's frightening," she once said, "to lose your anonymity."[133] Ironically, she would become the most photographed, copied and envied person on earth as "First Lady of the Western World."

Jacqueline Bouvier, born into wealth and social prominence, was educated at Miss Porter's School, Vassar and the Sorbonne in Paris. Her social experience, charm, beauty, self-assurance and aristocratic poise first captured America's imagination at her husband's inauguration as President in 1961 when televised inaugural balls enabled millions of Americans to be captivated by the youngest and most beautiful First Lady in generations. While the conservative Eisenhowers had brought stability to the nation following World War II, people were ready to break out of the post-war transition by the 1960s, and the youthful, vigorous, attractive Kennedys fit the feelings of the times. Dowdy became rowdy.

Mrs. Kennedy often said that her favorite First Lady was the uncommunicative Bess Truman. "Mrs. Truman was always just Mrs. Truman. Her central responsibility was to be Mrs. Truman."[134] Yet, try as she might, Jackie could never just be plain Mrs. Kennedy. Without trying, for example, she became a fashion arbiter, and not incidentally, an unwitting saleswoman for the American fashion business.

Her first priority, however, was to her children. Always. No matter what the occasion, she blocked time every day for play, games or reading, and remained firm in her efforts to protect them from outside influences while residing in the White House fishbowl. "If you bungle raising your children, I don't think whatever else you do well matters very much."[135] She delivered one baby stillborn and another died after a few days of life. Hence, her intensity of care and influence over surviving children Caroline and John was profound.

Perhaps that maternal consideration should be Jacqueline Kennedy's real legacy, although she shall surely be remembered for other things, such as her inspired work to transform the White House into a national historic object. She formed committees, scoured museums and storerooms, solicited gifts of historic furniture and American works of art, supervised painting, reupholstering and refurbishing, all intended to restore the White House to the glorious symbol of America's past and present. Not easy to please, she was a stern taskmaster with definite views. The results spoke for themselves as the White House was brilliantly restored under her influence. All Americans should be proud of her efforts.

Mrs. Kennedy was never comfortable with political activities, but promised her husband she would accompany him to Dallas in 1963, a trip that shall never be forgotten — the unreality of the President's assassination and the strength, courage and grace Jacqueline Kennedy showed under the most horrific circumstances. Without question, her poise and determination helped the nation emotionally survive that terrible experience.

If Mrs. Kennedy thought she might finally find the privacy she craved after the assassination, she was mistaken. Every activity, every vacation, every social event she attended was reported by the press, sometimes critically. Although the American people hoped that she would find happiness and inner peace, it would have to be on their terms. Thus, when Mrs. Kennedy married Greek shipping tycoon Ari Onassis, there was a palpable sense of shocked surprise, rage and disappointment throughout the nation.

After Ari Onassis' death, Jackie returned to New York where she found employment as a book editor. She lived in a 15-room cooperative apartment on Central Park and reveled in her son, daughter and grandchildren. A co-worker once described her: "She doesn't want to be known as the wife of the President of the United States or as the wife of one of the richest men in the world. She wants to be known as *herself.*"[136] As for herself, when asked her greatest achievement, she replied, "I think it is that after going through a rather difficult time, I consider myself comparatively sane."[137]

At times, the Kennedy presidency was compared with the mythical kingdom of Camelot. "Don't let it be forgot," Jackie told biographer Theodore White, "that there once was a spot, for one brief shining moment, that was known as Camelot."[138] In a memorial issue of *Look* magazine a year after President Kennedy's death, she wrote:

> *Now I think that I should have guessed it could not last. I should have known it was asking too much to dream that I might have grown old with him and see our children grow up together. So now he is a legend when he would have preferred to be a man.*[139]

When Jackie died in 1994, an era passed. Camelot had disappeared back into the mist . . . .

John F. Kennedy Presidential Library and Museum

BOSTON, MASSACHUSETTS

The Kennedy Library — stark, striking, imposing (Figure 85) — stands beside the sea that President Kennedy loved. The park-like surroundings and unique view of Boston's historic harbor provide a beautiful setting and the building designed by the internationally renowned architect, I. M. Pei, captures the modernity and vision of the man it honors. The interior, with huge picture windows and spacious galleries, is an aesthetic experience in perfect harmony with Kennedy's interest in the arts.

Planning for the Library began in December, 1963, in the sad days following the death of President Kennedy. From the very beginning, Jacqueline Kennedy was involved with its genesis — selection of the architect, consideration of the museum as great art, a place where people might search for truth, learn more about politics and government and especially the opportunity to reflect on the need to serve the public in some way.

Like other presidential libraries, the Kennedy Library is a research archive with a museum section representing the life of President Kennedy. The office of the President is illustrated by a combination of films, videotapes,

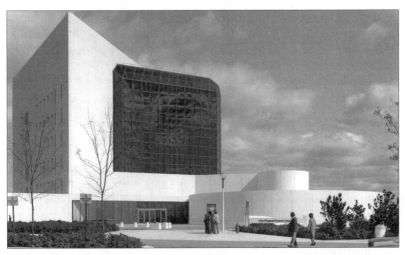

Figure 85. John F. Kennedy Presidential Library and Museum, Boston, Massachusetts. Photograph courtesy John F. Kennedy Presidential Library and Museum.

audio recordings, photographs, letters, speeches and artifacts. There are twenty-one exhibits covering President Kennedy's administration and his family life including several devoted to First Lady Jacqueline Kennedy. In one, her role in restoring the history of the White House with period furniture and decorations is highlighted, including presentation of the famous 1962 televised tour of the White House wherein she instilled national pride in our political and architectural heritage. Another gallery, "White House Room," displays personal items that include Mrs. Kennedy's *Inquiring Photographer* camera and her baby brush, all displayed in a closet with original *trompe l'oeuill* doors from the White House living quarters. All of the exhibits are permanent except those in the "Ceremonial Room" where the exhibit is changed every six months. Those exhibits will relate to ceremonial occasions at the White House and the value of those occasions as a stage to highlight cultural values and the arts, interests particularly important to Mrs. Kennedy.

The intention of the museum is to place the Kennedy story into the broad perspective of world and American history. The Library's self-description expresses the hope that "visitors will take from the Museum a deeper appreciation of our system of government and a greater awareness of the benefits and responsibilities of living in a free society."[140]

DIRECTIONS: By car from south of Boston: Northbound, take the Southeast Expressway (I 93/US 1/SR 3) to Dorchester, then take Exit 14 to Morrissey Boulevard and follow the historical markers to the library. **From the North and Boston:** Take the Southeast Expressway to Exit 15, then follow the historical markers (Figure 86). **By Rapid Transit:** Take the MBTA Red Line to the JFK/UMass Station where free shuttle buses transport visitors to the library. The shuttle buses run every 20 minutes between 8 AM and museum closing. Take the bus marked "JFK."

PUBLIC USE: Season and hours: Daily, 9 AM-5 PM. Closed Thanksgiving Day, Christmas Day, New Year's Day. **Admission fee:** Yes, with discounts for groups, students and seniors. **Food service:** A café is open 9 AM-5 PM. Picnics are allowed on the grounds. **Gift shop. For people with disabilities:** Fully accessible.

FOR ADDITIONAL INFORMATION: Contact: John F. Kennedy Presidential Library and Museum, Columbia Point, Boston, Massachusetts 02125, (617) 514-1600 *or* (866) JFK-1960. **Web site:** *www.jfklibrary.org*. **Read:** (1) Mary Van Rensselaer Thayer. 2007. *Jacqueline Kennedy*. (2) William and Christina Tree Davis. 1980. *The Kennedy Library*.

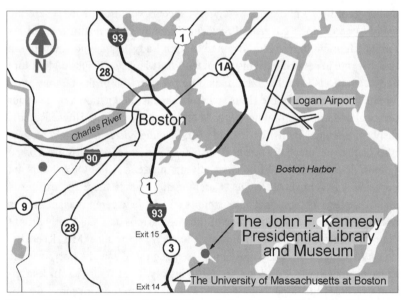

Figure 86. Location of the John F. Kennedy Presidential Library and Museum in Boston, Massachusetts.

Claudia Alta Taylor "Lady Bird" Johnson

First Lady, 1963–1969

Born: December 22, 1912, Karnack, Texas
Died: July 11, 2007, Stonewall, Texas

You can't make her mad, I've never seen her lose her temper.
— Daughter Lynda[141]

She's as gentle and serene as the cypress trees; quiet, deep-rooted, protected.
— Press Secretary Liz Carpenter[142]

She's soft and kind and understanding.
— Husband Lyndon[143]

That's the greatest woman I have ever known.
— Speaker Sam Rayburn[144]

Lady Bird carried Texas for us!
— Bobby Kennedy[145]

I make her sound like a combination of Elsie Dinsmore and the Little Colonel . . . but this is the problem with Bird. When you talk about her, you make her too good to be true.
— Congresswoman Lindy Boggs[146]

And so it goes. Her family and friends spared nothing in their praise of a woman who was a paragon of patience, equanimity and common sense, surely not easy as husband Lyndon was often impatient, demanding, imperious, profane and vulgar. Yet the sweet-tempered young lady from East Texas learned to deal with her impetuous husband with rare skill. In the first place, she believed in him. When they first met, she found him "terribly, terribly interesting . . . the most outspoken, straight-forward, determined young man. I knew I had met something remarkable, but I didn't quite know what."[147]

Psychologists might say she saw much of her father in him. As a successful farmer-merchant in a small Texas town, her father was personally driven, and drove his employees. Claudia's mother died when she was five, and her father became responsible for a little girl with whom he had no experience, nor much time for. Therefore, she spent a great deal of her childhood with her maiden Aunt Effie, who instilled in Lady Bird an appreciation of the beauty in music, arts and nature, but not much in practical matters. Her nickname was given to her by a nurse who claimed that she was as pretty as a Ladybird.

Lyndon proposed to Lady Bird on their second date and took her to meet his parents on the third. When it was time to return to Washington, where he was working as a congressional aide, he drove first to Karnack to meet her father. After dinner, Mr. Taylor told Lady Bird, "Daughter, you've been bringing home a lot of boys. This time you brought a man."[148] With that approval, Lyndon began a bombardment of letters, flowers and phone calls from Washington, and when he returned to Texas, he insisted they not wait. "We either get married now or we never will."[149] They married in Saint Mark's Episcopal Church in San Antonio and after the ceremony, as the couple rushed off on a Mexican honeymoon, the minister sighed, "I hope that marriage lasts."[150] If only he knew.

When Lyndon ran for Congress in 1937, Lady Bird asked her father for an advance on her future inheritance. With the help of that loan, later repaid, the campaign was successful and Lady Bird became a Washington wife, a job to which she quickly adapted. She conducted constituents' tours, assisted in Lyndon's office and often made suggestions on speeches and campaign strategy. In 1943, she purchased a radio station in Austin with the remainder of her inheritance, worked diligently to learn the business and supervised its expansion into a highly profitable radio/television enterprise.

In 1954, Lyndon, then a member of the United States Senate, was elected Majority Leader. At that time, Lady Bird began to speak in public. The once shy, behind-the-scenes marital anchor became a political force in her own right. Then, in 1955, Johnson suffered a massive heart attack. Lady Bird remained with him in the hospital for five weeks, converting her suite into an office. "Lyndon wanted me around 24 hours a day. He wanted me to laugh a lot, and always to have lipstick. During those days we rediscovered the meaning and freshness of life."[151]

Lyndon was back in the Senate by January 1956 — busy, impulsive and ornery as ever. In 1961, when he became John F. Kennedy's Vice President, the Johnsons entered a new phase of life. They traveled widely as representatives of the United States, and Lady Bird often found herself pinch-hitting for Jacqueline Kennedy at dinners, receptions and awards ceremonies the First Lady either could not or did not wish to attend.

Lady Bird was riding in the Dallas motorcade when President Kennedy was assassinated. Her first thought was of Mrs. Kennedy's welfare, and it was with incredulity and somber feelings of realization that she was now First Lady. The move into the White House was overwhelming, but Lady Bird adjusted brilliantly. "My first job," she decided, "was to make this home a place where Lyndon can operate productively, and to add to his operation in every way that I can, because I have never felt so much need on his part, and so much compassion on my part for him."[152] Chief Usher West noted that she soon ran the house "rather like the chairman of the board of a large corporation."[153]

A hyperactive CEO at that. She involved herself in women's affairs and in 1964 became extremely active in her husband's reelection campaign. She received particularly high marks for a solo whistle stop tour through the South, a trip some considered physically dangerous due to LBJ's controversial stand on civil rights.

During his second term, she turned her major effort to the beautification of America, an effort that culminated with passage of the Highway Beautification Act of 1965, popularly called the "Lady Bird Act."

In 1969, the Johnsons retired to their ranch where the former President died in 1973. Mrs. Johnson mourned, but recovered with a schedule almost as crowded as she had experienced as First Lady. She became heavily involved with fundraising and planning of the LBJ Library in Austin, served on the Board of Regents of the University of Texas and joined boards of several large corporations and charitable organizations, especially those involved with her favorite cause — the conservation, preservation and beautification of America's natural resources. A special place in her heart was the Lady Bird

Johnson Wildflower Center in Austin, Texas, a site dedicated to protect and preserve North America's native plants and natural landscapes.

In 2007, at the age of ninety-four, Lady Bird Johnson passed away peacefully at home, surrounded by her family. Until the end, although in frail health, she remained dedicated to her strong belief in America, an America she honored with passion. Mrs. Johnson once told an interviewer, "I sometimes look back and almost say to myself: 'Gee, was that really me? Did it all happen to me? It was a wonderful life.'"[154] It was a wonderful life she shared with the American people — and they are richer for it.

Lyndon B. Johnson National Historical Park and Lyndon B. Johnson State Park and Historic Site

JOHNSON CITY AND STONEWALL, TEXAS

A unique cooperative effort between the Lyndon B. Johnson National Historical Park and Lyndon B. Johnson State Park and Historic Site memorializes and dramatizes Lyndon Johnson's presence, stature and legacy in the vast and beautiful Texas Hill Country that he loved. The National Historical Park consists of two distinct areas, one in Johnson City and the other at Stonewall.

In 1913, when Lyndon was five, the family moved into a comfortable vernacular house located on Elm Street in Johnson City. Almost a quarter century later, Johnson delivered his first political speech — declaring his congressional candidacy in 1937 — from the front porch of this home. This structure has been restored and furnished to represent the period of Johnson's youth. The National Park Service visitor center (Figure 87A), located a block from the Elm Street house, features historic exhibits and two films, one of which is a biographical look at the life of Lady Bird.

The famous LBJ Ranch is located fourteen miles to the west of Johnson City near Stonewall. The state park visitor center lies immediately south of the LBJ Ranch, just across the Pedernales River. Here, visitors can pick up a driving permit, map and CD to assist in self-guided driving tours of the ranch that include the one-room schoolhouse where Johnson began his education, the reconstructed birthplace house, and a stop at the Johnson family cemetery, final resting place for the active, larger-than-life President and Mrs.

Johnson. The primary destination of the tour is the ranch's airplane hangar which features exhibits, a film and a bookstore/gift shop where tickets are sold for a ranger-guided tour of the Texas White House (Figure 87B) which opened to the public in 2008. Rooms currently available for visitation include

Figure 87. (**A**) National Park Service visitor center, Johnson City, Texas. Photograph courtesy Johnson City Chamber of Commerce. (**B**) The Texas White House, Lyndon B. Johnson National Historical Park, Stonewall, Texas. Photograph courtesy National Park Service.

the President's office, the living room and the dining room (Plate XV), all restored to their 1963–1968 appearance. The remainder of the home is still in the process of restoration and will be opened to the public in the future.

DIRECTIONS: Johnson City is 50 miles west of Austin, Texas. From Austin, take US Highway 290 westbound to Johnson City and the eastern section of the LBJ National Historical Park (Figure 88A). The Stonewall section of the National Historical Park and the Lyndon B. Johnson State Park and Historic Site are 14 miles farther west, near Stonewall (Figure 88B).

PUBLIC USE: Season and hours: *Johnson City visitor center*, 8:45 AM-5 PM. Guided tours of the LBJ Boyhood Home are conducted every thirty minutes. *Stonewall visitor center*: Open 8 AM-5 PM. Self-guided driving tours of the LBJ Ranch are available from 9 AM-5:30 PM seven days a week. Guided tours of the Texas White House are conducted 10 AM-4:30 PM. The Johnson City and Stonewall sites are closed Thanksgiving Day, Christmas Day, New Year's

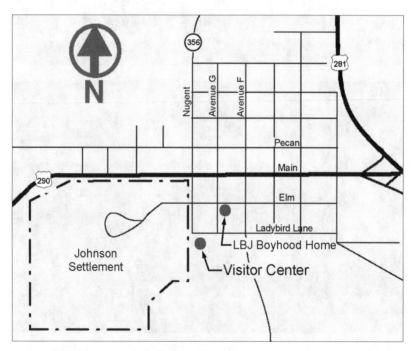

Figure 88A. Location of the National Park Service Visitor Center, Lyndon B. Johnson Boyhood Home, and Johnson Settlement — all parts of the Lyndon B. Johnson National Historical Park in Johnson City, Texas.

Day. **Admission fee:** Yes, for the tour of Texas White House only. **Food service:** There are picnic areas at each site. **Gift shops. For people with disabilities:** Accessible.

FOR ADDITIONAL INFORMATION: Contact: Lyndon B. Johnson National Historical Park, Box 329, Johnson City, Texas 78636, (830) 868-7128 *or* Lyndon B. Johnson State Park and Historic Site, P. O. Box 238, Stonewall, Texas 78671, (830) 644-2252. **Web site:** *National Park: www.nps.gov/lyjo; State Park: www.tpwd.state.tx.us/spdest/findadest/parks/lyndon_b_johnson/.* **Read:** (1) Lady Bird Johnson. 1970. *A White House Diary.* (2) Robert Dallek. 2005. *Lyndon B. Johnson: Portrait of a President.*

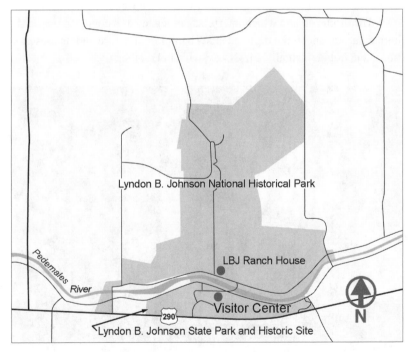

Figure 88B. Location of the LBJ Ranch House at Lyndon B. Johnson National Historical Park and the Visitor Center at Lyndon B. Johnson State Park and Historic Site, Stonewall, Texas.

Lyndon Baines Johnson Library and Museum

AUSTIN, TEXAS

It's all here, the story of our time...with the bark off.

-Lyndon B. Johnson, at the dedication

The Lyndon Baines Johnson Library and Museum (Figure 89), similar to the other presidential facilities built since FDR's administration, consists of separate library and museum divisions. The library section, available for use primarily for scholarly research, contains some thirty-five million documents related to Johnson and his presidency. The museum provides public exhibits of historical and cultural interest, including sequential displays that enable visitors to follow the political life of Lyndon Johnson from his tenure as a young congressman to his terms as President of the United States. One of the most popular exhibits of the museum is a special section devoted to Lady Bird Johnson and which interprets her legacy as a congressional wife, humanitarian, unofficial diplomat and champion of nature and its preservation. And, not incidentally, First Lady, wife and mother.

Figure 89. Lyndon Baines Johnson Library and Museum, Austin, Texas. Photograph courtesy Lyndon Baines Johnson Library and Museum.

Lyndon Johnson was responsible for some of the most sweeping and far-reaching social legislation in our history, but was finally victimized by the nation's division over the conflict in faraway Viet Nam. As President Johnson remarked at the dedication of the facility:

I hope that visitors who come here will achieve a better understanding of the presidency and that the young people who come here will get a clearer understanding of what this nation tried to do in an eventful period of history.

DIRECTIONS: The library and museum is on the campus of the University of Texas, 1 block from I 35. Exit I 35 at 26th Street and proceed westbound to Red River Street. Turn left on Red River Street and continue to the library and museum (Figure 90).

PUBLIC USE: Season and hours: *Museum:* Daily, 9 AM- 5 PM. Closed Christmas Day. *Library:* Monday-Friday, 9 AM-5 PM. Closed all federal holidays. **Gift Shop. For people with disabilities:** Accessible.

FOR ADDITIONAL INFORMATION: Contact: Lyndon Baines Johnson Library and Museum, 2313 Red River Street, Austin, Texas 78705, (512) 721-0200. **Web site:** *www.lbjlib.utexas.edu.* **Read:** Gordon Hall. 1967. *Lady Bird and Her Daughters.*

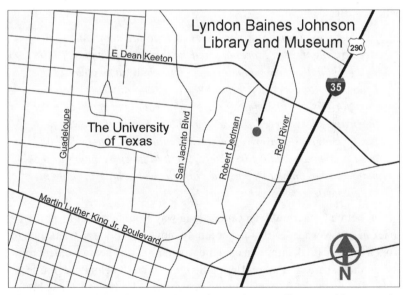

Figure 90. Location of the Lyndon Baines Johnson Library and Museum in Austin, Texas.

Thelma Catherine Ryan "Pat" Nixon

First Lady, 1969–1974

Born: March 16, 1912, Ely, Nevada
Died: June 22, 1993, Park Ridge, New Jersey

In his *Memoirs*, Richard Nixon recalled his wife on the day of his resignation as President:

> *She was wearing dark glasses to hide the signs of the two sleepless nights of preparations and the tears that [daughter] Julie said had finally come that morning. I knew how much courage she had needed to carry her through the days and nights of preparations for this abrupt departure. Now she would not receive any of the praise she deserved. There would be no round of farewell parties by congressional wives, no testimonials, no tributes. She had been a compassionate First Lady. She had given so much to the nation and so much to the world. Now she would have to share my exile. She deserved so much more.*[155]

Thelma Catherine Ryan came a long way from her birth in a miner's shack in Ely, Nevada. Early on, her family moved to southern California to work a ten-acre truck farm — a hard life wherein she and her two older brothers did their share, and more. Her mother died when Thelma was fourteen, and she assumed the responsibility of housekeeper for her father and brothers. When she was about to graduate from high school, her father became terminally ill, so she added nursing to her skills. He died in 1930 and as he'd always called her his Saint Patrick's Day baby, she changed her name to Patricia in his memory.

Hard work and adversity, however, did not dilute her childhood dreams of travel to faraway places nor achieving a college education. She enrolled at Fullerton Junior College in Southern California where she supported herself as a cleaning lady and bank clerk. She interrupted college to drive an elderly couple to New York in exchange for bus fare home, but instead of returning immediately, she remained in New York to work as a stenographer, book-keeper and sometimes X-ray technician at a tuberculosis hospital run by the Sisters of Mercy. "I wanted to reach out and help them. That is what gives one the deepest pleasure in the world — helping someone."[156]

She returned to Los Angeles two years later to enter the University of Southern California. To put herself through school, she held a variety of jobs — movie extra, store clerk, dental assistant and telephone operator. On campus, she could be found everywhere. Scholar Dr. Frank Baxter remembered her looking weary in his Shakespeare class:

> *There seemed to be plenty of reason for it. If you went to the cafeteria, there was Pat at the serving counter. An hour later, you'd go to the library and there was Pat checking out books. And later in the evening, there was Pat working on some student research program. Yet, with it all, she was a good student, alert and interested. She stood out from the empty-headed overdressed little sorority girls of that era like a good piece of literature on a shelf of cheap paperbacks.*[157]

She graduated in 1937, *cum laude*, with a teacher's certificate and an offer to teach typing and shorthand at Whittier High School, although that was hardly enough activity for a workaholic who also put on plays, coached the cheerleaders and served as faculty advisor to the Pep Committee. Still not busy enough, she won a role in *The Dark Tower*, a drama being produced by the Whittier Community Players and it was at the theater that she met young attorney Richard Nixon, who was dazzled by the beautiful young lady. She was less impressed with him, and when she rejected his offer of a date, he shocked her by boldly stating that she should reconsider because he was going to marry her one day.

Nixon's pursuit was long and persistent. Pat was not ready to settle down and continued to date other men, but was not totally uninterested — she admired Nixon's enormous energy and ambition and enjoyed their walks and talks. As they became more serious, she told her friends, "He's going to be president someday."[158] By the time he formally proposed, she was deeply in love. They married on June 21, 1940, at the Mission Inn in Riverside, California, and settled in a little garage apartment near Nixon's law office. World War II took them to Washington and a number of naval stations in the United States before Lieutenant Nixon shipped out to the South Pacific. Pat worked for the OPA in San Francisco awaiting his return.

After the war, Nixon entered politics despite Pat's discomfort with this decision. Daughter Tricia had arrived in 1946, finances were tight and Pat was not particularly interested in politics. She realized, however, that it was the life he wanted and finally agreed — under two conditions: home would be a refuge where she could provide the children with a normal life and, two, she would never be called on to deliver a political speech. So much for good intentions.

Pat Nixon was a trouper. "She didn't want politics ever. She hated the idea of ever facing another campaign. Every time Nixon entered one she was in deep despair," their friend Earl Mazo said.[159] Mrs. Nixon proved to be a good politician's wife but continued to shun the limelight. When he was Vice President to Dwight Eisenhower, however, they moved to a large fieldstone house where housekeepers, babysitters and servants were employed to manage the chores Pat had once handled, and their official duties precluded any thought of privacy. Pat's gracious public smile and imperturbable demeanor were deceiving as she was quick-witted and friends claimed that when out of the public eye she laughed, joked and even teased her solemn husband. If she had a temper, it was never displayed in public.

The Nixons made a number of goodwill trips — to the Far East, Africa, England and Russia, where she impressed State Department officials and foreign dignitaries. As a former schoolteacher, she was a good pupil. She studied up on the countries, visited schools and hospitals and insisted on meeting with women's groups everywhere. President Eisenhower congratulated Nixon after one trip, saying "Dick, I've heard some pretty good reports on you." Then he turned to Mrs. Nixon and said, "But the reports on you, Pat, have been wonderful!"[160]

The foreign trips were never easy. In 1958, the Nixons were the target of violent anti-US demonstrations in Latin America. An out-of-control mob in Caracas, Venezuela, came close to killing the couple during the motorcade from the airport to the American Embassy. Demonstrators spit on them, threw garbage and rocks and even attacked the cars with baseball bats. By all reports, Mrs. Nixon remained calm. A Secret Service man thought she "displayed more guts than any man I've ever seen."[161]

Pat was terribly disappointed when her husband lost the presidential election to John F. Kennedy in 1960, although she welcomed a return to private life. She was distraught when he ran for California governor in 1962, but, as usual, assisted in the campaign. After his defeat, she was quoted as being happy to be out of the rat race, telling a Hollywood producer, "You think people in the movie business are competitive, but they are not mean. In politics, they are the most vicious people in the world."[162] For all of her loathing, she reluctantly approved her husband's entry into the presidential race in 1968 as she realized how important it was for him, and was herself convinced that he was a man uniquely capable of solving the problems, both internal and external, that faced the nation.

He was elected, and to her surprise, she enjoyed being First Lady. Some thought there was "a new Mrs. Nixon." *Newsday* remarked, "Pat Nixon has suddenly emerged from an icy cocoon of literal anonymity and proven herself a living, breathing, thinking, lovely woman."[163] Not really, for she had always been that. She continued her lifelong pattern of hard work, sharing and giving to others. She even went on a solitary campaign tour in 1972. It had taken twenty-four years and many campaigns, but she seemed to have, according to a friend, "gotten the feel, the instinct if you will, that all political people need to possess if they want to survive."[164]

The Nixons retired to their California home, La Casa Pacific, upon his resignation from the presidency. Mrs. Nixon went into seclusion, although the disgrace brought them closer. He said:

> *At least we have the chance to spend a lot of time together. We've discovered, in this time of crisis, that we need each other. We've grown closer than ever before . . . I don't know what history will say about me, but I know it will say that Pat Nixon was truly a wonderful woman.*[165]

In 1968, Pat Nixon suffered a stroke that left her partially paralyzed. In 1980, the Nixons moved to New York and then northern New Jersey to be near their children and grandchildren. In 1993, Pat passed away quietly — with dignity and class. Just as she had lived her life.

Nixon Presidential Library and Museum

YORBA LINDA, CALIFORNIA

Richard Nixon was born in a small farmhouse that has been restored on the exact spot where it was built by his father in 1912. The house (Figure 91), part of a nine-acre complex of gardens and buildings that showcase the life and career of one of our most controversial presidents, stands at one end of the "First Lady's Garden" that features seasonal plantings and a 130-foot-long reflecting pool of quiet beauty.

At the other end of the pool stands the magnificent Main Gallery of the Nixon Presidential Library and Museum housing a motion-picture theater, amphitheater and 14,000 square feet of museum galleries highlighting Nixon's political career and legacy. For example, *Road to the Presidency* focuses on his early congressional and vice presidential campaigns, and *Structure of Peace* tells of the President as an architect of peace and includes a piece of concrete from the Berlin Wall. *Pat Nixon: Ambassador of Goodwill* is a moving tribute to the beloved First Lady. She was his trusted advisor and, as First

Figure 91. Richard Nixon's Birthplace (restored) and The First Lady's Garden at the Nixon Presidential Library and Museum, Yorba Linda, California. Photograph courtesy Nixon Presidential Library and Museum.

Lady, she was a globe-trotting ambassador of peace to 78 nations through-out the world, she promoted volunteerism and she inaugurated the White House candlelight tours. A "treasures" case contains personal gifts from the President and more lavish gifts from heads of state. A separate gallery is appropriately named *Gowns* and features a display of dresses and gowns worn by Mrs. Nixon and her daughters — Tricia's wedding gown, Julie's bridesmaid dress and Pat Nixon's mother-of-the-bride dress. There is also a light blue garter worn by Julie as part of "something old" passed down to her by First Lady Mamie Eisenhower.

Outside the Main Gallery is the most recent addition to the complex — The Loker Center, a $12-million building, one room of which is an exact replica of the White House East Room, America's "Grand Ballroom," the venue for special occasions such as state dinners, presidential speeches and press conferences. Also on the exterior is the actual presidential helicopter, "The Flying Oval Office," used by presidents Kennedy, Johnson, Nixon and Ford.

Richard and Pat Nixon are buried at the head of the reflecting pool near the birthplace house. Richard Nixon's gravestone reads, "The greatest honor history can bestow is the title of peacemaker." Mrs. Nixon's reads, "Even when people can't speak your language, they can tell if you have love in your heart."

DIRECTIONS: From Los Angeles: Drive southbound on I 5 to Route 91 and exit eastbound, proceeding to Route 57. Exit northbound on Route 57 and proceed to Yorba Linda Boulevard. Exit eastbound onto Yorba Linda to the library and museum. **From San Diego:** Drive northbound on I 5 to Route 57. Exit northbound on Route 57 and proceed to Yorba Linda Boulevard. Exit eastbound onto Yorba Linda Boulevard to the library and museum (Figure 92).

PUBLIC USE: Season and hours: Monday-Saturday, 10 AM-5 PM; Sunday, 11 AM-5 PM. Closed Thanksgiving Day and Christmas Day. **Admission fee:** Yes, with discounts for groups, students and seniors. Children ages six and un-der, free. **Gift shop. For people with disabilities:** Fully accessible.

FOR ADDITIONAL INFORMATION: Contact: Nixon Presidential Library and Museum. 18001 Yorba Linda Boulevard, Yorba Linda, California 92886, (714) 993-3393. **Web site:** *www.nixonlibrary.org.* **Read:** (1) Julie Nixon Eisenhower. 1986. *Pat Nixon: The Untold Story.* (2) Stephen E. Ambrose. 1987. *Nixon.*

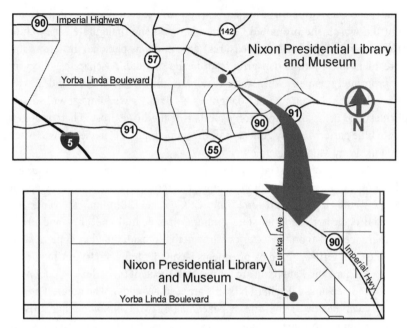

Figure 92. Location of the Nixon Presidential Library and Museum in Yorba Linda, California.

Elizabeth Bloomer Warren Ford

First Lady, 1974–1977

Born: April 8, 1918, Chicago, Illinois

In a speech to the American people following his inauguration in 1974, President Gerald R. Ford said, "The long American nightmare is over."[166] In the wake of the Watergate scandal, people yearned for honesty in government and responded to the decent man who now led the nation. From his political history in the Congress, they knew what to expect — a scrupulously direct and forthright administration that would lead them from the morass of the then-existing flawed national leadership.

What they might not have expected was Betty Ford, dutiful congressional wife, described by Press Secretary Ron Nessen as "a silent, smiling, plastic politician's wife who blossomed in the White House into an outgoing, witty and warm public personality with strong and independent views."[167] Mrs. Ford did not wholly agree. She felt she hadn't really changed, it was just that when she became First Lady, people began listening to her. And listen they did, for she was totally forthright and honest, whether she agreed with her husband or not. Shades of Eleanor Roosevelt!

Her support of the Equal Rights Amendment, the Supreme Court decision regarding abortion — *Roe v. Wade*, giving women the right to choose — plus liberal views on pre-marital sex and use of marijuana offended many people, including members of the President's staff, but hindsight showed she may have helped more than hurt. For example, the nation was surprised when she went public about her battle with breast cancer that included a mastectomy, but the attention and publicity she received persuaded many women to seek early testing and/or treatment.

Elizabeth Bloomer was an ebullient, assertive young woman, born in Chicago and raised in Grand Rapids, Michigan. To the annoyance of her two older brothers, she was a tomboy, but at eight years of age she joined a dance class and discovered her great passion. By her teens, she was teaching dance and working as a model, all the while doing well in her studies. For two summers after high school, she attended the famous Bennington School of the Dance in Vermont, where she fell under the spell of legendary choreographer Martha Graham. In 1939, she moved to New York City to study with Graham, who advised Betty that while she had a promising future in dance, she must give up everything else to concentrate on her art. Betty tried, but began to wonder if she had the single-mindedness and dedication that Graham's professionalism required. She returned to Grand Rapids to consider her options, and decided not to pursue it. Instead, she became "The Martha Graham of Grand Rapids." She trained her own troupe, taught modern dance and worked as a fashion coordinator, window designer, model trainer and sometimes buyer for Herpolscheimer's department store.

In 1942, Betty entered into an unsuccessful marriage that ended in divorce. At about the time the divorce was finalized, she was introduced to local attorney Gerald Ford. Reluctant to enter into another relationship so quickly, she hesitated, but the romance became serious, and she accepted Ford's marriage proposal in early 1948. Their engagement wasn't made public, however, until he'd announced his candidacy for Congress. Until the wedding, scheduled for October, she helped in his campaign headquarters, partly, she said, so she might see her fiancé once in a while. She was learning a bitter lesson — being a politician's wife meant sharing him with voters, constituents, meetings and public appearances. It is apparently true that candidate Ford left his own wedding-rehearsal dinner to deliver a speech and made it to the wedding ceremony itself with little time to spare.

When Jerry was elected, Betty enjoyed life in Washington, but never did get used to her husband's absences that forced her to bring up their children single-handedly, cook, clean, take care of the family finances, help out in the office, entertain constituents and indulge in other important political activities. When Jerry was named House Minority Leader in 1968, his absences grew even longer and put a serious strain on their marriage. The emotional toll, along with an excruciatingly painful pinched nerve and attendant arthritis, drove Betty to seek psychiatric help. In eighteen months of therapy, she developed self-confidence and a sense of self-worth. Author Paul Boller wrote:

> *She also learned to reserve some private space of her own, in which she could find an outlet for her own feelings and interests apart from her responsibilities to her husband and children. She convinced her husband, too, that it would be better for both of them if he retired from office after running once more in 1974.*[168]

Such is fate. In 1973, Vice President Spiro Agnew resigned in disgrace and Gerald Ford was appointed by President Nixon to replace him. Eight months later, Richard Nixon himself resigned and Ford assumed the presidency. The Fords moved into the White House where their natural warmth was a refreshing change from the solemnity and bunker mentality of the Nixon administration. Betty continued to pursue her interests in the arts, worked with handicapped children and the elderly, and emerged as a vigorous feminist and champion of the Equal Rights Amendment. She worked hard for women's rights and effectively lobbied her husband to appoint more women to high political office.

Mrs. Ford loved her role as First Lady. She saw Jerry more than ever and, most important, became a personality in her own right. Press aide Sheila Weidenfeld said:

> *She began to realize she was special, not because she was Mrs. Gerald R. Ford, but because she was Betty Ford, a woman with special personality traits. People admired her honesty, her sparkle, her frankness. What's more, as First Lady, she had national influence. She could push causes in which she believed. For the first time in her life she was in the spotlight because of her own characteristics.*[169]

Gerald Ford lost his bid for a full term in office. In the post-White House years Betty went public with news of her dependence on pain-killing drugs and alcohol. By doing so, she aimed to encourage those needing help to be open about their problems. "I draw strength from that," she said. "I think that doing constructive things and helping people is probably the best cure in the world for your personal problems."[170]

She was briefly hospitalized for her dependence problems, but upon her release she became almost as busy as she'd been in the White House. She helped people searching for aid and advice, and gave her time to arthritis and cancer research activities. She helped found the Betty Ford Center for Drug and Alcohol Rehabilitation in Rancho Mirage, California, the premier facility devoted to the assistance and rehabilitation of those afflicted with one of America's most serious social problems. What a glorious legacy for the straightforward, honest and caring Betty Ford.

Gerald R. Ford Presidential Museum

GRAND RAPIDS, MICHIGAN

The Gerald R. Ford Presidential Museum (Figure 93) is a handsome triangular building situated on the west bank of the Grand River, right in downtown Grand Rapids, the city that Gerald Ford represented in Congress for twenty-five years. The museum was dedicated in 1981 with presidents Ford and Reagan, the Prime Minister of Canada and the President of Mexico in attendance. The museum was renovated and rededicated in 1997.

Visits to the Ford Museum begin with screening of a twenty-minute orientation film, *A Time to Heal: Gerald R. Ford's America*, then progress to

Figure 93. Gerald R. Ford Presidential Museum, Grand Rapids, Michigan. Photograph courtesy Gerald R. Ford Presidential Museum.

a 1970s gallery complete with disco scenes and a multi-screen tribute to the Age of Aquarius. The Ford Museum doesn't just show history, it drops visitors into the middle of it. A recreated Ford Oval Office presents a typical day in the life of the President with a sound and light show and the Cabinet Room is a faithful reproduction of the one in the White House. Visitors may sit around the table and interact with video presentations of crises President Ford and his cabinet members confronted — The *SS Mayaguez* crisis, the Watergate scandal and others.

A special gallery devoted to Betty Ford highlights Mrs. Ford's involvement with the Equal Rights Amendment and her battle with cancer, and there is a tape of her first television interview with Morley Safer. Four of her gowns are displayed as are a number of state gifts and others presented at the time of the nation's bicentennial. There is a replica of a dining room table from the White House, set as if for a state dinner. And, finally, visitors enter a simulated White House to tour eleven rooms created through the wonder of holographic technology.

DIRECTIONS: Grand Rapids is in western Michigan, 75 miles west of Lansing. **From Lansing:** Take I 96 to I 196; use the Ottawa Street Exit in Grand Rapids and continue southbound to Pearl Street. Turn right on Pearl Street and proceed 3 blocks to the museum. **From the south:** Take US Route 131 northbound and exit at Pearl Street. Turn right on Pearl Street and continue directly to the museum on the left (Figure 94).

PUBLIC USE: Season and hours: Daily, 9 AM-5 PM. Closed Thanksgiving Day, Christmas Day, New Year's Day. **Admission fee:** Yes, with discounts for groups, students and seniors. **Museum shop. For people with disabilities:** Fully accessible.

FOR ADDITIONAL INFORMATION: Contact: Gerald R. Ford Presidential Museum, 303 Pearl Street NW, Grand Rapids, Michigan 49504, (616) 254-0400. **Web site:** *www.fordlibrarymuseum.gov*. **Read:** Betty Ford. 1978. *The Times of My Life.*

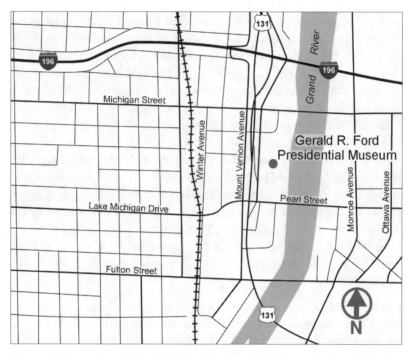

Figure 94. Location of Gerald R. Ford Presidential Museum in Grand Rapids, Michigan.

Eleanor Rosalynn Smith Carter

First Lady, 1977–1981

Born: August 18, 1927, Plains, Georgia

In 1845, Sarah Polk became the first First Lady to share her husband's political ambition, serving as his private secretary and closest confidante. Mary Lincoln, Helen Taft and Florence Harding consciously promoted and even encouraged, some say pushed, their husbands to become President. Edith Wilson became "acting president" during her husband's incapacity, and Eleanor Roosevelt, Franklin's "eyes and ears," became a persuasive voice in national and international affairs in her own right.

Yet, perhaps none — until Hillary Clinton — wielded more controversial influence on her husband than Rosalynn Carter. She and husband Jimmy were a true team; he called her "almost a perfect extension of himself."[171] Mrs. Carter put it more succinctly. "We co-ordinate."[172] Jimmy invited her to cabinet meetings and shortly after his inauguration, sent her on a goodwill mission to South America intended to promote human rights and democracy. She studied the history and culture of the countries on the agenda, and although the trip was considered a success, it was roundly criticized in some quarters because she was not an elected official. One reporter asked if the trip was an appropriate exercise of her position as First Lady. "I am the person closest to the president," she replied, "and if I can explain his policies and let the people know of his great interest and friendship, I intend to do so."[173]

Jimmy and Rosalynn Carter grew up in Plains, Georgia, sharing the small-town values of hard work, church, family, school and concern for others.

Rosalynn was a dutiful, caring daughter whose life was transformed by the death of her father when she was thirteen. Her mother was forced to work, and eldest child Rosalynn assumed adult responsibilities — supervision of the household and care of her younger sister and two brothers. With all of that, she had an active social life and graduated from Plains High School as valedictorian in 1944. After graduation, she moved on to Georgia Southwestern College in Americus.

Ruth Carter was Rosalynn's best friend and although the Smiths and Carters had known each other for years, it was not until Rosalynn's sophomore year in college that Ruth was perceptive enough to arrange a more formal meeting between her Naval Academy midshipman brother, Jimmy, and Rosalynn. After their second date, Jimmy told his mother that Rosalynn was the girl he was going to marry. Rosalynn wasn't quite so sure, although their romance blossomed via frequent letter writing. On his next leave, Jimmy proposed, but Rosalynn wasn't ready to settle down. The visits and letters continued, and when he proposed again in February, 1946, she was ready. They married upon his graduation from the Naval Academy and hers from Georgia Southwestern. She was almost nineteen.

The next seven years were full of joy — and frustration. Navy life meant frequent separations, loneliness, constant moves and adjustment. She learned to run a household and rear the children — at that time there were three — by herself and, by doing so, gained self-confidence as they moved from Norfolk to New London to San Diego to Schenectady to Philadelphia. She was proud of Jimmy's work with the Navy's nuclear program, and proud, too, of her own strength of character and ability to provide a stable home life essential to his happiness and career.

When his father died in 1953, Jimmy decided to resign his commission and return to Plains to run the family's wholesale peanut-farming business. Rosalynn was distraught at the thought of a return to small-town life that would jeopardize her new-found freedom and independence. In her biography, she describes a "battle that lasted for days," [174] but she was unable to change her husband's decision. She was miserable back in Plains, but when he asked for help in managing the peanut business, she agreed and emerged as an astute, progressive businesswoman. As her knowledge of the business grew, Jimmy relied on her advice. "We grew together," [175] she said as they began a long and fruitful interdependence.

In 1962, Jimmy was elected to the Georgia State Senate, the beginning of his political career. During his political campaigns, Rosalynn toured extensively. She made speeches, handed out literature and attended luncheons, barbeques and teas. When he was elected Governor of Georgia in 1968, she entered the Governor's mansion with trepidation, but assumed her new responsibilities with energy and passion. She learned how to entertain important people and took special interest in working on behalf of retarded children, a cause she continued to sponsor when she resided in the White House.

Jimmy was elected President in 1976. As First Lady, Rosalynn took on more causes — problems of the elderly, the Equal Rights Amendment, the plight of American cities and others. *The Washington Star* summarized her activities during her first fourteen months in the White House:

> *She visited eighteen foreign nations and twenty-seven American cities; held 259 private and 50 public meetings; made fifteen major speeches; held twenty-two press conferences; gave thirty-two interviews; attended 83 official receptions; held twenty-five meetings with special groups. And all of that in addition to her social responsibilities!*[176]

The Carter administration, beset by an energy crisis and the Iranian hostage situation, lost the reelection bid in 1980, a defeat that embittered Mrs. Carter. She became depressed, and it was some time before she regained her old energy and zest. But eventually the Carters resumed their cooperative adventure in life. Back in Plains they indulged in their favorite activities — walking, reading, fishing and cooking. They wrote books and became involved in Habitat for Humanity, a non-profit Christian organization that builds low-cost housing for the poor. Naturally, they were involved in planning the Carter Library in Atlanta.

The Carters still reside in Plains, where they visit friends and remain active in civic affairs and especially in their church. They are good, simple folks; Rosalynn describes herself as "an ordinary woman, who never for one moment doubted she was anything but an ordinary woman, who did the very best she could, and took advantage of every opportunity that came her way."[177]

Jimmy Carter National Historic Site

PLAINS, GEORGIA

The rural Southern culture of Plains revolves around farming, church and school — deep, lasting influences on the characters of Jimmy and Rosalynn Carter. The Jimmy Carter National Historic Site was established not only to interpret his life, but to preserve the history and heritage of a small, rural Southern community.

The historic site of seventy-seven acres lies mostly within the Plains Historic Preservation District that covers most of the town. Plains High School, which Jimmy Carter and Rosalynn Smith attended, has been converted to a visitor center/museum containing a restored principal's office, a classroom, and three rooms of museum exhibits pertaining to the local history of President Carter — his childhood, presidency and post-presidency. A special gallery, *Rosalynn Carter: First Lady from Plains, Georgia*, provides visitors with a glimpse into the life of Rosalynn, documenting the life of a once-shy, small-town girl from rural southwest Georgia who grew up to inspire a nation and command the attention of the world as a strong, confident First Lady working alongside the most powerful leader in the free world.

A film narrated by Charles Kuralt presents an overview of the Carters' lives as told by friends and family and, since the Carter home (Figure 95) is not open for public visitation, the museum provides a sixteen-minute tour on

Figure 95. The Carter home on the Carter Compound, Jimmy Carter National Historic Site, Plains, Georgia. Photograph courtesy National Park Service.

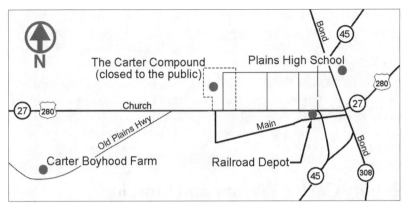

Figure 96. Location of selected venues within Jimmy Carter National Historic Site, Plains, Georgia.

videotape. In addition to the High School and the Carter home, the historic site, which is operated by the National Park Service, includes Jimmy Carter's boyhood farm and the Plains railroad depot.

The Plains Preservation District also includes Rosalynn Carter's childhood home and the United Methodist Church where Jimmy and Rosalynn were married. The Maranatha Baptist Church on Buena Vista Road is their present church home and it is where the former President conducts regular Sunday school classes and Rosalynn participates in many other church activities.

When the young couple returned from Navy duty, they lived in Public Housing Unit 9A on Church Street, and the "Haunted House" on Old Plains Highway was their home from 1956 to 1961. Those sites are not open to the public but may be viewed from the road. The famous Seaboard Railroad depot, the location of Carter's 1976 campaign headquarters, is open as a museum.

Guided walking tours of Plains provided by the National Park Service are available upon request. Ranger-led bus tours, also available, require advance reservations. A tour of Plains, with its ordinary homes and friendly, industrious people, is witness to the true spirit and community of America.

DIRECTIONS: From Atlanta, Georgia, take I 75 southbound to US Route 19; follow US Route 19 southwest to Americus, Georgia, and turn westbound on US Route 280 to Plains (Figure 96).

PUBLIC USE: Season and hours: *Plains High School Visitor Center and Museum:* 9 AM-5 PM. *Plains Depot Museum:* 9 AM-4:30 PM. *Jimmy Carter Boyhood Farm:* 10 AM-5 PM. Closed Thanksgiving Day, Christmas Day, New Year's Day. **Gift shop. For people with disabilities:** Fully accessible.

FOR ADDITIONAL INFORMATION: Contact: Jimmy Carter National Historic Site, 300 N. Bond Street, Plains, Georgia 31780, (229) 824-4104 *or* The Georgia Welcome Center, 1763 Highway 280 West, Plains, Georgia 31780, (229) 824-7477. **Web site:** *www.nps.gov/jica.* **Read:** Rosalynn Carter. 1984. *First Lady from Plains.*

Jimmy Carter Library and Museum

ATLANTA, GEORGIA

The Jimmy Carter Library and Museum (Figure 97), one of thirteen presidential libraries managed by the National Archives and Records Administration, is part of The Carter Presidential Center, a sprawling complex of interconnected modern buildings set in a grove of Georgia pines and flowering plants affording a breathtaking view of the Atlanta skyline. The library, which houses Carter's presidential papers, is a research facility utilized primarily by scholars and historians. The museum section differs from other presidential museums in that a large portion is devoted to the Carters' post-presidency years, both Jimmy's and Rosalynn's. The impact of the Carters after their White House residency is unique and profound and exhibits are designed to show connections between their roots in Georgia, his agenda as President, their shared determination to work for peace and human rights, and her advocacy for improvement in mental health which has lasted far beyond the White House years.

Except for the existing replica of the Oval Office, the museum has a brand-new look — high tech and family-friendly. Interactive exhibits with multiple touch-screen stations take visitors to countries around the world where the Carters have worked. Visitors also discover the multi-faceted work of The Carter Center, the non-profit organization which the Carters founded in 1982, now widely recognized for its bold initiatives to resolve conflicts, advance democracy and human rights and prevent disease in more than 70 countries.

In an attempt to make the entire museum a teaching tool, the museum is interwoven with kid-friendly and education-oriented exhibits created to both

Figure 97. Jimmy Carter Library and Museum, Atlanta, Georgia. Photograph courtesy Jimmy Carter Library and Museum.

inspire and challenge young people to choose careers to help people around the word, as well as make the world a better place.

In announcing plans for the museum's restoration, President Carter said:

> *Rosalynn and I hope the new museum will be a teaching tool not only for students of history, but for people of all ages eager to learn about the world beyond their own borders, where for 27 years The Carter Center has worked to build hope for suffering people.*[178]

Although her presence is felt throughout the museum as President Carter's helpmeet and advisor, there are two individual galleries devoted to Rosalynn Carter (Plate XVI), one concentrating on her early years, the other on her White House experiences. The latter emphasizes her efforts on behalf of mental health, carried over from her work as First Lady and her continuing involvement with the Rosalynn Carter Institute for Caregiving.

DIRECTIONS: From the north or south: Take I 75/85 to Exit 248C, the Freedom Parkway, then follow the historical markers. **From the east or west:** Take I 20, exiting at Moreland Avenue northbound, following Moreland Avenue northbound about 2 miles to Freedom Parkway. Turn left on Freedom Parkway and follow the historical markers (Figure 98).

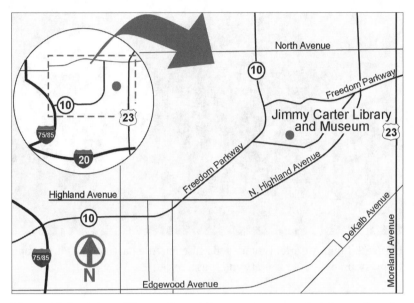

Figure 98. Location of Jimmy Carter Library and museum in Atlanta, Georgia.

PUBLIC USE: Season and hours: *Museum:* Monday-Saturday, 9 AM-4:45 PM; Sunday, 12 M-4:45 PM. *Library*: Monday-Friday, 8:45 AM-4:30 PM. Closed Thanksgiving Day, Christmas Day, New Year's Day. **Admission fee:** For museum only. Children under 16, free. **Food service:** There is a full-service restaurant. **Museum shop. For people with disabilities:** Fully accessible.

FOR ADDITIONAL INFORMATION: Contact: Jimmy Carter Library and Museum, 441 Freedom Parkway, Atlanta, Georgia 30307, (404) 865-7100. **Web site:** *www.jimmycarterlibrary.gov.* **Read:** Douglas Brinkley. 1998. *The Unfinished Presidency: Jimmy Carter's Journey beyond the White House.*

Nancy Davis Reagan

First Lady, 1981–1989

Born: July 6, 1923, New York, New York

In an earlier section of this book, First Lady Elizabeth Monroe was described as:

> *A remarkably beautiful woman, with a much-admired taste in dress and decoration. In public, her formal manners left an impression of coldness and reserve, but in private she was a devoted wife and doting mother, possessing to the full the domestic virtues then so highly prized.*[179]

Author Harry Scammon might as easily been describing modern-day First Ladies Jacqueline Kennedy or Nancy Reagan, and while it may be unfair to compare them, Jacqueline Kennedy and Nancy Reagan were remarkably similar. Products of wealth, social position and fine education, each was, in her time, also a fashion trend-setter.

Nancy Reagan, unfortunately, lived to regret it. Avoiding the simplicity of the Carter White House, she opted to return a sense of pride and dignified class to the presidency when husband Ronald was elected President in 1980. With funds raised in the private sector, she refurbished and rejuvenated the White House living quarters and purchased a new set of White House china. For her personal use she borrowed — and returned — gowns and jewelry from America's top designers. In a wink, high fashion was back in style, as was vocal, sometimes very nasty, criticism of the First Lady. Mrs. Reagan was assaulted in the press for her excessive expenditures at a time of recession and unemployment. Her use of designer clothing, whether borrowed or paid for, was criticized as tasteless and improper. Her protestations that the White House was a special place and deserved the best of everything fell on deaf ears. Comedians fell into line with quips about what was perceived as her obsession with fashion and society. She once asked the President what to do about the comments and he suggested, "Forget it!"[180] Easier said than done.

People were prone to forget that Nancy Reagan, raised in comfortable circumstances, took an elegant mode of living for granted. She was hardly putting on airs. She was what she was — a graduate of Chicago's Girl's Latin School and Smith College; famous as a former movie actress and Beverly Hills wife and hostess. Her closest friends lived in Bel Air and were considered Hollywood royalty. She moved easily and confidently in those circles when Ronald Reagan was president of the Screen Actors Guild, then presided efficiently and comfortably as First Lady of California when he served as governor. She caused an early brouhaha when she refused to have her family live in the aging governor's mansion in Sacramento, a building that had been declared unsafe for habitation in 1941! Her intransigence and attendant publicity led to the construction of a new mansion; her contribution to the safety of subsequent governors and their families was surely appreciated by them.

Nancy Reagan has been quoted as saying that her life "really began with Ronnie,"[181] and, indeed, she devoted her life to her husband's career and well-being. After their wedding, she abandoned her own budding film career to focus her life on husband and children.

The strongest influence in Nancy Davis' life was her stepfather, Dr. Loyal Davis, a prominent Chicago neurosurgeon. Nancy's mother had married Dr. Davis when Nancy was seven, and he adopted Nancy formally a few years later. Dr. Davis was an active ultra-conservative with considerable influence on the political beliefs of Nancy and husband Ronald, who thought as one, and they progressed to become a formidable political team. Many pundits considered Ronald Reagan a nice guy who was essentially lazy and pliable. The steel and power, according to some critics, was Nancy, often called the most influential First Lady since Edith Wilson. Mrs. Reagan demurred. In a speech in 1988, she said, "Although I don't get involved with policy, it's silly to suggest that my opinion should not carry some weight with the man I've been married to for 35 years!" In the same talk, she had some advice for future First Ladies:

> *Be yourself. Do what you're interested in and don't be afraid*
> *to look after your husband . . . Don't think the White House is*

going to be a glamorous, fairy-tale life. It's very hard work with high highs and low lows. Since you're under a microscope, everything is magnified, so just keep your perspective and your patience.[182]

In 1994, Ronald Reagan announced publicly that he was victimized by Alzheimer's Disease. For the next ten years, the entire Reagan family coped with the debilitating illness that took his life in 2004. Through their ordeal, the entire nation watched as Nancy Reagan tended her husband with solicitude. Her courage, patience and forthrightness impressed the nation as a dramatic expression of love and devotion. She worked unselfishly with the Alzheimer's Association, the nation's premier organization mandated to increase awareness of, and find a cure for, the disease. Her dedication to this effort actually increased after the President's death.

Ronald Reagan Presidential Library and Museum

Simi Valley, California

The Ronald Reagan Presidential Library and Museum (Figure 99), a Spanish mission-style complex of 153,000 square feet, stands high in the rugged mountains of southern California, with command of spectacular, sweeping views of the surrounding valleys and foothills. The library portion of the complex is archival, housing all of President Reagan's papers and records, for use by scholars and historians.

A public exhibit area of the museum portions includes the "First Lady's Gallery" which features a photo montage of Nancy Reagan's life, plus representative gowns and jewelry she wore while serving as First Lady, and there are displays of gifts from world leaders and others that recount the former President's personal and political history. A replicated Oval Office, accurate to the pictures on the walls and knickknacks on the President's desk, is popular, as is a rear verandah dramatized by a section of the Berlin Wall that was presented to President Reagan by the German people in 1990. Its commemorative plaque reads, "for his unwavering dedication to humanitarianism and freedom over communism throughout his presidency."[183]

President Reagan once stated that he hoped to share Air Force One with the American people, a wish that came true when the Air Force One

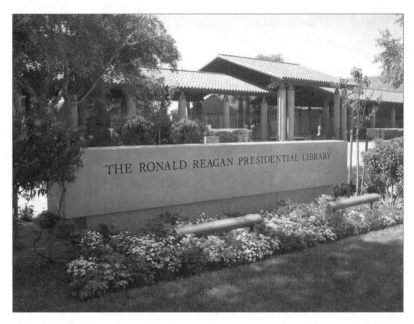

Figure 99. Ronald Reagan Presidential Library and Museum, Simi Valley, California. Photograph courtesy The Ronald Reagan Presidential Foundation.

Pavilion opened in 2005. The Boeing 707 used by the President during his eight years in office was retired and flown to southern California where it is displayed in a dramatic, glass-enclosed pavilion raised one-story above the floor on specially-designed pedestals, giving the impression of actual flight. A tour of the plane's interior includes a look at the President's and First Lady's private cabins, his office, galleys, cockpit and the communications center.

When the Library was constructed, twin crypts designed as a resting place for the Reagans were installed on the verandah; they feature a view of the foothills and the Pacific Ocean to the West, a fitting site for the rugged outdoorsman president and his beloved partner. The President was laid to rest there on June 11, 2004.

The museum galleries were closed for renovation in the spring of 2010. Reopening is scheduled for February 6, 2011, the 100th anniversary of Ronald Reagan's birth. During the renovation process, the replicated Oval Office, the Berlin Wall and the Air Force One displays will remain open.

DIRECTIONS: From Santa Barbara and points north: Take the Ventura Freeway (US Route 101) southbound to Route 23. Exit Route 23 onto Olsen Road (which soon becomes Madera Road) eastbound for 2 miles to Presidential Drive and the entrance to the Library. **From Los Angeles and points south:** Take the San Diego Freeway (I 405) northbound to Route 118 West. Exit onto Madera Road southbound and proceed 3 miles to Presidential Drive (Figure 100).

PUBLIC USE: Season and hours: Daily, 10 AM-5 PM. Closed Thanksgiving Day, Christmas Day, New Year's Day. **Admission fee:** Yes, with discounts for seniors. Children, free. **Gift shop. Food service:** There are two restaurants: Reagan's Country Café and the Ronald Reagan Pub snack shop. **For people with disabilities:** Fully accessible.

FOR ADDITIONAL INFORMATION: Contact: Ronald Reagan Presidential Library and Museum, 40 Presidential Drive, Simi Valley, California 93065, (805) 577-4000 *or* (800) 410-8354. **Web site:** *www.reaganlibrary.com.* **Read:** (1) Garry Wills. 1987. *Reagan's America: Innocents at Home.* (2) Nancy Reagan. 1989. *My Turn: The Memoirs of Nancy Reagan.*

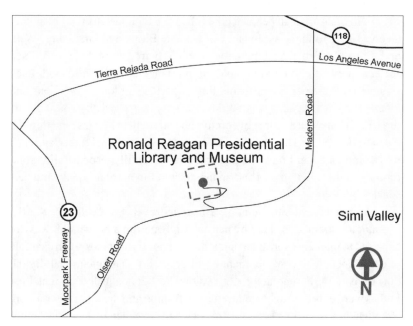

Figure 100. Location of Ronald Reagan Presidential Library and Museum at Simi Valley, California.

Barbara Pierce Bush

First Lady, 1989–1993

Born: June 8, 1925, New York, New York

In the first chapter in this book, there is a quote by Martha Washington, "My heart is made up, my heart is in the cause; George is right; the general is always right."[184]

Did the American people come full circle with the election of another George (Bush) and the ascendancy of his wife Barbara to First Lady? Well, both she and Martha Washington were white-haired and full-figured. Each suffered the loss of a child or children in infancy or early childhood. Each was married to an active husband, thus experiencing long separations and loneliness. Each husband was a military officer in grave danger during wartime. Each lady was a source of comfort and strength to her husband through the most difficult and trying times of his military and political career, and each was a product of her time, with a strong sense of family responsibility, solid training in the social graces and an innate belief in marital fidelity and personal propriety.

Yet times and situations have changed over two centuries. Martha Washington, trained to stand by her husband and run a household, was not expected to publicly express an opinion. If her public behavior set an example or caused people to copy her manners or dress, it was unintentional. By the time Barbara Bush came along, expectations were dramatically different. First Ladies were expected to be trendsetters in fashion and the art of entertaining although they were not necessarily expected to have their own political opinions. They were expected to be family-oriented and at the same time political helpmeets appearing on the campaign trail looking bright and well-groomed as well as attentive to and interested in the candidate's speech — no matter how many times she'd heard it. And she might have to make a speech herself.

Barbara Bush may be as close to a perfect modern First Lady as we shall ever know. Unlike Martha Washington, she did not necessarily believe that George was always right. She had her own firm opinions, although they were mostly kept private. She supported George's endeavors while maintaining her own personality. "I don't fool around with his office, and he doesn't fool around with my household," she once said.[185] That attitude worked throughout their marriage, and as far as she was concerned, there was no good reason to change in the White House.

Barbara and George grew up in affluent, socially proper circumstances, she in trendy Westchester County, New York, he in equally trendy Greenwich, Connecticut. She dropped out of Smith College to marry young naval officer Bush in 1945, eventually moving to the oil fields of Texas after his service in World War II. They began a roller coaster ride of travel — she's been quoted as having set up housekeeping in twenty-eight homes in twenty-seven cities, all the while bringing up five children. Over the course of their life journey, there was hard work, loneliness, tragedy, financial success and great joy.

Mrs. Bush loved being First Lady as she enjoyed entertaining and socializing and thrived on foreign travel. The nation loved her earthiness and ability to laugh at herself — she once said, "My mail tells me that a lot of fat, white-haired, wrinkled ladies are tickled pink. I mean, look at me. If I can be a success, so can they."[186] Such self-deprecation played into the hearts of the American public, although few realized that her modesty was bittersweet. In 1953, the Bush's four-year-old daughter Robin died of leukemia after agonizing, harrowing and painful months of treatment. It was during that ordeal that Mrs. Bush's hair turned white. In Robin's memory, the Bushes established the Bright Star Foundation, devoted to the study of, and search for, a cure for leukemia. Mrs. Bush also remains an active participant with the Leukemia Society of America.

Mrs. Bush is equally well-known for her efforts on behalf of literacy. Using her First Lady position as a "bully pulpit," she established the Barbara Bush Foundation for Family Literacy, designed to support reading programs around the country. She said:

I spent the summer thinking about what would help the most people possible. And it suddenly occurred to me that every single thing I worry about — things like teenage pregnancies, the breakup of families, AIDS and the homeless — everything would be better if more people could read, write and understand.[187]

She is proud of her family relationships. In an imaginary interview with himself in his biography, *Looking Forward,* George Bush wrote:

Q: Going back to 1948, the year you left college and went to Texas. Out of all the things you've done since then — in Congress, the UN, China, the CIA, the vice-presidency — what single accomplishment are you proudest of?

GB: The fact that our children still come home.[188]

What a compliment and what a legacy. Is Barbara Bush genuine? Well, would any other First Lady say, "I married the first man I ever kissed. When I tell this to my children, they just about throw up."[189] In retirement, the Bushes remain active in many causes, commuting between their homes in Texas and Kennebunkport, Maine. In 2001, Barbara Bush entered an exclusive club, joining Abigail Adams as the only First Ladies whose eldest sons became the country's chief executive.

George Bush Presidential Library and Museum

COLLEGE STATION, TEXAS

The George Bush Presidential Library and Museum complex, located on the campus of Texas A&M University, is administered by the National Archives and Records Administration. The library/archives building is filled with millions of documents, hundreds of hours of video footage, and thousands of rolls of film pertaining to George Bush's vice-presidential and presidential years.

The museum building (Figure 101) is a magnificent edifice with a majestic fifty-foot-high rotunda of Texas limestone, marble and granite. The museum is heavily computerized, featuring a multitude of interactive audio/visual presentations such as replicas of the Bush Oval Office and the President's office at Camp David. A World War II Avenger torpedo bomber hanging from the ceiling and a slab of the Berlin Wall are moving reminders of the scope of service to the nation performed by President Bush.

Figure 101. George Bush Presidential Library and Museum, College Station, Texas. Photograph courtesy George Bush Presidential Library and Museum.

After viewing a brief orientation film narrated by the Bushes, a self-guided tour passes by more than thirty displays featuring some of their life experiences, including but not confined to their early lives, their courtship and marriage, a family scrapbook, World War II and the beginning of a new life in Texas (joy, success — and tragedy), George Bush's congressional days and subsequent ambassadorship to the United Nations, Chairman of the Republican Party, Chief of Liaison to Peking (a video slide show of that tenure comes from Barbara Bush's private collection), Director of the CIA, the vice presidency and the presidency. Two of the galleries are devoted exclusively to Mrs. Bush, one concentrating on her childhood and formative years, the other on her experiences as First Lady and her efforts on behalf of literacy, AIDS prevention and volunteerism — efforts that have continued well past the White House years (Plate XVI).

In the spring of 2002, the museum dedicated the Barbara Bush Botanical Garden, a four-acre panoply of antique roses located to the rear of the museum. Future plans call for expansion to include additional flowers indigenous to the area.

DIRECTIONS: College Station is in southeastern Texas about 80 miles north-west of Houston. **From Houston:** Take I 45 northbound to Conroe and turn left on Route 105 to Navasota, turning right on Route 6 to Bryan/College Station (Business 6/Texas Avenue). Turn left off of Texas Avenue onto Harvey Mitchell Parkway and proceed 4 miles to George Bush Drive. Turn right and proceed 0.25 mile to the entrance on the left. **From Dallas:** Take I 45 south-bound to Madisonville, then Route 21 westbound to College Station. Continue to Harvey Mitchell Parkway and turn left. Proceed 6 miles to George Bush Drive and turn left for 0.25 mile to the entrance (Figure 102).

PUBLIC USE: Season and hours: Monday-Saturday, 9:30 AM-5 PM; Sunday, 12 M-5 PM. Closed Thanksgiving Day, Christmas Day, New Year's Day. **Admission fee: Gift shop. For people with disabilities:** Fully accessible, with wheelchairs available.

FOR ADDITIONAL INFORMATION: Contact: George Bush Presidential Library and Museum, 1000 George Bush Drive West, College Station, Texas 77845, (979) 691-4000. **Web site:** *http://bushlibrary.tamu.edu.* **Read:** Donnie Radcliffe. 1989. *Simply Barbara Bush.*

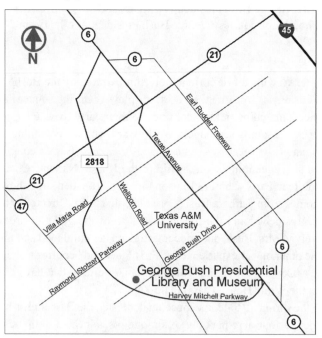

Figure 102. Location of George Bush Presidential Library and Museum on the campus of Texas A&M University, College Station, Texas.

Hillary Diane Rodham Clinton

First Lady, 1993–2001

Born: October 26, 1947, Park Ridge, Illinois

On January 3, 2001, Hillary Clinton entered the annals of American political history when she was sworn in as United States Senator from New York, the first First Lady to achieve national elective office. During the senatorial campaign and literally moments after her opponent conceded the election, rumors and speculation began as regards her political future, stature and influence in the Democrat party and especially her chances for the Democratic presidential nomination in 2008.

While she was considered the front runner for that nomination, she was defeated in a close, protracted and sometimes bruising primary contest with the eventual nominee, Barack Obama. It was a difficult defeat, although in perspective it was the most dramatic showing by a woman on a national political level in our nation's history. And why not? After all, Mrs. Clinton is highly intelligent, strongly motivated and politically shrewd. Her commitment to the welfare of the nation, especially to children, was well documented through her eight years as First Lady. Experience as her husband's primary advisor as well as international travel, natural intelligence and personal grace provided invaluable experience in observing — and participating in — domestic and foreign affairs. Mrs. Clinton has been compared favorably with the most active First Ladies in our nation's history: Abigail Adams, Sarah Polk, Helen Taft, Edith Wilson, Eleanor Roosevelt and Rosalynn Carter. Heady company.

Hillary Diane Rodham and her two younger brothers grew up in a close-knit family in the Chicago suburb of Park Ridge, with a middle-class background that established within the ambitious young woman a life-long commitment to family, work and service. She once wrote, "We all have an obligation to give something of ourselves to our community."[190] A brilliant student, Hillary graduated from Wellesley College in 1969, then entered Yale Law School where she met fellow student Bill Clinton. Political activists and soul mates, they soon became a formidable political team and married in 1975 when serving as law professors at the University of Arkansas. Bill entered politics and won the race for Arkansas Attorney General and, in 1978, was elected Governor, serving in that position for twelve years. As First Lady of Arkansas, Mrs. Clinton worked tirelessly on behalf of children and families and was named the Arkansas Woman of the Year in 1984 in recognition of her professional and personal accomplishments.

Upon taking office as President in 1993, Bill Clinton made health care reform a major priority and asked the First Lady to chair a Task Force on National Health Care Reform, a job that became a political mine field. Mrs. Clinton was subjected to severe criticism for her participation in political and legislative matters as she was not an elected official. Forced to resign her chairmanship, Mrs. Clinton continued to advocate improvement of health care quality and her commitment to children led her to champion efforts on their behalf: immunization programs, health insurance coverage, innovative prenatal care and raising awareness of the dangers of tobacco and drugs. Her book, *It Takes a Village and Other Lessons Children Teach Us,* was a national call for all segments of society to take increased responsibility for children.

In addition to her domestic responsibilities, the First Lady served as a goodwill ambassador during a number of foreign trips. From Europe to Asia, from Africa to Latin America, Mrs. Clinton carried a message of human rights, health care and economic rights for women around the world.

The Clinton administration was clouded by a moral crisis that resulted in the impeachment of the President. Through the darkest days of the constitutional arguments and media frenzy, Mrs. Clinton remained steady and resolute. It could not have been easy for her as graphic reports of extramarital presidential dalliances were daily fodder in the media, but Mrs. Clinton never responded to questions regarding the situation. She continued her duties stoically, and then surprised the nation by establishing residence in New York State where she announced her candidacy for United States Senator.

Rumors flew again. Was this her way of separating herself from her husband? We may never know, except that Hillary Clinton, a brilliant politician, prevailed, served with distinction and went on to conduct the brilliant but unsuccessful presidential primary campaign in 2007–2008.

Losing that election was a bittersweet experience for Hillary Clinton although, as expected, she did not fade away from patriotic responsibility. President-elect Barack Obama, recognizing her experience and dedication to the nation, appointed her Secretary of State where she utilizes her knowledge of and friendship with nations around the globe to further positive American interests.

Then there is 2016. Well, only time will tell.

Clinton House Museum

Fayetteville, Arkansas

In the mid-1970s, Bill Clinton and Hillary Rodham were teaching law at the University of Arkansas in Fayetteville. He had proposed marriage more than once, but she was not ready to settle down. But one day, driving around town and admiring houses, she evinced interest in a modest house near the campus. In secret, he purchased it and said, "Remember that house you liked so much? Well, I just bought it and now you have to marry me because I can't live there alone."[191] On October 11, 1975, they married in the living room before a gathering of family and friends.

The Clinton home (Figure 103), owned by the University of Arkansas and managed by the City of Fayetteville, opened for public visitation in 2005. It is an unpretentious, one-bedroom, 1800-square-foot house that epitomizes the word "cozy," a perfect starter home for a young couple embarking on careers in law and politics. As a museum, it contains photographs, displays and memorabilia from Bill Clinton's early political career in Arkansas, numerous mementos of his eight years as President and on-loan pieces from the Clinton Presidential Library collection in Little Rock. The bedroom is utilized as a media room showing fascinating commercials from Clinton's congressional campaign and those for Attorney General of Arkansas.

The living room features a replica of Hillary's wedding dress and a display case contains pictures of the wedding and a copy of their wedding license. All of the rooms are representative of a young couple beginning

Figure 103. Clinton House Museum, Fayetteville, Arkansas. Photograph courtesy Clinton House Museum.

married life without much furniture. In the living room, for example, they owned a couple of director's chairs and little else.

The back yard has been beautified with "The First Ladies' Garden" that features 44 varieties of flowers considered favorites of the ladies who have lived in the White House. The flower beds are framed by two glorious flowering trees, a dogwood and a cherry, all engendering an atmosphere of quiet tranquility.

DIRECTIONS: From I 540, take Exit 62 (Route 180) eastbound to Route 112 (Razorback Road), go northbound 0.25 mile on Route 112 to Leroy Pond Drive, then turn right onto Leroy Pond Drive for another 0.25 mile. When it dead ends at California Boulevard, turn left and proceed to #930 (Figure 104).

PUBLIC USE: Season and hours: Monday-Saturday, 8:30 AM-4:30 PM. Closed Thanksgiving Day and day after, Christmas Day, New Year's Day, Memorial Day, July 4, Labor Day. **Admission fee. Gift shop. For people with disabilities:** Not accessible.

FOR ADDITIONAL INFORMATION: Contact: Museum Director, Clinton House Museum, 930 California Boulevard, Fayetteville, Arkansas 72701, (877) 245-6445. **Web site:** *www.clintonhousemuseum.org*. **Read:** Donnie Radcliffe. 1993. *Hillary Rodham Clinton.*

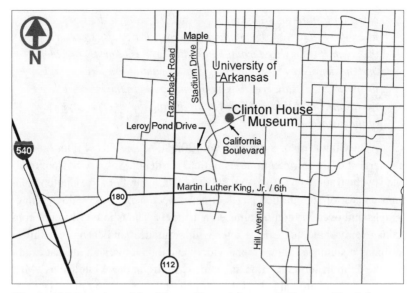

Figure 104. Location of the Clinton House Museum in Fayetteville, Arkansas.

William J. Clinton Presidential Library and Museum

LITTLE ROCK, ARKANSAS

On November 18, 2004, former President Bill Clinton and Senator Hillary Clinton joined President George W. Bush and former presidents George H. W. Bush and Jimmy Carter and their wives in ceremonies to dedicate the William J. Clinton Presidential Center in Little Rock, Arkansas.

The $165-million complex, built on a 31-acre riverfront tract, is one phase of a significant redevelopment and revitalization program in Little Rock, its centerpiece the unusual, state-of-the-art William J. Clinton Presidential Library and Museum, its basic form a glass bridge symbolizing President Clinton's theme of "Building a Bridge to the 21st Century" (Figure 105).

As *Newsweek* described the building:

> *Like Clinton himself, the library is larger than life: bold and dramatic. Yet, as he wanted, it is also people-friendly and light. It*

campaigns hard for your vote of 'Wow!' The long glass box canti-
levers 90 feet to the edge of the Arkansas River . . . Its structure —
the supports that slice through the building — is honestly revealed,
and the details are crisp and elegant. An outer glass screen shades
the main glass wall, creating an airy veranda in the best Southern
tradition. The inside is filled with light and has an expansive view
of the river and the city.[192]

The Clinton library/museum, with 20,000-square-feet of floor space, is
the largest of the thirteen libraries in the Presidential Library System operated by the National Archives and Records Administration. The Clinton holdings consist of 76.8 million pages of paper documents, 1.85 million photographs and over 75 thousand museum artifacts. The Clinton Museum contains twenty-three thematic alcoves with permanent and changing exhibits
utilizing documents, photographs, videos and interactive stations that exam-
ine the Clinton administration and showcase life in the White House. Mrs.
Clinton was an integral part of the administration and many displays show
her participation; one alcove, "The World of the First Lady," for example, is

Figure 105. William J. Clinton Presidential Library and Museum, Little Rock,
Arkansas. Photograph courtesy William J. Clinton Foundation.

devoted to Hillary Clinton and her many contributions to the Clinton presidency. It contains three monitors with continuously-running film, plus artifacts and personal items such as her best-selling book *It Takes a Village* and the Grammy Award she won for the book's audio version. Another alcove, "State Events," is devoted to displays and photographs associated with state dinners and other important social events. Mrs. Clinton's second inaugural gown and another worn at a state dinner for the President of China are featured. A separate display case is filled with historical artifacts from the Rodham family such as Hillary's childhood toys and other memorabilia.

There are replicas of the Oval Office and the Cabinet Room, a multipurpose Great Hall seating 220, classrooms and an 80-seat theater. Surrounding the main building is an impressive park that features the University of Arkansas Clinton School of Public Service, housed in a restored passenger train depot. The park also contains walking/bicycle trails, an amphitheater, picnic areas and Tyler Denton Field where kickball and other sports can be played.

DIRECTIONS: From I 30 in downtown Little Rock's River Market district, take Exit 141A and follow signs to the Clinton Presidential Library at 1200 President Clinton Avenue (Figure 106).

PUBLIC USE: Season and hours: Monday-Saturday, 9 AM-5 PM; Sunday, 1 PM-5 PM. Closed Thanksgiving Day, Christmas Day, New Year's Day. **Admission fee. Museum shop:** Located in a separate building west of I 30 at 610 President Clinton Avenue. **Food service:** Indoor-Outdoor Café. **For people with disabilities:** Accessible.

FOR ADDITIONAL INFORMATION: Contact: William J. Clinton Presidential Library and Museum, 1200 President Clinton Avenue, Little Rock, Arkansas 72201, (501) 374-4242. **Web site:** *www.clintonlibrary.gov.* **Read:** Kati Marton. 2001. *Hidden Power: Presidential Marriages That Shaped Our Recent History.*

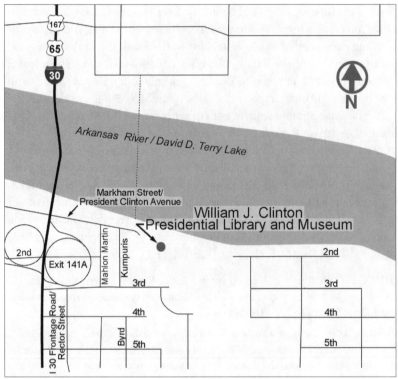

Figure 106. Location of William J. Clinton Presidential Library and Museum in Little Rock, Arkansas.

Laura Welch Bush

First Lady, 2001–2009

Born: November 4, 1946, Midland, Texas

Prior to the Republican National Convention in 2000, Judy Keen of *USA Today* wrote "Calm amid the Chaos," one of the first articles written about Laura Bush, and there may never be a better description. After all, teaching second graders was among her life experiences! Family matriarch Barbara Bush loves her quiet daughter-in-law: "Laura was an only child and is not like most only children. She should be rotten, but she's not. I think she thinks we're a very funny family. She's always got a little bit of a twinkle, like, 'I can't believe these people.'"[193]

Laura Welch was raised in Midland, Texas. She graduated from Southern Methodist University with a degree in education and she earned a master's degree in library science from the University of Texas. She worked as a teacher and librarian in Houston and Austin before returning home to work at the JFK Elementary School in Midland. She resided in the Chateaux Dijon Apartments, coincidentally the residence of George W. Bush, but it was not until 1977 that mutual friends got them together at a backyard barbeque. Three months later, they married.

The marriage was not without difficulties. In 1982, Laura, pregnant with twin daughters, developed toxemia and went into shock. She was dangerously close to losing the unborn babies and perhaps her own life, but thankfully they survived. Then, in 1986, she was the catalyst for her husband's decision to terminate a drinking problem. It was in 1994, however, when George won the Texas governorship and they moved into the governor's mansion, that Laura blossomed as her own person. She set participation priorities — literacy, breast cancer awareness and early child development — causes she continued to champion as America's First Lady.

Mrs. Bush was a reluctant celebrity, thrust into a public persona not of her choosing. Yet she rose to the occasion when terrorists attacked the World Trade Center and the Pentagon on September 11, 2001, forever changing America's personality and endangering its basic freedoms and way of life. Her calm demeanor as she stood by her husband's side when he spoke and traveled around the nation were important psychological demonstrations of courage under fire.

Laura Bush, quiet, reserved, private and gentle, is certainly different from her extroverted mother-in-law, but she brought to the White House the same intensity, love of family, intelligence and grace. Her feet remained firmly on the ground. "We find a lot of refuge in each other and the family. We had a long time in marriage before we got into politics, and we know that there is life on the other side of it."[194]

That life continues to be busy, productive and devoted to others. Mrs. Bush's most proactive association is with the Laura Bush Foundation for America's Libraries, its mission to support the education of our nation's neediest students by helping schools expand, diversify and update the book collections of school libraries. Since 2001, the foundation has distributed millions of dollars in grants to schools throughout the country. What a legacy for a former school librarian!

Michelle LaVaughn Robinson Obama

First Lady, 2009–

Born: January 17, 1964, Chicago, Illinois

The excitement engendered by Mrs. Obama's entrance into the White House was palpable, although there was little doubt that she would be a very interesting First Lady. Her background of accomplishment in academia and the law and her sense of responsibility to her city and, especially, its sometimes disenfranchised citizens augured well for her tenure in the nation's capital.

Michelle Robinson grew up on the South Side of Chicago, raised in a conventional two-parent home wherein the father worked, the mother stayed at home and the family ate meals together. Her father, a city water plant employee, Democrat precinct captain and victim of multiple sclerosis, was an inspiration to Michelle and her brother Craig, currently men's basketball coach at Oregon State University. A brilliant student, she graduated from prestigious Whitney Young High School before majoring in sociology with a minor in African-American studies at Princeton University where she graduated *cum laude* in 1985. She obtained a Juris Doctor degree from Harvard Law School in 1988. Returning home, she joined the law firm Sidley Austin where she met and married fellow attorney Barack Obama. In 1993 she became Executive Director for the Chicago office of Public Allies, an organization that encouraged young people to work on social issues in non-profit groups and government agencies. In 1998 Michelle served as the Associate Dean of Student Services at the University of Chicago where she developed the University's Community Service Center, and in 2002 she began working for the University of Chicago Hospitals, rising to the position of Vice President for Community and External Affairs.

Essence magazine listed Mrs. Obama among "25 of the World's Most Inspiring Women" in 2006, and a year later *Vanity Fair* listed her among "10 of the World's Best Dressed People," an honor repeated in 2008. That same year, she made *People* magazine's best dressed list, praised for her "classic and confident" look. And she was not yet First Lady!

Add to that resume her well-known love of family, personal and extended. She brought natural charm to the White House, coupled with a realistic attitude. She told *Good Morning America:*

> *It is so hard to project out realistically what life will be for me as a woman, for me as a mother when Barack becomes president. It's hard to know. What I do know is that given the many skills that I have on so many levels, I will be what I have to be at the time. And it really will depend on what the country needs, what my family needs, what Barack needs. So I want to be flexible enough so whatever is needed of me, that's what I will do.*[195]

Her first priority is her family as she sets aside quality time each day for her young daughters in an effort to give them a sense of normalcy and privacy in the fishbowl that is the White House. But as one of her husband's closest advisers, she may be compared to earlier First Ladies who had political influence: Sarah Polk, Helen Taft, Florence Harding, Eleanor Roosevelt, Rosalynn Carter and Hillary Clinton. Others recall the fashion sense of Dolley Madison, Jackie Kennedy and Nancy Reagan; the family devotion of Frances Cleveland or Lucretia Garfield; the outspokenness of Betty Ford or Barbara Bush.

Like her predecessors, she has "causes." Time will tell whether her interest in and experience with affirmative action, the plight of inner cities or other national problems will be on her agenda although she has already begun an important program delineating the problem of childhood obesity. It is safe to say, however, that Michelle Obama is her own person. Her life, already one of high and inspiring accomplishment, can only be enhanced by her continuing service to the nation as First Lady.

The White House

W<small>ASHINGTON</small>, DC

On November 1, 1800, when President John Adams moved into "The President's House," he wrote to his wife in Massachusetts, "The building is in a state to be habitable, and now we wish for your company."[196] Abigail arrived on November 16 to a cold, damp and chilly unfinished structure; there was inadequate firewood, a lack of running water and the outdoor privy had not been completed. Abigail, familiar with harsh New England winters and hard farm life, coped. She managed to make six rooms livable, even to the extent of hanging the presidential laundry in what is now the East Room.

The Adams were in the house only briefly as the President was defeated for reelection, but in that short time they made an indelible mark and left prescient reminders of what the house was to become. Abigail was quoted, "This house is built for ages to come,"[197] and John initiated what was to become a presidential tradition by leaving a note for his successor: "I pray heaven to bestow the best blessings on this house, and all that shall hereafter inhabit it. May none but honest and wise men rule under this roof."[198]

Through the years, The President's House (Figure 107) has led four lives: it has been, simultaneously, the office of the President, a museum of American art treasures, the People's House and a family home — home to newlyweds, old married folks, widowers and one bachelor. Proposals, marriages, births, deaths and christenings have taken place under its roof. It has known the experience of Teddy Roosevelt's children roller-skating across the floor, pillow fights of the Garfield boys and the courtship of Lynda Johnson by Charles Robb in the third-floor solarium. In short, the White House is in some ways not very different from houses all across the nation, for it has been the home — temporary and less private, surely — of a genuine American family.

Figure 107. The south front of the White House, Washington, DC. Photograph courtesy National Park Service.

The White House has been home and office to Presidents since 1800. While George Washington initiated its construction, approved its architectural design and urged its utilization as a combination home and office, he never lived there. Men (and women) battle to move in, but sometimes discover that residency can be less than rewarding. Harry Truman called it a "glamorous prison"[199] but Gerald Ford said it was "the best public housing I've ever seen."[200] First Lady Mary Todd Lincoln referred to it as "that white sepulcher"[201] and Edith Roosevelt likened the arrangement to a shopkeeper "living above the store."[202] Most residents have decried the lack of privacy, one exception being Barbara Bush, who noted after two years in residence, "You'd have to be a little crazy not to like this."[203]

Barbara Bush, with her patrician background and long experience as a political wife, was particularly well-equipped to handle the requirements of White House residency. Others were intimidated, overwhelmed or inexperienced. In the years prior to the Civil War, many First Ladies had never even been to Washington, DC. Others, too ill to participate, turned social affairs over to friends or other family members, and some were content to focus on their large families although it was difficult to balance and maintain that divide between public and private responsibilities. Lucy Hayes, Caroline Harrison and Edith Roosevelt, for example, nevertheless undertook public projects for the historic preservation of elements of "the people's house."

First and foremost in the minds of each First Lady, without exception, was to maintain a haven of familiarity, comfort and escape for their husbands from the pressures of presidential responsibility. As each new administration takes office, arrangements are made for the second floor living quarters to reflect their taste and personal requirements. Betty Ford insisted that she and Gerald have one private room, making sure that it contained some of their favorite things — the President's old blue leather chair, for example, and other items brought from home. Valuable White House antiques were lovely, but she and the President needed some place to call their own.

Extended families create a different problem — overcrowding. Lucy Hayes, Edith Roosevelt, Letitia Tyler, Mary Lincoln, Eliza Johnson, Julia Grant, Lucretia Garfield, Jacqueline Kennedy, Pat Nixon, Rosalynn Carter and Hillary Clinton brought a number of children and other family members to share limited space. Frances Cleveland gave birth to baby Esther in the White House, necessitating conversion of a living room to a nursery. The Clevelands despaired over the arrangements and lack of privacy and bought a large house about three miles from the mansion, sleeping at 1600 Pennsylvania Avenue only from December to March when the social calendar peaked.

The White House has evolved since 1800 from a distinguished but less than imposing 20-or-so rooms to a 132-room mansion tended by a staff of over one hundred. In 1790, Congress passed the Residence Act which authorized a house for the President as part of a "Grand Columbian Federal City" to be built "at some place on the Potomac between the mouth of the eastern branch and the Conogocheague."[204] Thus, the District of Columbia was conceived. The design for the "President's House" was opened to an architectural competition won by Irish-born James Hoban whose winning entry was based on the Dublin home of the Duke of Leinster.

During the competition, Thomas Jefferson championed a design featuring a red brick façade. If he had prevailed, we might be referring to the Brick House or the Red House. The building was torched by the British during the War of 1812 but much of the outer walls was preserved, and the stone covered with white paint when the house was rebuilt. "The White House" did not become the mansion's official name until the presidency of Theodore Roosevelt.

Thomas Jefferson, the second occupant, made many changes. For example, the west colonnade that faces the Rose Garden is a Jefferson legacy. From then on, presidents — and their wives — have redecorated, personalized, restored or expanded the White House, each leaving an individual imprint.

During Andrew Johnson's tenure, his daughter and hostess, Martha Johnson Patterson, supervised changes when the house was refurbished from its Civil War shambles. President and Mrs. Rutherford B. Hayes, a couple of wealth and taste, redecorated the house extensively with an eye to enhancing tradition rather than eliminating it. On the other hand, Chester A. Arthur got rid of much of the historic furniture and hired Louis Comfort Tiffany to furnish the house in lavish Victorian style. President Taft, who desired more space, built the first Oval Office, and his wife Helen ordered an oversized bathtub to accommodate the 300-pound President. With Franklin Roosevelt's presidency, the White House received an indoor swimming pool, a wheelchair ramp — and the East and West wings.

In the late 1940s, an engineering study, prompted when the legs of Margaret Truman's piano went through a second floor ceiling, found that the White House was structurally unsound — literally falling down — and a major renovation effort was initiated. The Truman family moved to Blair House across Pennsylvania Avenue while the structure was made safe. With the addition of the Truman Balcony to the improvements, the White House had arrived at its present-day form.

First Ladies often indulged in decorative changes to the non-office workings of the White House. Dolley Madison hired an outside consultant to help her select curtains and furniture. James and Elizabeth Monroe, first occupants of the White House following the fire damage during the War of

1812, brought a French elegance to the décor and furniture that has lasted for almost two centuries. Several pieces from the Monroe era are still displayed in the Blue Room. Mary Lincoln spent lavishly for the White House, and was roundly criticized for her efforts during wartime. Lucy Hayes and Caroline Harrison supervised important redecoration efforts.

For the first century, however, little attention was given to the preservation of the White House historical record. Edith Roosevelt made an important contribution when she initiated a project to display portraits of herself and former First Ladies in the White House, and in the 1920s Grace Coolidge set an important precedent when she appointed the first advisory committee to select furnishings and artwork for the mansion. It was not until Jackie Kennedy became First Lady, however, that the White House as a museum came about. Almost immediately upon her husband's election, she announced that her "cause" as First Lady would be to make the White House "a showcase of American art and history."[205] She succeeded brilliantly by forming the White House Historical Association, its purpose to increase "the understanding, appreciation, and enjoyment of the Executive Mansion."[206] An inventory of the White House holdings showed "furniture, 1942; ceramics, 15,661; glassware, 3145; metal ware, 13,092; lighting fixtures, 1121; paintings, 338; prints and drawings, 451; and sculpture, 69." Museums and private homes were scoured for White House treasures. Her imprint and contribution was recognized in 1988 when the American Association of Museums concluded that the White House had moved beyond being simply a home and office but had become the nation's oldest important showcase for the arts and it was accredited as a museum.

Seat of government. Home to presidents. Center of the free world. All of those terms are used to describe the White House — the house that hosts more tourists each year than any other, the house that all Americans view with respect and consider their own. Home, also, to the dreams, aspirations and faith of an entire nation of people. It is the President's home — and ours.

DIRECTIONS: The White House is on Pennsylvania Avenue, between 15th and 16th streets, easily reached by the Metro subway system. The White House is a 3-block walk from the Farragut North, McPherson Square and Metro Center stations, all stops on the Blue and Orange lines. Metro Center is also served by the Red Line.

PUBLIC USE: Season and hours: Due to security concerns, The White House is open on a restricted basis for self-guided tours, although some areas such as the Oval Office and the family living quarters are closed. Tours begin in the East Wing and proceed by the Library and the Vermeil Room, then up the staircase to the State Floor, where visitors may view the East Room, the Green, Blue and Red rooms, the State Dining Room and the Entrance Hall.

Tours for groups of ten or more people may be arranged only through one's Member of Congress and are accepted up to six months in advance. These self-guided tours will be scheduled approximately one month before the requested date, from 7:30 AM to 12:30 PM, Tuesday through Friday. For the enjoyment of White House visitors and other tourists, the National Park Service has opened a White House Visitor Center at the corner of 15^(th) Street and "E." The center, with exhibits and video displays, is open 7:30 AM-4 PM. No admission fee. **Gift shop. For people with disabilities:** Fully accessible.

FOR ADDITIONAL INFORMATION: Contact: The White House, 1600 Pennsylvania Avenue, Washington, DC. Tours: (202) 456-7041. **Web site:** *www.whitehouse.gov*. **Read:** William Seale. 1986. *The President's House: A History*.

Section III

Additional Information

Burial Sites of the First Ladies

Martha Washington: Mount Vernon, Virginia

Abigail Adams: First Parish Church, Quincy, Massachusetts

Martha Jefferson: Monticello, Charlottesville, Virginia

Dolley Madison: Montpelier, Orange, Virginia

Elizabeth Monroe: Hollywood Cemetery, Richmond, Virginia

Louisa Adams: First Parish Church, Quincy, Massachusetts

Rachel Jackson: The Hermitage, Nashville, Tennessee

Hannah Van Buren: Kinderhook Cemetery, Kinderhook, New York

Anna Harrison: William Henry Harrison State Park, North Bend, Ohio

Letitia Tyler: Cedar Grove Plantation, Kent County, Virginia

Julia Tyler: Hollywood Cemetery, Richmond, Virginia

Sarah Polk: Capitol Hill, Nashville, Tennessee

Margaret Taylor: Zachary Taylor National Cemetery, Louisville, Kentucky

Abigail Fillmore: Forest Lawn Cemetery, Buffalo, New York

Jane Pierce: Old North Cemetery, Concord, New Hampshire

Harriet Lane: Green Mount Cemetery, Baltimore, Maryland

Mary Lincoln: Oak Ridge Cemetery, Springfield, Illinois

Eliza Johnson: Andrew Johnson National Cemetery, Greeneville, Tennessee

Julia Grant: Grant's Tomb, New York, New York

Lucy Hayes: Spiegel Grove, Fremont, Ohio

Lucretia Garfield: Lake View Cemetery, Cleveland, Ohio

Ellen Arthur: Albany Rural Cemetery, Albany, New York

Frances Cleveland: Princeton Cemetery, Princeton, New Jersey

Caroline Harrison: Crown Hill Cemetery, Indianapolis, Indiana

Ida McKinley: McKinley National Memorial, Canton, Ohio

Edith Roosevelt: Youngs Memorial Cemetery, Oyster Bay, New York

Helen Taft: Arlington National Cemetery, Arlington, Virginia

Ellen Wilson: Myrtle Hill Cemetery, Rome, Georgia

Edith Wilson: Washington National Cathedral, Washington, DC

Florence Harding: Harding Memorial, Marion, Ohio

Grace Coolidge: Plymouth Notch Cemetery, Plymouth, Vermont

Lou Hoover: Herbert Hoover National Historic Site, West Branch, Iowa

Eleanor Roosevelt: Home of Franklin D. Roosevelt National Historic Site, Hyde Park, New York

Elizabeth Truman: Harry S Truman National Historic Site, Independence, Missouri

Mamie Eisenhower: Eisenhower Center, Abilene, Kansas

Jacqueline Kennedy: Arlington National Cemetery, Arlington, Virginia

Claudia "Lady Bird" Johnson: Johnson Family Cemetery, Stonewall, Texas

Thelma "Pat" Nixon: Nixon Presidential Library and Museum, Yorba Linda, California

End Notes

1. Deborah Jones Sherwood. 2003. *The First Ladies*. New York: Barnes and Noble, 12.
2. Ibid., 184.
3. *The First Ladies, Part I; Public Expectations*. PBS, 10/25/04.
4. Noel B. Gerson. 1975. *The Velvet Glove: A Life of Dolly Madison*. Nashville: Thomas Nelson, 12.
5. *The First Ladies, Part I; Public Expectations*. PBS, 10/25/04.
6. Anonymous. 1998. *The Manuscript Society News*, 19(2: Spring): 64.
7. Carl Sferrazza Anthony, ed. 2003. *"This Elevated Position . . ." A Catalogue and Guide to the National First Ladies' Library and the Importance of First Lady History*. Canton: National First Ladies' Library, 160.
8. "The Dedication." First Ladies' Library web site, *www.firstladies.org*.
9. Laura Bush speech as quoted on White House web site: *www.whitehouse.gov/news/release/2003/o9/20030906-12.hytml*.
10. Anonymous. 1998. *The Manuscript Society News*, 19(2: Spring): 62.
11. Anthony, 74
12. Paul F. Boller, Jr. 1988. *Presidential Wives*. New York: Oxford University Press, 5.
13. Cranston Jones. 1962. *Homes of the American Presidents*. New York: Crown Publishers, 30.
14. Douglas Southall Freeman. 1948–1952, 1957. *George Washington: A Biography*. Seven volumes. New York: Scribner's, 6: 452-453.
15. Joseph J. Ellis. 2004. *His Excellency, George Washington*. New York: Alfred A. Knopf, 189.
16. Joseph E. Fields, ed. 1994. *Worthy Partner: The Papers of Martha Washington*. Westport: Greenwood Press, 223, 224.
17. Boller, 7
18. Lynne Withey. 1981. *Dearest Friend: A Life of Abigail Adams*. New York: Touchstone Books; Sadler, 30.
19. National Park Service brochure.
20. Ibid.
21. Boller, 31.
22. Adrienne Koch and William Peden, eds. 1944. *Autobiography*, in *The Life and Selected Writings of Thomas Jefferson*. New York: The Modern Library, 53.
23. Irving Brant. 1942–1962. *James Madison*. Six volumes. Indianapolis: Bobbs-Merrill, 5: 450.
24. L. B. Cutts, ed. 2006. *Memoirs and Letters of Dolley Madison*. Whitefish: Kessinger Publishing, 15.
25. Boller, 37.
26. Montpelier brochure.
27. Ibid., attribution not confirmed.
28. Hillary Clinton. 1998. "Discovering Montpelier." *The Friends of Montpelier Newsletter*, Summer 1990, 5.
29. Harry Ammon. 1990. *James Monroe: The Quest for National Identity*. Charlottesville: University Press of Virginia, 61, 62.
30. Monroe, James. 1959. *The Autobiography of James Monroe*. Syracuse: Syracuse University Press, 49.

31. Will of Jay Johns, 1974, as included in Ash Lawn-Highland Statement of Purpose, April, 1990.

32. Paul C. Nagel. 1997. *John Quincy Adams.* New York: Alfred A. Knopf, 416.

33. Paul C. Nagel. 1987. *The Adams Women: Abigail and Louisa Adams, Their Sisters and Daughters.* New York: Oxford University Press, 287.

34. Sadler, 54.

35. Ladies' Hermitage Association, The. *Andrew Jackson's Hermitage.* 1987. Nashville: The Ladies' Hermitage Association, 21.

36. Ibid., 40.

37. Ibid., 44.

38. Obituary from *"Albany Argus,"* February, 1819, written by John Chester, Minister of First Presbyterian Church of Albany.

39. Sadler, 68.

40. Laura Carter Holloway. 1870. *The Ladies of the White House.* New York: United States Publishing Company, 382, 383.

41. Robert Seager II. 1963. *And Tyler, Too: A Biography of John and Julia Tyler.* New York: McGraw-Hill, 196, 200.

42. Boller, 83.

43. Ibid.

44. Ibid., 84.

45. Anonymous. 1952. "Letters of Mrs. James K. Polk to her Husband." *Tennessee Historical Quarterly,* 11(June): 180.

46. Bill Harris. 1997. *Homes of the Presidents.* Godalming, Surrey, United Kingdom: CLB International, 66.

47. Mary Ormsbee Whitton. 1948. *First First Ladies.* Freeport: Books for Library Press, 215–216.

48. Boller, 95.

49. Ibid., 97.

50. Ibid., 96.

51. Sadler, 89.

52. Wheatland rack card.

53. Sadler, 101.

54. Jones, 111.

55. Boller, 110.

56. Ishbel Ross. 1973. *The President's Wife: Mary Todd Lincoln: A Biography.* New York: Putnam, 108.

57. Elizabeth Keckley. 1968. *Behind the Scenes: Thirty Years a Slave and Four Years in the White House.* New York: G. W. Carleton & Co., 103, 104.

58. Ross, 105, 106.

59. Emily Todd Helm. 1898. "Mary Todd Lincoln." *McClure's Magazine,* 11(September): 42, 43.

60. Boller, 120.

61. Lately Thomas. 1968. *The First President Johnson.* New York: William Morrow, 245.

62. Sadler, 113.

63. Mary Clemmer Ames. 1880. *Ten Years in Washington: Life and Scenes in the Nation's Capital, as a Woman Sees Them.* Hartford: A. D. Worthington & Co., as quoted in Boller, 130.

64. Ibid., 128.

65. Ishbel Ross. 1959. *The General's Wife: The Life of Mrs. Ulysses S. Grant.* New York: Dodd Mead, 142.

66. Boller, 143.

67. John Y. Simon, ed. 1975. *The Personal Memoirs of Julia Dent Grant.* New York: Putnam, 196, 197.

68. Ibid., 161.

69. Thomas A. Campbell, Jr. 1979. "The U. S. Grant Home State Historic Site." *Historic Illinois,* 1(5: February): 1–4.

70. Ibid.

71. Galena fund-raising brochure for Julia Grant statue.

72. Emily Apt Geer. 1995. *First Lady: The Life of Lucy Webb Hayes.* Fremont: The Rutherford B. Hayes Presidential Center, 138.

73. Harris, 86.

74. Sadler, 124, 125, quoting Journalist Laura Holloway.

75. Charles R. Williams, ed. 1922– 1926. *Diary and Letters of Rutherford B. Hayes.* Five volumes. Columbus: Ohio State Archaeological and Historical Society, 5: 97.

76. Sadler, 133.

77. Boller, 160.

78. Thomas C. Reeves. 1975.

Gentleman Boss: The Life of Chester Alan Arthur. New York: Alfred A. Knopf, 84.

79. Irwin Hood Hoover. 1974. *Forty-Two Years in the White House.* Boston: Greenwood Publishing Group, 12, 14.

80. Furman, 258.

81. Harry J. Sievers, S.J. 1960. *Benjamin Harrison, Hoosier Warrior.* New York: University Publishers, 167.

82. Boller, 180, 181.

83. Charles S. Olcott. 1916, 1963. *The Life of William McKinley.* Two volumes. Syracuse: Syracuse University Press, 2: 316.

84. Charles Willis Thompson. 1929. *Presidents I Have Known and Two Near Presidents.* Indianapolis: Bobbs-Merrill, 17.

85. Boller, 188.

86. First Ladies Library brochure.

87. Ibid.

88. Ibid.

89. Michael Teague. 1981. *Mrs. L: Conversations with Alice Roosevelt Longworth.* Garden City: Doubleday, 5.

90. Boller, 197.

91. Sylvia Jukes Morris. 1980. *Edith Kermit Roosevelt: Portrait of a First Lady.* New York: Coward, McCann and Geoghegan, 516.

92. Jones, 165.

93. Furman, 266.

94. Letter to author from Curator Paula Beazley, November 26, 2003.

95. William H. Harbaugh. 1993. *The Theodore Roosevelts' Retreat in the South Albemarle: Pine Knot 1905–1908.* Charlottesville: Albemarle County Historical Society, 11.

96. Henry F. Pringle. 1998. *The Life and Times of William Howard Taft.* Two volumes. Newtown: American Political Biography Press, 1: 79.

97. *New York Times.* May 23, 1943, 43.

98. Ray Stannard Baker. 1946. *Woodrow Wilson: Life and Letters.* Eight volumes. New York: Charles Scribner's, 2: 57.

99. Boller, 221.

100. Mrs. Ernest P. Bicknell. 1914. "The Home-Maker of the White House." *Survey,* 33(October 3): 22.

101. Allen S. Link. 1956. *Wilson: The New Freedom.* Princeton: Princeton University Press, 462.

102. Carl Sferrazza Anthony. 1998. *Florence Harding.* New York: William Morrow, 261.

103. Ishbel Ross. 1961. *Grace Coolidge and Her Era.* New York: Dodd Mead, 68.

104. Boller, 262.

105. *Champlain College Bulletin.*

106. Ruth Dennis.1986. *The Homes of the Hoovers.* West Branch: Herbert Hoover Presidential Library Assocation, 2.

107. Ibid., 43.

108. From letter quoted in internet biography on Herbert Hoover Presidential Library web site: *www.hoover.archives.gov.*

109. Eleanor Roosevelt. 1949, 1975. *This I Remember.* New York: Greenwood Publishing Group, 348, 349.

110. Boller, 299.

111. National Park Service brochure.

112. Ibid.

113. Frances Perkins. 1946. *The Roosevelt I Knew.* New York: Viking, 64.

114. Franklin D. Roosevelt memorandum, December 26, 1937, as quoted in United States Department of Interior brochure, reprint 1957.

115. Campobello brochure.

116. National Park Service brochure.

117. Harry S. Truman. 1955, 1956. *Memoirs.* Two volumes. Garden City: Doubleday, 5.

118. Margaret Truman. 1956. *Souvenir: Margaret Truman's Own Story.* New York: McGraw Hill, 83, 84.

119. Margaret Truman. 1986. *Bess W. Truman.* New York: Macmillan, 11.

120. Boller, 316.

121. Sadler, 226.

122. Margaret Truman, with Margaret Cousins. 1956. *My Own Story.* London. Eyre and Spottiswoode, as quoted in Sadler, 226.

123. William G. Clotworthy. 2003.

Homes and Libraries of the Presidents. Blacksburg: McDonald & Woodward, 241.

124. Mamie Eisenhower. 1970. "My Memories of Ike." *Reader's Digest,* 96(February): 70.

125. Dorothy Brandon. 1954. *Mamie Doud Eisenhower: A Portrait of a First Lady.* New York: Scribner's, 47.

126. Alden Hatch. 1954. *Red Carpet for Mamie.* New York: Holt, 167.

127. Boller, 339.

128. Boller, 342.

129. J. B. West. 1973. *Upstairs at the White House: My Life with the First Ladies.* New York: Coward, McCann and Geoghegan, 131, 132.

130. Steve Neal. 1978. *The Eisenhowers: Reluctant Dynasty.* Garden City: Doubleday, 401.

131. National Park Service brochure.

132. Ibid.

133. Marianne Means. 1963. *The Women in the White House.* New York: Random House, 267.

134. Ibid.

135. Ralph G. Martin. 1983. *A Hero for Our Time: An Intimate Story of the Kennedy Years.* New York: Macmillan, 79.

136. Stephen Birmingham. 1978. *Jacqueline Bouvier Kennedy Onassis.* New York: Grosset and Dunlap, 198.

137. Boller, 371.

138. Peter Collier and David Horowitz. 1984. *The Kennedys: An American Drama.* New York: Summit, 318.

139. Boller, 368.

140. JFK Library brochure.

141. Marie Smith. 1964. *The President's Lady: An Intimate Biography of Mrs. Lyndon B. Johnson.* New York: Random House, 91.

142. Liz Carpenter. 1970. *Ruffles and Flourishes.* Garden City: Doubleday, 14.

143. Boller, 379.

144. Frances Spatz Leighton and Helen Baldwin. 1964. *They Call Her Lady Bird.* New York: McFadden-Bartell, 182, 183.

145. Boller, 386.

146. Ibid., 379.

147. Ibid., 380, 381.

148. Smith, 40.

149. Ibid., 381.

150. Ibid., 382.

151. Leighton and Baldwin, 94, 95.

152. Boller, 387.

153. West, 283, 284.

154. Ruth Montgomery. 1964. *Mrs. LBJ.* New York: Avon, 182.

155. Richard M. Nixon. 1978. *Memoirs.* New York: Grosset and Dunlap, 1086.

156. Fawn Brodie. 1981. *Richard Nixon: The Shaping of his Character.* New York: Norton, 152.

157. Boller, 398.

158. Julie Nixon Eisenhower. 1986. *Pat Nixon: The Untold Story.* New York: Simon and Schuster.

159. Lester David. 1978. *The Lonely Lady of San Clemente.* New York: Thomas Y. Crowell, 18.

160. J. Eisenhower, 143.

161. Brodie, 371.

162. Ibid., 451.

163. Boller, 408.

164. David, 161.

165. Helen McCain Smith. "Ordeal! Pat Nixon's Final Days in the White House." *Good Housekeeping,* 83(July): 127.

166. Kati Marton. 2001. *Hidden Power.* New York: Random House, 200.

167. Ron Nessen.1978. *It Sure Looks Different from the Inside.* Chicago: Playboy Press, 28.

168. Boller, 422.

169. Sheila Rabb Weidenfeld. 1979. *First Lady's Lady: With the Fords in the White House.* New York: Putnam, 217.

170. Phyllis Battelle. 1981. "Betty Ford and Finding Courage in Pain." *Ladies Home Journal,* 98(January): 46.

171. Ralph G. Martin. 1979. "When Jimmy Carter Married Her, He Married Magic." *Ladies Home Journal,* 96(March): 99.

172. Boller, 434.

173. Rosalynn Carter. 1984. *First Lady from Plains.* New York: Houghton

Mifflin, 191.

174. Martin, 101.

175. Carter, 41.

176. Ibid., 173, 174.

177. Jean Saunders Wixon. 1985. "Saga of an Ordinary Woman." *Modern Maturity Magazine*, 30(February/March): 70.

178. Jimmy Carter press conference, Atlanta, Georgia, March 2009 announcing reopening of museum following renovation.

179. Ammon, 61, 62.

180. Bill Adler. 1985. *Ronnie and Nancy: A Very Special Love Story.* New York: Crown, 186.

181. Anne Edwards. 1987. *Early Reagan: The Rise to Power.* New York: Morrow/Avon, 113.

182. Nancy Reagan. 1987. "Nancy Reagan Defends Her Rights in Advising the President." *New York Times*, May 5: 26. Nancy Reagan speech to the American Newspaper Publishers Association, May 4, 1987, as quoted in Boller, 464, 465.

183. Plaque on piece of Berlin Wall

184. Sadler, 22.

185. Donnie Radcliffe. 1989. *Simply Barbara Bush.* New York: Warner Books, 57.

186. Boller, 174.

187. Ellen Goodman. 1989. "Welcoming a Role Model." *Fort Worth Star-Telegram*, January 27, Section 1: 25.

188. George H. W. Bush, with Victor Gold. 1987. *Looking Forward.* New York: Knopf Doubleday, 213.

189. Radcliffe, 140

190. Luann Paletta. 1990. *World Almanac of First Ladies.* New York: World Almanac Publishing: 156.

191. Clinton House Museum Tour Guide pamphlet.

192. Cathleen McGuigan. 2004. "Bill's New Bridge." *Newsweek,* September 5.

193. Judy Keen. 2000. "Laura Bush: Calm amid the chaos." *USA Today*, July 31.

194. Ibid.

195. Liza Mundy. 2008. *Michelle.* New York: Simon and Schuster, 197.

196. C. Brian Kelly. 1999. *Best Little Stories From the White House.* Nashville: Cumberland House, 36.

197. Ibid, 37.

198. Ibid, 37.

199. Hugh Sidey. 1992. "Two Centuries and Counting." *Time*, October 19: 48.

200. Kelly, 70.

201. Sidey, 48.

202. Betty Boyd Caroli. 1992. *Inside the White House.* New York: Canopy Books, 23.

203. Ibid.

204. John E. Ferling. 1988. *The First of Men: A Life of George Washington.* Knoxville: University of Tennessee Press, 394.

205. Caroli, 128.

206. Ibid., 124.

Acknowledgements

It is not hard to make a list of people who have been helpful in the preparation of this book. It is more difficult to adequately thank them for their generosity. As much as I would love to thank each personally, let me merely say that each is a professional, dedicated to the perpetuation of part of America's glorious history and study of its great personalities.

Mount Vernon: Dawn Bonner, Emily Dibella, Mary V. Thompson. *Abigail Adams Birthplace*: Cathy Torrey. *Adams NHP*: Elizabeth Agati, Caroline Keinath. *Todd House*: Jane Cowley, Philip Sheridan, Isabel Ziegler. *Montpelier*: Alison Deeds, Elizabeth Loring. *Greensboro Historical Museum*: Adrienne Byrd, Linda Evans, Fred Goss. *Ash Lawn-Highland*: Carolyn Holmes. *James Monroe Museum and Memorial Library*: Meghan Budinger. *The Hermitage*: Marsha Mullin. *Grouseland*: Dennis Latta, Dan Sarell. *Sherwood Forest*: Harrison, Payne and Kay Tyler. *Fillmore House Museum*: Esther Kopp, Diane Meade. *The Pierce Manse*: Caroline Amport, Joan Davis. *Wheatland*: Patrick Clarke. *Mary Todd Lincoln House*: Gwen Thompson. *Lincoln Home NHS*: Kathy DeHart, Tim Townsend. *President Lincoln's Cottage at the Soldiers' Home*: Erin Mast, Frank Milligan. *Abraham Lincoln Presidential Library and Museum*: Dave Blanchette. *Andrew Johnson NHS*: Serisha Boyett, Leah Giles, Kendra Hinkle, Jim Small. *Ulysses S. Grant NHS*: Pam Sanfilippo. *Grant's Farm*: Pier Scott. *Ulysses S. Grant Home State Historic Site*: Terry Miller. *Grant Cottage SHS*: Beverly Clark, Dave Hubbard. *Lucy Hayes Heritage Center*: Paul and Shirley Thacker. *Rutherford B. Hayes Presidential Center*: Tom Culbertson, Gilbert Gonzalez. *James A. Garfield NHS*: Sherda Williams. *President Benjamin Harrison Home*: Jennifer Capps, Phyllis Geeslin. *First Ladies NHS*: Pat Krider, Mary Rhodes. *William McKinley Presidential Library & Museum*: Christopher Kenney, Joyce Yut. *Sagamore Hill NHS*: Mark Koziol, Amy Verone. *Pine Knot*: Paula Beazley. *Edith Bolling Wilson Birthplace Museum*: Leslie King. *Woodrow Wilson House Museum*: Frank Auletta, Marie Danch. *The Harding Home*: Melinda Gilpin, Sherry Hall.

Goodhue Home: Shelley Richardson. *Herbert Hoover NHS* and *Herbert Hoover Presidential Library and Museum*: Janlyn Slach. *Home of Franklin D. Roosevelt NHS* and *Franklin D. Roosevelt Presidential Library and Museum*: Clifford Laube, William Urbin. *Roosevelt Campobello International Park*: Harold Bailey, Ron Beckwith, Anne Newman. *Eleanor Roosevelt NHS*: Sarah Olson. *Harry S Truman NHS*: Eileen Andes, Mike Ryan. *Mamie Doud Eisenhower Birthplace*: Suzanne Caswell, Charles Irwin. *Eisenhower NHS*: Carol Hegeman. *Dwight D. Eisenhower Presidential Library and Museum*: Samantha Kenner, Timothy Rives, Matthew Thompson. *John F. Kennedy Presidential Library and Museum*: Allan Goodman, James Hill, James Wagner. *Lyndon B. Johnson NHP* and *Lyndon B. Johnson State Park and Historic Site*: Sherry Justus, Gus Sanchez. *Johnson City Chamber of Commerce*: Belinda Nagy. *Lyndon Baines Johnson Library and Museum*: Margaret Harman, Anne Wheeler. *Nixon Presidential Library and Museum*: Jonathan Movroydis, Sandy Quinn. *Gerald R. Ford Presidential Museum*: Don Holloway. *Jimmy Carter NHS*: Katherine Brock, Gabriel Laster. *Jimmy Carter Library and Museum*: Tony Clark, Deanne Congilee, Calvin Sylvester. *Ronald Reagan Presidential Library and Museum*: Melissa Giller. *George Bush Presidential Library and Museum*: Brian Blake, Bonnie Burlbaw, Tracy Paine. *Clinton House Museum*: Kate Johnson, Kelli Nixon. *William J. Clinton Presidential Library and Museum*: Skip Rutherford.

Many individuals and organizations generously provided photographs for use in this book. The photograph of the Saxton McKinley House on the front cover, home of the First Ladies National Historic Site and the National First Ladies' Library, was provided by the National First Ladies' Library. The color plates, identified by plate number and location on the page, are used through the courtesy of, and are credited to, the following: 1 top and bottom: Mount Vernon Ladies' Association; 2 top: National Park Service, Adams National Historical Park; 2 bottom: Montpelier Foundation; 3 top and bottom; Hal Conroy for Ash Lawn- Highland; 4 top: Ladies' Hermitage Association; 4 bottom; Paige Swope; 5 top: Grouseland Foundation; 5 middle and bottom; Leah Price for the Fillmore House Museum; 6 top: LancasterHistory.org, Lancaster County's Historical Society and President James Buchanan's Wheatland; 6 bottom: National Park Service, Lincoln Home National Historic Site; 7 Abraham Lincoln Presidential Library and Museum; 8 top: National Park Service, Andrew Johnson National Historic Site; 8 bottom: Galena State Historic Sites; 9 top: Shirley Thacker for the Lucy Hayes

Heritage Center; 9 bottom: Rutherford B. Hayes Presidential Center, Fremont, Ohio; 10 top and bottom: National First Ladies' Library; 11 top: National Park Service, Sagamore Hill National Historic Site; 11 bottom: Herbert Hoover Presidential Library and Museum; 12 top and bottom: National Park Service, Home of Franklin D. Roosevelt National Historic Site, W. D. Urbin; 13 top: Roosevelt Campobello International Park Commission; 13 bottom and 14 top and bottom: National Park Service, Eleanor Roosevelt National Historic Site, W. D. Urbin; 15 top: National Park Service, Harry S Truman National Historic Site, 15 middle: National Park Service, Eisenhower National Historic Site, 15 bottom: National Park Service, Lyndon B. Johnson National Historical Park; 16 top: Jimmy Carter Library and Museum; 16 bottom: George Bush Presidential Library and Museum. Credits for black-and-white images are given as parts of the captions for those images.

Thanks also to my computer guru Terry Noziglia, publisher Jerry McDonald and staff who have been patient (most of the time) and helpful (all of the time) through four books, and my daughter Amy Clotworthy. When she was a child, I dedicated my first book to her. Now I acknowledge her great work as my editor.

And to Jo — as always, with love.

Bibliography

Adler, Bill. 1985. *Ronnie and Nancy: A Very Special Love Story*. New York: Crown.

Akers, Charles W. 1980. *Abigail Adams: An American Woman*. Boston: Little, Brown.

Alexandria Convention and Visitors' Association. n.d. *Alexandria*. Alexandria: Alexandria Convention and Visitors' Association.

Allgor, Catherine. 2000. *Parlor Politics: In Which the Ladies of Washington Help Found a City and a Government*. Charlottesville: University Press of Virginia.

Ambrose, Stephen E. 1987. *Nixon*. Three volumes. New York: Simon and Schuster.

———. 1990. *Eisenhower: Soldier and President*. New York: Simon and Schuster.

Ames, Mary Clemmer. 1880. *Ten Years in Washington: Life and Scenes in the Nation's Capital, as a Woman Sees Them*. Hartford: A. D. Worthington & Co.

Ammon, Harry. 1990. *James Monroe: The Quest for National Identity*. Charlotesville: University Press of Virginia.

Anthony, Carl Sferrazza. 1998. *Florence Harding*. New York: William Morrow.

———, ed. 2003. *"This Elevated Position . . ." A Catalogue and Guide to the National First Ladies' Library and the Importance of First Lady History*. Canton: National First Ladies' Library.

Apostol, Jane. 1987. *South Pasadena, 1888–1988: A Centennial History*. Pasadena: Pasadena Historical Museum.

Ash Lawn-Highland. 1999. *Ash Lawn-Highland: A Guide*. Williamsburg: The College of William and Mary.

Auchincloss, Louis. 2001. *Theodore Roosevelt*. New York: Henry Holt.

Baker, Jean H. 1987. *Mary Lincoln*. New York: W. W. Norton.

Baker, Ray Stannard. 1946. *Woodrow Wilson: Life and Letters*. Eight volumes. New York: Charles Scribner's.

Baker, William S. 1982. *Itinerary of General George Washington from June 15, 1775 to December 23, 1783*. Philadelphia: J.B. Lippincott.

Bassett, Margaret. 1969. *Profiles and Portraits of American Presidents and Their Wives*. Freeport: Bond Wheelwright.

Battelle, Phyllis 1981. "Betty Ford and Finding Courage in Pain." *Ladies Home Journal,* January: 46.

Bauer, K. Jack. 1985. *Zachary Taylor: Soldier, Planter, Statesman of the Old Southwest.* Baton Rouge: Louisiana State University Press.

Bell, Carl Irving. 1980. *They Knew Franklin Pierce.* Springfield: April Hill Publishers.

Bicknell, Mrs. Ernest P. 1914. "The Home-Maker of the White House." *Survey,* 33(October 3): 22.

Birmingham, Stephen. 1978. *Jacqueline Bouvier Kennedy Onassis.* New York: Grosset and Dunlap.

Bober, Natalie S. 1995. *Abigail Adams, Witness to a Revolution.* New York: Simon and Schuster.

Boller, Paul F., Jr. 1988, 1998. *Presidential Wives.* New York: Oxford University Press.

Borneman, Walter R. 2008. *Polk.* New York: Random House.

Bourne, Miriam Anne. 1982. *First Family, George Washington and His Intimate Relations.* New York: W. W. Norton.

Brady, Patricia. 2005. *Martha Washington: An American Life.* New York: Viking.

Brandon, Dorothy. 1954. *Mamie Doud Eisenhower: A Portrait of a First Lady.* New York: Scribner's.

Brant, Irving. 1942–1962. *James Madison.* Six volumes. Indianapolis: Bobbs-Merrill.

———. 1970. *The Fourth President: A Life of James Madison.* Indianapolis: Bobbs-Merrill.

Brinkley, Douglas. 1998. *The Unfinished Presidency: Jimmy Carter's Journey beyond the White House.* New York: Viking Penguin.

———. 2009. The *Wilderness Warrior: Theodore Roosevelt and the Crusade for America.* New York: HarperCollins.

Brodie, Fawn. 1974. *Thomas Jefferson: An Intimate History.* New York: Norton.

———. 1981. *Richard Nixon: The Shaping of His Character.* New York: Norton.

Brown, Katherine L. 1991. *The Woodrow Wilson Birthplace*, 2nd ed. Staunton: The Woodrow Wilson Birthplace Foundation, Inc.

Brownstein, Elizabeth. 2005. *Lincoln's Other White House.* New York: John Wiley and Sons.

Bryan, Helen. 2002. *Martha Washington: First Lady of Liberty.* New York: John Wiley and Sons.

Buller, Jon, Susan Schade, Dana Regan, Sally Warner, and Jill Weber. 2005. *Smart About the First Ladies.* New York: Grosset and Dunlap.

Burns, James MacGregor, with Susan Dunn. 2004. *George Washington*. The American Presidents Series, edited by Arthur Schlesinger, Jr. New York: Henry Holt and Company.

Bush, George H. W., with Victor Gold. 1987. *Looking Forward*. New York: Knopf Doubleday.

Busch, Noel F. 1974. *Winter Quarters*. New York: Liveright.

Cahalan, Sally Smith. 1988. *James Buchanan's Wheatland*. Lancaster: The James Buchanan Foundation.

Caldwell, Mary French. 1936. *General Jackson's Lady*. Nashville: The Ladies' Hermitage Association.

Calhoun, Charles W. 2005. *Benjamin Harrison*. New York: Times Books.

Campbell, Thomas A., Jr. 1979. "The U.S. Grant Home State Historic Site." *Historic Illinois*, 1(5:February): 1–4.

Caroli, Betty Boyd. 1987. *First Ladies*. New York: Oxford University Press.

———. 1992. *Inside the White House*. New York: Canopy Books.

———. 1996. *America's First Ladies*. Pleasantville: Reader's Digest Association, Inc.

Carpenter, Liz. 1970. *Ruffles and Flourishes*. Garden City: Doubleday.

Carson, Barbara. 1990. *Ambitious Appetites*. Washington, DC: AIA Press.

Carter, Jimmy. 1988. *An Outdoor Journal*. New York: Bantam Books.

Carter, Rosalynn. 1984. *First Lady from Plains*. New York: Houghton Mifflin.

———. 2010. *Within Reach: Ending the Mental Health Crisis*. New York: Rodale.

Chidsey, Donald Barr. 1959. *Valley Forge*. New York: Crown.

Chitwood, Oliver Perry.1990. *John Tyler: Champion of the Old South*. Newtown: American Political Biography Press.

Clark, Mary Higgins. 1968, 2002. *Mount Vernon Love Story*. New York: Simon and Schuster.

Cleaves, Freeman. 1990. *Old Tippecanoe: William Henry Harrison and His Time*. Newtown: American Political Biography Press.

Cleere, Gail S. 1989. *The House on Observatory Hill*. Washington, DC: Oceanographer of the Navy, U.S. Government Printing Office.

Clinton, Catherine. 2008. *Mary Lincoln*. New York: HarperCollins.

Clinton, Hillary. 1998. "Discovering Montpelier." *The Friends of Montpelier Newsletter*, Summer 1990: 5.

Clotworthy, William G. 1994, 2003. *Homes and Libraries of the Presidents*. Blacksburg: McDonald & Woodward.

———. 2008. *Homes and Libraries of the Presidents*. Third edition. Granville: McDonald & Woodward.

————. 1998. *Presidential Sites*. Blacksburg: McDonald & Woodward.

————. 2002. *In the Footsteps of George Washington*. Blacksburg: McDonald & Woodward.

Colbert, Nancy A. 1998. *Lou Henry Hoover: The Duty to Serve*. Greensboro: Morgan Reynolds.

Coleman, Elizabeth Tyler. 1955. *Priscilla Cooper Tyler and the American Scene*. Tuscaloosa: University of Alabama Press.

Collier, Peter, and David Horowitz. 1984. *The Kennedys: An American Drama*. New York: Summit.

Comstock, Helen. 1965. *The 100 Most Beautiful Rooms in America*. New York: Viking.

Cook, Blanche Wiesen. 1999. *Eleanor Roosevelt*. Two volumes. New York: Viking Penguin.

Coolidge, Calvin. 1929. *The Autobiography of Calvin Coolidge*. New York: Cosmopolitan Book Corporation. Reprinted by the Calvin Coolidge Memorial Foundation, Plymouth, Vermont, 1989.

Coolidge, Grace Goodhue. 1992. *Grace Coolidge: An Autobiography*. Edited by Lawrence E. Wikander and Robert H, Ferrell. Published posthumously. Worland: Wyoming: High Plains Publishing Company.

Cruse, Katherine W. 1994. *An Amiable Woman: Rachel Jackson*. Nashville: The Ladies' Hermitage Association.

Cutts, L. B., ed. 2006. *Memoirs and Letters of Dolley Madison*. Whitefish: Kessinger Publishing.

Dallek, Robert. 2005. *Lyndon B. Johnson: Portrait of a President*. New York: Oxford University Press.

David, Lester. 1978. *The Lonely Lady of San Clemente*. New York: Thomas Y. Crowell.

Davis, William, and Christina Tree. 1980. *The Kennedy Library*. Exton: Schiffer Publishing.

Dennis, Ruth. 1986. *The Homes of the Hoovers*. West Branch: Herbert Hoover Presidential Library Association.

DePauw, Linda Grant. 1975. *Founding Mothers: Women in America in the Revolutionary Era*. Madison: Demco Miller.

Edwards, Anne. 1987. *Early Reagan: The Rise to Power*. New York: Morrow/Avon.

Eisenhower, Julie Nixon. 1986. *Pat Nixon: The Untold Story*. New York: Simon and Schuster.

Eisenhower, Mamie. 1970. "My Memories of Ike." *Reader's Digest,* 96(February): 70.

Eisenhower, Susan. 1996. *Mrs. Ike*. New York: Farrar, Strauss and Giroux.

Elder, Betty D. 1980. *A Special House*. Columbia: James K. Polk Memorial Association.

Elliot, William Griffis. 1915. *Millard Fillmore*. Ithaca: Andrews and Church.

Ellis, Joseph J. 2001. *Founding Brothers*. New York: Alfred A. Knopf.

———. 2004. *His Excellency, George Washington*. New York: Alfred A. Knopf.

Ferling, John E. 1988. *The First of Men: A Life of George Washington*. Knoxville: University of Tennessee Press.

Ferris, Robert G., series ed. *The Presidents*. Washington, DC: United States Department of the Interior, National Park Service.

Fields, Joseph E., ed. 1994. *Worthy Partner: The Papers of Martha Washington*. Westport: Greenwood Press.

Flexner, James Thomas. 1974. *Washington: The Indispensable Man*. Boston: Little, Brown.

Ford, Betty. 1978. *The Times of My Life*. New York: Harper and Row.

Freeman, Douglas Southall. 1948–1952, 1957. *George Washington: A Biography*. Six volumes. New York: Scribner's (Volume 7 edited posthumously by J. A. Carroll and Mary Ashworth).

Freidel, Frank. 1977. *Our Country's Presidents*. Washington, DC: National Geographic Society.

Furman, Bess. 1951. *White House Profile: A Social History of the White House, Its Occupants and Its Festivities*. Indianapolis: Bobbs-Merrill.

Gara, Larry. 1991. *The Presidency of Franklin Pierce*. Lawrence: University Press of Kansas.

Geer, Emily Apt. 1995. *First Lady: The Life of Lucy Webb Hayes*. Fremont: The Rutherford B. Hayes Presidential Center.

Gerlinger, Irene. 1970. *Mistresses of the White House*. Freeport: Books for Libraries Press.

Gerson, Noel B. 1975. *The Velvet Glove: A Life of Dolly Madison*. Nashville: Thomas Nelson.

Gingrich, Virginia F. 1994. *The Story of the Church at the Crossroads*. Canton: Church of the Savior United Methodist.

Goodman, Ellen. 1989. "Welcoming a Role Model." *Fort Worth Star-Telegram,* January 27, Section 1: 25.

Graff, Henry F. 2002. *Grover Cleveland*. New York: Henry Holt.

Grant, Ulysses S. 1990. *Memoirs and Selected Letters 1839–1865*. New York: The Library of America.

Green, Fitzhugh. 1986. *George Bush: An Intimate Portrait*. New York: Hippocrene Books.

Griffis, William Elliot. 1915. *Millard Fillmore*. Ithaca: Andrews and Church.

Hagedorn, Hermann, and Gary Roth. 1977. *Sagamore Hill: A Historic Guide*. Oyster Bay: Theodore Roosevelt Association.

Hall, Gordon. 1967. *Lady Bird and Her Daughters*. Philadelphia: Macre Smith Company.

Halliday, E. M. 2001. *Understanding Thomas Jefferson*. New York: HarperCollins.

Hamilton, Holman. 1966. *Zachary Taylor: Soldier in the White House*. Hamden: Audubon Books.

Hamilton, Neil A. 2001. *Presidents: A Biographical Dictionary*. New York: Checkmark Books.

Harbaugh, William H. 1993. *The Theodore Roosevelts' Retreat in Southern Albemarle: Pine Knot 1905–1908*. Charlottesville: Albemarle County Historical Society.

Harris, Bill. 1997. *Homes of the Presidents*. Godalming, Surrey, United Kingdom: CLB International.

———. 2005. *The First Ladies Fact Book*. Norwalk: Easton Press.

Hatch, Alden. 1954. *Red Carpet for Mamie*. New York: Holt.

Hawthorne, Nathaniel. 1993. *Franklin Pierce*. New York: Tichnor, Reed and Fields.

Hay, Peter. 1988. *All the Presidents' Ladies*. New York: Penguin.

Heald, Edward T. 1992. *The Condensed Biography of William McKinley*. Canton: Stark County Historical Society.

Hecksher, August. 1985. "Historic Houses: Campobello." *Architectural Digest*, March: 220–228.

———. 1991. *Woodrow Wilson*. New York: Maxwell Macmillan International.

Helm, Emily Todd. 1898. "Mary Todd Lincoln." *McClure's Magazine*, 11(September). 42, 43.

Henning, Arthur. 1971. *Miss Florence and the Artists of Old Lyme*. Essex: Pequot Press.

Heymann, C. David. 1989. *A Woman Named Jackie*. New York: Carol Communications.

Hogarth, Paul. 1976. *Walking Tours of Old Philadelphia*. Barre: Barre Publishing.

Holloway, Laura Carter. 1870. *The Ladies of the White House*. New York: United States Publishing Company.

Holmes, David L. 2003. *Religion of the Founding Fathers*. Charlottesville: Ash Lawn–Highland Publishing.

———. 2006. *The Faiths of the Founding Fathers*. New York: Oxford University Press.

Holt, Marilyn Irwin. 2007. *Mamie Doud Eisenhower: The General's First Lady*. Lawrence: University Press of Kansas.

Hoogenboom, Ari. 1995. *Rutherford B. Hayes: Warrior and President*. Lawrence: University Press of Kansas.

Hoover, Herbert. 1951. *The Memoirs of Herbert Hoover.* Three volumes. New York: The MacMillan Company.

Hoover, Irwin Hood. 1974. *Forty-Two Years in the White House*. Boston: Greenwood Publishing Group.

Hudson, Patricia L. 1990. "Old Hickory's House." *Americana,* 17(6): 32–38.

Hunt, Conover. 1989. *The Sixth Floor: John F. Kennedy and the Memory of a Nation.* Dallas: SMU Press and the Sixth Floor Museum.

Irving, Washington. 1994. *George Washington: A Biography*. New York: Da Capo Press.

James, Marquis. 1940. *Andrew Jackson: Portrait of a President*. New York: Bobbs-Merrill.

Jensen, Amy L. 1970. *The White House and Thirty-Five Families*. New York: McGraw-Hill.

Johnson, Lady Bird. 1970. *A White House Diary*. New York: Holt, Rinehart and Winston.

Jones, Cranston. 1962. *Homes of the American Presidents*. New York: Crown Publishers.

Kane, Joseph Nathan. 1999. *Presidential Fact Book*. New York: Random House.

Keckley, Elizabeth. 1968. *Behind the Scenes: Thirty Years a Slave and Four Years in the White House*. New York: G. W. Carleton & Co.

Kelly, C. Brian. 1992, 1999. *Best Little Stories From the White House*. Nashville: Cumberland House.

Kelley, Kitty. 1991. *Nancy Reagan*. New York: Simon and Schuster.

Ketcham, Ralph. 1990. *James Madison: A Biography*. Charlottesville: University Press of Virginia.

Klapthor, Margaret. 1975. *The First Ladies*. Washington, DC: White House Historical Association.

Klein, Philip Shriver. 1963. *President James Buchanan*. University Park: Pennsylvania State University Press.

Koch, Adrienne, and William Peden, eds. 1944. *The Life and Selected Writings of Thomas Jefferson.* New York: The Modern Library.

Kochman, Rachel M. 1980. *Presidents: Birthplaces, Homes, and Burial Sites*. Osage: Osage Publications.

Ladies Hermitage Association, The. 1987. *Andrew Jackson's Hermitage.* Nashville: The Ladies' Hermitage Association.

Lambert, Darwin. 1971. *Herbert Hoover's Hideaway: The Story of Camp Hoover on the Rapidan River in Shenandoah National Park*. Luray: Shenandoah Natural History Association.

Langston-Harrison, Lee. 1992. *Images of a President: Portraits of James Monroe*. Fredericksburg: The James Monroe Museum.

Lash, Joseph P. 1971. *Eleanor and Franklin*. New York: Norton.

Lately, Thomas. 1968. *The First President Johnson*. New York: William Morrow.

Law, Charles Cecil, *et al*. 1985. *Mount Vernon: A Handbook*. Mount Vernon: Mount Vernon Ladies' Association.

Leech, Margaret. 1959. *In the Days of McKinley*. New York: Harper and Row.

Leighton, Frances Spatz, and Helen Baldwin. 1964. *They Call Her Lady Bird*. New York: McFadden-Bartell.

Lengyel, Cornel Adam. 1964. *Presidents of the United States*. New York: Golden Press.

Levin, Phyllis Lee. 1987. *Abigail Adams*. New York: Mo Martin's Press.

Lindsley, James Elliott. 1974. *A Certain Splendid House*. Morristown: Washington Association of New Jersey.

Link, Allen S. 1956. *Wilson: The New Freedom*. Princeton: Princeton University Press.

Loane, Nancy. 2009. *Following the Drum: Women at the Valley Forge Encampment*. Dulles: Potomac Books.

Lombardi, Frank. 1987. "Nancy Reagan Defends Her Rights in Advising the President." *New York Times*, May 5: A26.

Lossing, Benson J. 1886. *Mary and Martha: The Mother and the Wife of George Washington*. New York: Harper and Brothers.

MacDonald, Rose Mortimer Ellzey. 1937. *Nelly Custis, Child of Mount Vernon*. New York: Ginn.

Martin, Joseph Plumb. 1962. *Private Yankee Doodle, A Narration of some of the Adventures, Dangers and Sufferings of a Revolutionary Soldier*. George F. Scheer, ed. New York: Little, Brown.

Martin, Ralph G. 1979. "When Jimmy Carter Married Her, He Married Magic." *Ladies Home Journal,* 96(March): 99.

———. 1983. *A Hero for Our Time: An Intimate Story of the Kennedy Years*. New York: Macmillan.

Marton, Kati. 2001. *Hidden Power: Presidential Marriages That Shaped Our Recent History*. New York: Pantheon.

Mayo, Edith P., general ed. 1996. *The Smithsonian Book of First Ladies*. New York: Henry Holt.

McLaughlin, Jack. 1988. *Jefferson and Monticello: The Biography of a Builder*. New York: Henry Holt.

McCullough, David. 1992. *Truman*. New York: Simon and Schuster.

———. 2001. *John Adams*. New York: Simon and Schuster.

McGuigan, Cathleen. 2004. "Bill's New Bridge." *Newsweek,* September 5.

Means, Marianne. 1963. *The Women in the White House*. New York: Random House.

Meserve, Dorothy, and Philip Kunhardt, Jr. 1985. *Twenty Days*. Newcastle: Newcastle Publishing.

Mitchell, Stewart, ed. 1947. *New Letters of Abigail Adams, 1798–1801*. American Biography Series. Boston: Reprint Services Corp.

Monroe, James. 1959. *The Autobiography of James Monroe*. Syracuse: Syracuse University Press. First paperback edition, 1990. Charlottesville: University Press of Virginia.

Montgomery, Ruth. 1964. *Mrs. LBJ*. New York: Avon.

Moore, Virginia. 1979. *The Madisons*. New York: McGraw-Hill.

Morris, Edmund. 1979. *The Rise of Theodore Roosevelt*. New York: Coward, McCann and Geohegan.

Morris, Sylvia Jukes. 1980. *Edith Kermit Roosevelt: Portrait of a First Lady*. New York: Coward, McCann and Geohegan.

Mundy, Liza. 2008. *Michelle.* New York: Simon and Schuster.

Nagel, Paul C. 1983. *Descent from Glory: Four Generations of the John Adams Family*. Boston: Little, Brown.

———. 1987. *The Adams Women: Abigail and Louisa Adams, Their Sisters and Daughters*. New York: Oxford University Press.

———. 1997. *John Quincy Adams*. New York: Alfred A. Knopf.

Neal, Steve. 1978. *The Eisenhowers: Reluctant Dynasty*. Garden City: Doubleday.

Neff, Kelly J. 1997. *Dear Companion: The Inner Life of Martha Jefferson*. Hampton Roads: Hampton Roads Publishing Co., Inc.

Nelson, Anson, and Fanny Nelson. 1892. *Memorials of Sarah Childress Polk*. New York: A. D. F. Randolph.

Nessen, Ron. 1978. *It Sure Looks Different From the Inside*. Chicago: Playboy Press.

Nevins, Allan. 1966. *Grover Cleveland: A Study in Courage*. New York: Dodd, Mead.

Newton, Arvin. 1963. *Longfellow: His Life and Work*. Boston: Little, Brown.

Nichols, Roy F. 1958. *Franklin Pierce: Young Hickory of the Granite Hills*. Philadelphia: University of Pennsylvania Press.

Niven, John. 1983. *Martin Van Buren: The Romantic Age of American Politics*. New York: Oxford University Press.

Nixon, Richard. 1978. *Memoirs*. New York: Grossett and Dunlap.

Nolan, Jeannette Covert. 1958. *Dolley Madison*. New York: Julian Messner, Inc.

Olcott, Charles S. 1916, 1963. *The Life of William McKinley*. Two volumes. Syracuse: Syracuse University Press.

Owens, Kenneth N. 1963. *Galena, Grant and the Fortunes of War: A History of Galena, Illinois during the Civil War*. DeKalb: Northern Illinois University.

Pearson, Eleanor Fox. 1942. "Dolley Madison: She Was a Rose of Rare Beauty." *Greensboro (NC) Daily News*, May 24.

Perkins, Frances. 1946. *The Roosevelt I Knew*. New York: Viking.

Peskin, Allen. 1978. *Garfield*. Kent: Kent State University Press.

Pinsker, Matthew. 2003. *Lincoln's Sanctuary: Abraham Lincoln and the Soldiers' Home*. New York: Oxford University Press.

Pitkin, Thomas M. 1973. *The Captain Departs: Ulysses S. Grant's Last Campaign*. Carbondale: Southern Illinois University Press.

Poggiali, Leonard. 1993. "Conditional Surrender: The Death of U. S. Grant and the Cottage on Mount McGregor." *Blue and Gray Magazine*, 10(February): 60–65.

Pollamine, Barbara. 1993. *Great and Capitol Changes: An Account of the Valley Forge Encampment*. Gettysburg: Thomas Publishing.

Powell, J. M. 1993. *Bring Out Your Dead*. Philadelphia: University of Pennsylvania Press.

Preston, Daniel. 2001. *Life of James Monroe With a Chronology*. Charlottesville: Ash Lawn-Highland Publishing.

Pringle, Henry Fowles. 1939. *The Life and Times of William Howard Taft: A Biography*. New York: Farrar and Rinehart.

———. 1998. *The Life and Times of William Howard Taft*. Two volumes. Newtown: American Political Biography Press.

Pryor, Helen B. 1969. *Lou Henry Hoover: Gallant First Lady*. New York: Silver Burdett.

Radcliffe, Donnie. 1989. *Simply Barbara Bush*. New York: Warner Books.

———. 1993. *Hillary Rodham Clinton*. New York: Warner Books.

Rayback, Robert J. 1959. *Millard Fillmore*. Buffalo: Buffalo Historical Society.

Reagan, Nancy. 1989. *My Turn: The Memoirs of Nancy Reagan*. New York: Random House.

Reeves, Thomas C. 1975. *Gentleman Boss: The Life of Chester Alan Arthur*. New York: Alfred A. Knopf.

Remini, Robert V. 1977. *Andrew Jackson and the Course of American Empire, 1767–1821*. New York: Harper and Row.

———. 1988. *Andrew Jackson*. Three volumes. Baltimore: Johns Hopkins University Press.

———. 2002. *John Quincy Adams*. American Presidents Series. New York: Henry Holt.

Roberts, Bruce. 1990. *Plantation Homes of the James River*. Chapel Hill: University of North Carolina Press.

Roberts, Cokie. 2004. *Founding Mothers*. New York: HarperCollins.

———. 2008. *Ladies of Liberty*. New York: HarperCollins.

Roosevelt, Eleanor. 1949, 1975. *This I Remember*. New York: Greenwood Publishing Group.

———. 1978. *Autobiography of Eleanor Roosevelt*. New York: Barnes and Noble Books.

Roosevelt, Theodore. 1975. *Autobiography of Theodore Roosevelt*. New York: Da Capo Press.

Ross, Ishbel. 1959. *The General's Wife: The Life of Mrs. Ulysses S. Grant*. New York: Dodd Mead.

———. 1961. *Grace Coolidge and Her Era*. New York: Dodd Mead.

———. 1973. *The President's Wife: Mary Todd Lincoln — A Biography*. New York: Putnam.

———. 1975. *Power with Grace: The Life Story of Mrs. Woodrow Wilson*. New York: Putnam.

Russell, Jan Jarboe. 1999. *Lady Bird*. New York: Scribner's.

Ruttenber, E. M., and L. H. Clark. 1881. *History of Orange County, New York. 1683–1881*. Newburgh: Journal Printing House and Book-binding.

Sadler, Christine. 1963. *America's First Ladies*. New York: Macfadden-Bartell Corporation.

Saunders, Frances Wright. 1985. *First Lady Between Two Worlds: Ellen Axson Wilson*. Chapel Hill: University of North Carolina Press.

Schactman, Tom. 1981. *Edith and Woodrow: A Presidential Romance*. New York: Putnam.

Seager, Robert, II. 1962. *And Tyler, Too: A Biography of John and Julia Tyler*. New York: McGraw-Hill.

Seale, William. 1986. *The President's House: A History*. Two volumes. Washington, DC: The White House Historical Association.

———. 1988. *Virginia's Executive Mansion*. Richmond: Citizen's Advisory Council for Interpreting and Furnishing the Executive Mansion for the Virginia State Library and Archives.

Sellers, Charles. 1966. *James K. Polk, Continentalist: 1843–1846*. Princeton: Princeton University Press.

Shephard, Jack. 1980. *Cannibals of the Heart: A Personal Biography of Louisa Johnson Adams and John Quincy Adams*. New York: McGraw Hill.

Sherwood, Deborah Jones. 2003. *The First Ladies: Their Lives and Legacies*. New York: Barnes and Noble.

Shirley, Connie.1992. "Powerful Pages of History." *Texas Highways,* October: 40–45.

Shulman, Holly C., and David B. Mattern, eds. 2003. *The Selected Letters of Dolley Payne Madison*. Charlottesville: University of Virginia Press.

Sibert, Jacquelyn, managing ed. 1993. *The Presidents*. Indianapolis: Funk and Wagnalls Special Edition. Indianapolis: Curtis Publishing Company.

Sidey, Hugh. 1992. "Two Centuries and Counting." *Time,* October 19.

Sievers, Harry J., S.J. 1959. *Benjamin Harrison, Hoosier Statesman. From the Civil War to the White House, 1865–1888*. New York: University Publishers.

———. 1960. *Benjamin Harrison, Hoosier Warrior*. New York: University Publishers.

———. 1997. *Benjamin Harrison, Hoosier President*. Newtown: American Political Biography Press.

Simon, John Y., ed. 1975. *The Personal Memoirs of Julia Dent Grant*. New York: Putnam.

Smith, Helen McCain. 1976. "Ordeal! Pat Nixon's Final Days in the White House." *Good Housekeeping,* 83(July).

Smith, Marie. 1964. *The President's Lady: An Intimate Biography of Mrs. Lyndon B. Johnson*. New York: Random House.

Taft, Helen Herron. 1914. *Recollections of Full Years*. New York: Dodd, Mead.

Teague, Michael. 1981. *Mrs. L: Conversations with Alice Roosevelt Longworth*. Garden City: Doubleday.

Temple, Wayne C. 1984. *By Square and Compasses: The Building of Lincoln's Home and its Saga*. Bloomington: Ashlar Press.

Thane, Elswyth. 1960. *Washington's Lady*. New York: Crowell-Collier.

———. 1968. *Mount Vernon Family*. New York: Crowell-Collier.

———. 1970. *Dolley Madison*. New York: Crowell-Collier.

Thayer, Mary Van Rensselaer. 2007. *Jacqueline Kennedy*. Whitefish: Kessinger Publishing Company.

Thomas, Lately. 1968. *The First President Johnson*. New York: William Morrow.

Thompson, Charles Willis. 1929. *Presidents I Have Known and Two Near Presidents*. Indianapolis: Bobbs-Merrill.

Trefousse, Hans L. 1989. *Andrew Johnson*. New York: W. W. Norton.

Truman, Harry S. 1955, 1956. *Memoirs*. Two volumes. Garden City: Doubleday.

Truman, Margaret. 1956. *Souvenir: Margaret Truman's Own Story*. New York: McGraw Hill.

———. 1994. *Bess W. Truman*. New York: Macmillan.

Truman, Margaret, with Margaret Cousins. 1956. *My Own Story*. London: Eyre and Spottiswoode.

Turner, Justin, and Linda Turner, eds. 1972. *Mary Todd Lincoln: Her Life and Letters*. New York: Alfred A. Knopf.

Upton, Harriet Taylor. 1890. *Our Early Presidents: Their Lives and Children*. Boston: Best Books.

Wall, Charles C., Christine Meadows, John H. Rhodehamel, and Ellen McAllister Clark. 1974, 1985. *Mount Vernon: A Handbook*. Mount Vernon: Mount Vernon Ladies' Association.

Ware, Susan, ed. 1988. *Forgotten Heroes: Myra Colby Bradwell, Champion of Women's Legal Rights*. Essay by Jean Harvey Baker, Society of American Historians, 103–110. New York: Simon and Schuster.

Walker, Turnely. 1953. *Roosevelt and the Warm Springs Story*. New York: A. A. Wynn.

Washington, George, edited by John H. Rhodehamel. 1997. *George Washington: Writings*. Washington, DC: Library of America.

Watson, Robert P. 2000. *The Presidents' Wives*. Boulder: Lynne Rienner.

Weidenfeld, Sheila Rabb. 1979. *First Lady's Lady: With the Fords in the White House*. New York: Putnam.

West, J. B. 1973. *Upstairs at the White House: My Life with the First Ladies*. New York: Coward, McCann and Geoghegan.

Whitton, Mary Ormsbee.1948. *First First Ladies*. Freeport: Books for Library Press.

Wills, Garry. 1987. *Reagan's America: Innocents at Home*. New York: Doubleday.

Williams, Charles R., ed. 1922–1926. *Diary and Letters of Rutherford B. Hayes*. Five volumes. Columbus: Ohio State Archaeological and Historical Society.

Wilson, Edith Bolling. 1939. *My Memoir*. Indianapolis: Bobbs-Merrill.

Withey, Lynne. 1981. *Dearest Friend: A Life of Abigail Adams*. New York: Touchstone books.

Woodward, W. E. 1946. *George Washington: The Image and the Man*. New York: The Liveright Publishing Company.

Wootton, James E. 1987. *Elizabeth Kortright Monroe*. Charlottesville: Ash Lawn Publishing.

Xinis-Fishman, Paula, ed. 1990. *Monroe On*. Charlottesville: Ash Lawn-Highland.

Young, Joanne. 1973. *Washington's Mount Vernon*. New York: Holt, Rinehart and Winston.

Index